Vatican II:

Keeping the Dream Alive

Vatican II:

Keeping the Dream Alive

Denis Hurley OMI

Cluster Publications

2005

ISBN 1-875053-48-4

First published in 2005

Published by Cluster Publications
P.O. Box 2400
Pietermaritzburg 3200
South Africa
Tel. & fax: (033) 345 9897
E-mail: cluster@futurenet.co.za
Internet: http://www.hs.unp.ac.za/theology/cluspub.htm

Cluster Publications is a non-profit publishing enterprise of the Pietermaritzburg Cluster of Theological Institutions, aiming to produce good scholarship and accessible and inexpensive resources for contemporary theology.

Typesetting by Lou Levine of *Stylish Impressions* – (033) 3869584
Cover design by *Justin James Design*

Front cover picture: Community of Sant'Egidio, Rome
Back cover picture: von Galli, Mario and Moosbrugger, Bernhard, *The Council and the Future*, McGraw Hill, New York, 1966

Printed by Interpak Books (Pty) Ltd, Pietermaritzburg, South Africa

Contents

Reflections on Vatican II

Preface

Albert Nolan OP

How quickly we forget. The Second Vatican Council has already disappeared into the mists of past history. There are fewer and fewer Catholics today who can remember those heady days when the Church took a giant step forward. For generations of Catholics since then the Council is simply a non-event. And what a terrible loss that is proving to be.

The struggle against apartheid is beginning to suffer the same fate. There are young people today, black and white, who have no memory of apartheid and cannot imagine what all the fuss was about. The government is trying hard to preserve the memory of past struggles, but the participation of the Church in these struggles is almost entirely forgotten, even by those who were so much a part of it.

How quickly we forget people too. Archbishop Denis Hurley stood like a giant in the Church and society for so many years – not only in South Africa and not only in the Catholic Church. Today, so soon after his passing, there is the danger that he too might be forgotten as we become more and more a people with very little historical consciousness.

We do not want to be people who live in the past and who remain nostalgic about past events. The challenges we confront are here and now, but we are certain to flounder and to repeat the mistakes of the past, unless we know and appreciate what has gone before us. The present can only be understood in the light of those past events and the personalities who helped directly or indirectly to shape the Church and society of today.

What we have in this book is Archbishop Denis Hurley's Second Vatican Council memoir and a few essays about what has happened since. Its publication 40 years after the Council is timely and challenging. Not only because we so easily forget the past, but also because we can so easily misunderstand and be misled about the past – with disastrous results.

I travel fairly extensively and I try to listen to what people are saying in

South Africa and elsewhere especially in the Catholic Church. What I find more worrying than forgetfulness about the past, is the extraordinary ignorance among so many, especially young people, about the history of the Church. At best, the Second Vatican Council is ignored; at worst, it is completely misunderstood.

Some of the people I have spoken to think that Vatican II simply changed the liturgy and gave priests and religious more freedom than they had had before. What they do not seem to know anything about is the very rich pastoral theology, ecclesiology and spirituality of the Council documents.

Hurley's memoir of the proceedings at the Council, his answers to questions about it and his own interventions during the Council sessions will help the reader to appreciate something of its profound insights. Serious students of Catholic teaching should take the time to read the Vatican documents themselves – and perhaps this book will encourage them to do so.

In South Africa there is yet another form of ignorance. On the whole we do not, and perhaps never did, appreciate the tremendous role played by Archbishop Denis Hurley at the Council.

The Archbishop was not only a saintly man, he was also exceptionally gifted in a number of ways. He was a clear thinker and a good writer. He was well read in all the latest theology of that time. He devoured each new book as it came out, grasping its meaning and relevance for the Church immediately and with great excitement. Hurley was a real intellectual and a profound theologian with a sharp critical mind. This comes across very clearly in these memoirs.

One of the things I always admired in him was his genuine openness to new ideas. He had no trouble accepting the discoveries and insights of the Jesuit palaeontologist, Teilhard de Chardin. Just as he was immediately able to accept the insights of feminist theologians and others in more recent times. Spiritually and intellectually he lived up to his own episcopal motto: "Where the Spirit is, there is freedom".

He was a man of immense courage. He did not hesitate to speak out at the Council no matter how unpopular it might make him with the conservatives or with anyone else. It was he who spoke out in praise of Teilhard during one of his interventions.

It was no surprise therefore to hear that he made a deep impression on the other Council fathers as well as the observers and journalists. I discovered this first-hand because I happened to be in Rome during the first session of the Council. As a postgraduate student at the Angelicum I lived with some of the *periti* or experts as well as some Dominican journalists. Each day they would come home with the latest news of what had happened at the Council that day. I cannot tell you how often the name of a certain Archbishop Denis Hurley cropped up.

He was clearly a key player in the drama that unfolded day by day and one of the leading progressives. One can see that for oneself by reading between the lines of this memoir.

Months before the Council began his talents were acknowledged in that he was elected as a member of the Central Preparatory Commission. He was deeply critical of the workings of the Commission. He speaks of himself as "barging in where angels fear to tread". Not all his suggestions were accepted, but he had nevertheless a considerable influence on the decisions of the Commission.

Later, he was elected to the Commission for Seminaries, Academic Studies and Catholic Schools where his ideas on seminary training were widely appreciated by both conservatives and progressives. However, his attempt to have the years of philosophy and theology integrated into one holistic curriculum were not accepted in the end. What he writes about this makes very interesting reading for us today.

During the Council Hurley made some crucially important interventions. He had many interests and concerns but one that stands out was his concern that the approach in all the documents of the Council be at all times pastoral. He felt that abstract theological statements would not be of much value to the Church in its everyday life.

Hurley spoke of the Council as "the great revolution that was taking place in the Catholic Church" and of his participation in it as "the greatest experience of my life".

The result is that his memoir about that period in his life makes the Second Vatican Council come alive for the reader. We can experience with him the daily struggles, the ups and downs, the hopes and disappointments and the excitement at being part of an event of such historic importance.

There would be no better way of learning to appreciate the Council and the great personalities who shaped it than by reading this memoir.

In his essay, "Denis Hurley and the Reception of Vatican II", Mervyn Abrahams CSsR, Lecturer in Church History and Moral Theology at St Joseph's Theological Institute, takes up the story of the Archbishop's tireless attempts to bring the insights and decisions of the Council to the Church in South Africa and particularly to his own Archdiocese. He takes us through South Africa's liturgical and catechetical renewal, the establishment of lay ministries and parish pastoral councils, our involvement in social justice, the famous Pastoral Plan: Community Serving Humanity and the role Hurley played in all of this. We are reminded also of the international role he played especially as chairperson of ICEL, the International Commission on English in the Liturgy.

But the process will continue for a long time yet, says Abrahams. The implementation of the Council's vision has hardly begun.

Marie-Henry Keane OP, Prioress General of the Newcastle Dominican Sisters, writes about keeping the dream alive – the dream of the Second Vatican Council that became the dream of Hurley himself. "This great son of South Africa," she writes, "lives on in us".

Sue Rakoczy IHM, a professor at St Joseph's Theological Institute, gives us an overview of the struggles and conflicts in the Church today. "We are a dysfunctional Church," she writes. But then she offers us a very important insight about what has been missing and what is needed today: "the transformation of the inner life of the Church". The challenge is to radical holiness for all the baptised, not only bishops, priests and religious. She quotes Rahner's famous prophecy: "In the future we shall be mystics ... or we shall be nothing".

Have we been too concerned, I ask myself, with structures and plans and teachings, and too little with spirituality, contemplative prayer and union with God – for everyone? Not that structures and plans and teachings are not important, but without a deep spirituality they easily flounder and disappoint. One of the central insights of the Council, and of Archbishop Hurley himself, was the radical call to holiness addressed to all the baptised.

In his contribution, Chrys McVey OP, a member of the General Council of the Dominican Friars in Rome, sums it up by declaring that the Council was only partially successful and that much of its spirit and hopefulness never really materialised. What we need now, he writes is "trust and patience", qualities which Denis Eugene Hurley had in great abundance.

We owe a debt of gratitude to those who compiled and edited this book and to those who wrote the reflective essays, but above all we owe a debt of gratitude to our beloved Archbishop for the role he played during the Second Vatican Council and after, and for this memoir which reminds us of much that we might have forgotten (or informs us of much that we might indeed never have known), much that is still of importance to the Church of today.

The challenge of this book, addressed to all of us, is to take up the torch of the Second Vatican Council and to continue the work of *aggiornamento,* reform and spiritual renewal.

Foreword

Allan Moss OMI

I congratulate anyone who takes on the challenge of writing a book about a famous person. It warrants scholarly research, even better to have first-hand knowledge of the famous person. Paddy Kearney, together with relatives and friends of Archbishop Hurley and some scholars of high reputation, have undertaken such a task. Their efforts complement much of what the Archbishop himself has written. One of his favourite topics was the Second Vatican Council. Being one of the Council fathers and having participated in the debates that produced some of the most famous Church documents, he happily shared his experiences, and has done so very fully in the memoir published in this book.

It is my privilege to have known the archbishop personally, especially when he came to live with us at Sabon House when he retired. He lived simply in his room, not even having an office of his own. He cheerfully received people, including many important visitors, in these humble circumstances. He was also a prolific writer, covering a variety of topics, theological, philosophical, political – even sport! Living closely with him, he struck me most of all as a spiritual person, spending hours in prayer, in the chapel, taking part with his Oblate confreres in the Eucharist, Divine Office, and devotions. It witnessed to the great faith of a humble soul in the presence of God.

Although Archbishop Hurley was a great intellectual, he led a simple life of prayer. He was close to God and close to his people. He was a brilliant speaker and also a great listener, even to a simple person trying to make a point. People felt he was with them but he often confessed that he was not close enough to those who needed him. Nevertheless, one could see many of the beatitudes in him: he identified with the poor and the suffering; he was merciful and helped create institutions to serve the needy; he was a champion for justice.

Once when visiting the ancient Roman city of Ostia, I discovered that salt (*sal*) was part of a payment (*sal*ary) to a Roman soldier for his services. Here is a great warrior of Christ who served his Church long and faithfully. He must certainly be worth more than his weight in salt, or even in gold. Little wonder that so soon after his death some of the laity have already suggested that his cause for canonisation be introduced in Rome so that the long process can be commenced without delay.

I congratulate all involved in publishing this book which is a tribute to a great and holy man. Archbishop Hurley was a student in Rome and had a great love for the Latin language: I can imagine our Lord saying to him *"Vos estis sal terrae"*: "You are the salt of the earth" Mt 5:13. Not needing to hear Archbishop Hurley's response, because He will read his well-known smile and know that the humble man feels highly honoured by his God and by his people.

Introduction and Acknowledgments

Paddy Kearney

Shortly before his sudden death on 13 February 2004, Archbishop Denis Hurley visited Cluster Publications in Pietermaritzburg. He left with them the manuscript of his memoir on the Second Vatican Council, asking them to assess it for publication.

After the Archbishop's death it was discovered that the board of Cluster Publications had decided they would be willing to publish this significant account of the Council.

When the Archbishop's family were in Durban for his funeral on 28 February, they met with the Oblate Provincial, Father Allan Moss OMI, and agreed that the publication should go ahead. In order to situate the Archbishop's memoir in context, they requested that theologians be invited to write several additional essays for the same volume. These would reflect on the Archbishop's role in the Council, and the extent to which its decrees have been implemented, especially in South Africa. They would also look at the state of the Church 40 years after Vatican II and discuss whether there is now a need for a further Vatican Council and if so what its agenda might be.

It seemed appropriate in addition to publish extracts from speeches delivered by the Archbishop in the Council's plenary sessions, as well as a recent interview in which he reflected on the Council. Many thanks to Pastoral Press of Portland, Oregon in the U.S. for permission to reproduce this interview.

This collection is an important contribution to the many reflections on the Council taking place at present, in 2005, the 40th anniversary of the Council's conclusion.

The photograph which appears on the cover was taken in the Archbishop's last year. It reminds us that he wrote his memoir of the

Council in his last years and remained an enthusiastic promoter of Vatican II until the end.

I take this opportunity to thank all who assisted with this publication, especially those who contributed to it: Mervyn Abrahams CSsR, Philippe Denis OP, Alois Greiler SM, Marie-Henry Keane OP, Chrys McVey OP, Allan Moss OMI, Albert Nolan OP, John Page and Sue Rakoczy IHM.

Many thanks also to Martin Badenhorst OP for his thorough edit of the memoir and to Reverend Tony Gamley for sterling assistance with proofreading. Devoted former secretaries to Archbishop Hurley, Julie Mathias and Pat Maycock, have helped the process in every way possible. This book would not have been possible without Julie's patient and painstaking typing. A word of thanks also to Bruce Page of Independent Newspapers for his willingness to be consulted about questions of style. Gladys Weigner, friend of Bernard Moosbrugger – a great photographer of the Second Vatican Council, Gunther Simmermacher of *The Southern Cross*, and Petal O'Hea have given much help with illustrations.

The cover design and scanning of the illustrations was provided by Justin Waldman, and the layout of the book by Lou Levine. We owe them much for their creativity and patience.

The generosity of Cardinal Wilfrid Napier OFM and of Hans Wennink of Stichting Porticus have enabled Cluster Publications to make this book available at a very reasonable price.

In conclusion, many thanks to Nelly Mellis of Cluster Publications who never faltered in her conviction that this book should be published, and to Interpak Books (Pty) Ltd who did a fine job of printing.

Denis Eugene Hurley: 1915-2004

Paddy Kearney

Archbishop Denis Hurley loved to tease Nelson Mandela that he had lived on Robben Island long before that island's most famous prisoner. Born in 1915, the son of Irish immigrant parents, the young Denis grew up at a succession of lighthouses where his father was lighthouse keeper: Cape Point, Robben Island, East London and Clansthal (Umkomaas) along South Africa's lengthy coastline.

Having finished his schooling at St. Charles' Marist College, Pietermaritzburg, he was sent to Ireland for his basic training as an Oblate of Mary Immaculate, and then to Rome where he completed licentiates in philosophy at the Angelicum and theology at the Gregorian University, and where he was ordained in 1939.

His encounters in Rome with brilliant black students from other countries was an eye-opener for the young man who had grown up with typical white South African attitudes of that time. He also made a special study of the Catholic Church's social teaching and was much influenced by Joseph Cardijn's "see – judge – act" method, one of the major influences of his years overseas.

Returning to South Africa in July 1940 he was assigned to Durban's Emmanuel Cathedral, and just four years later his outstanding intellect and leadership qualities led to his being chosen at the age of 29 to head the new St. Joseph's Scholasticate in Pietermaritzburg, where young Oblates were prepared for the priesthood. He honed his public-speaking skills by regularly taking part in the city's parliamentary debating society.

On the retirement of Bishop Henri Delalle, the 31-year-old Father Hurley was chosen to succeed him and ordained bishop in 1947, the youngest Catholic bishop in the world at that time.

For his motto he selected *Ubi Spiritus, ibi libertas* "Where the Spirit is, there is freedom" 2 Cor 3:17, with its relevance to the South African situation clearly in mind. It was to provide a profoundly appropriate description of his entire ministry.

Just five years later the Vatican promoted him to the rank of archbishop, once again the youngest in the world. "I found myself in a lift that was going up" he said of this spectacularly rapid series of promotions.

In 1952 his colleagues elected him to chair the Southern African Catholic Bishops' Conference, a position he held until 1961. For the first time the Conference spoke out against apartheid in major joint statements drafted by Hurley in 1952 and 1957, the latter describing apartheid as "intrinsically evil" many years before the World Alliance of Reformed Churches was to declare it a "heresy".

In the early 1950s in response to Verwoerd's Bantu Education Act which deprived Church schools of government subsidies, Hurley spearheaded a campaign to raise funds to keep Catholic schools going – open defiance of apartheid policy.

Hurley began to be ever bolder in his opposition to apartheid, addressing significant protest meetings against successive pieces of legislation.

In the midst of one of the most repressive periods in South Africa's history, came an experience of an entirely different kind – the Second Vatican Council, a major policy-making conference of the world's 2,500 Catholic bishops (1962-1965), which was to be the great highlight of Hurley's life. Chosen by Pope John XXIII to be a member of the agenda-setting Central Preparatory Commission, he worked closely with some of Europe's leading cardinals to ensure that a progressive majority took control of the Council. In eloquent Latin he gave a number of ground-breaking addresses in the plenary sessions and became known as one of a small number of bishops who ensured the Council's success.

Back in South Africa after the Council, Hurley promoted its vision with great enthusiasm in his own archdiocese and throughout the country: fostering a new system of religious education for young people, developing an innovative, experience-based system of seminary formation for priests, making public worship more understandable and participatory, drawing lay people into structures of consultation and decision-making. The

Archdiocese of Durban became known internationally for its enthusiastic implementation of Vatican II resolutions.

The Council had helped to broaden his vision and made him aware that many third world bishops faced similar struggles. He discovered that the prophetic stance he had been taking enjoyed the support of the overwhelming majority of the world's bishops. This gave him a new confidence to adopt a sharper critique in his opposition to apartheid. In his capacity as president of the South African Institute of Race Relations he gave major anti-apartheid addresses in 1965 and 1966. Most notable was "Apartheid: Crisis of Christian Conscience" a masterly demolition of claims that "separate development" could in any way be justified as Christian.

But Hurley was moving away from purely academic opposition. At this time the apartheid regime was forcibly uprooting hundreds of thousands of black people to consolidate the black homeland areas. One of the most notorious of these removals was to a place in Natal called Limehill. When this removal was threatened not only did Hurley denounce the government's proposal, but he was present in solidarity on the day the removal took place, frequently visited the people to hear their problems, and published the names and ages of the small children who died as a result of the removal.

When in 1974 the government made it illegal to call for conscientious objection, despite the threat of severe penalties, Hurley openly supported the South African Council of Churches' resolution on the subject, identified himself with conscientious objectors and gave evidence on their behalf when they were brought to court.

Over the years Hurley was to make a number of calls for ecumenical church campaigns for a more just society, only to be disappointed by a poor response. In the process he learnt that the churches needed to be organised for an effective response. This meant structures, budgets and full-time staff for justice work. Thus he founded Diakonia in 1976 to help Durban churches pool their efforts through an ecumenical structure and in 1979 supported the establishment of the Pietermaritzburg Agency for Christian Social Awareness (PACSA).

Having publicly backed the integration of Church schools from the early 50s, Hurley was delighted when in 1976 some nuns began to simply admit Black pupils to previously white schools, despite what the law said.

His vigorous defence of their action helped prevent the government from closing the schools.

Elected president of the SACBC for two further terms (1981-1987) Hurley was scathing in his criticism of police and army misconduct in the Vaal Triangle and in Namibia.

Remarks he made about the "Koevoet" special police unit in Namibia led to his appearing in the dock for defamation, an event that caused an international stir. The charges were dropped when it became clear the state would be severely embarrassed by the evidence Hurley's legal team had assembled.

With the backing of Durban's Legal Resources Centre in 1985 he successfully applied for the release of a detainee held under laws that allowed indefinite detention without access to lawyers, family or friends. Until that time it had also been the law that not even a court could intervene and order the release of a detainee.

Workers too enjoyed Hurley's powerful support. He let them meet in church premises to keep united during the massive textile workers' strikes of 1980 and in 1985 donated Church land to dismissed workers to farm so that they could make an income during the protracted strikes. "We want to throw the moral weight of the Church behind their struggle", he said.

There was a price for Hurley's high-profile opposition to apartheid: much criticism from inside and outside the Church. KwaZulu-Natal MPC, Brian Edwards, called him "an ecclesiastical Ché Guevara"; Minister of Justice Jimmy Kruger, seriously considered banning him; President P W Botha angrily wagged his finger at him during a meeting with a bishops' delegation. Hurley's house was petrol-bombed with no-one ever claiming responsibility.

Truth and Reconciliation Commission investigations revealed that along with four other Church leaders, including Desmond Tutu, he was regarded as one of the state's "most wanted" political opponents – against whom the security police had to resort to smears and dirty tactics because banning and detentions were not an option for such high-level clerics.

But Hurley was also criticised by the left, for example, for declining to endorse the Kairos Document (1985) and the Road to Damascus (1989), statements of liberation theology which he felt were too soft on the use of violence. Some were also disappointed about his reluctance to be associated with South African Communist Party flags in Durban's freedom march on 22 September 1989.

One of Hurley's last efforts while in office as archbishop was to inspire and lead the drawing up of a major national Church programme entitled "Community Serving Humanity" which draws on Latin American models of small groups meeting regularly for bible-sharing, prayer, reflection and social action.

Having completed 45 years as Bishop of Durban, almost the whole period of Nationalist Party rule, Hurley was succeeded by Wilfrid Napier in 1992, by that time being the Catholic Church's longest-serving bishop in the world. The cities of Durban and Pietermaritzburg honoured him as a freeman. He chose to become parish priest of Emmanuel Cathedral, one of Durban's poorest and most difficult inner-city parishes where he remained until 2002 when he decided to retire and to devote more time to his memoirs.

From 1993-1998 Hurley was Chancellor of Natal University, one of 10 universities which had awarded him honorary doctorates. He was also decorated by the governments of France, Italy and South Africa, having received the Order of Meritorious Service (Class 1) from President Nelson Mandela.

Many have asked why Hurley was not made a cardinal. The reason isn't hard to find. Just as he openly criticised apartheid, so he took positions, for example, on birth control and the ordination of women, which were not popular with the Vatican. In addition, perhaps his extensive anti-apartheid work had been seen as too political in Vatican circles.

But Hurley was not one to adjust his message for the sake of personal advancement. For the first 14 years of his life he had observed his disciplined and responsible father work at several lighthouses, ensuring that they never failed to warn and guide passing ships. Young Denis was absorbing the lesson of a lifetime – to courageously, consistently and with the utmost clarity, let his own light shine. And with this light he helped guide the Catholic Church into the modern world and bring South Africa safely to its new democracy. His writings and example continue to challenge both Church and society.

Denis Hurley:
Memories of Vatican II[*]

* Endnotes on pgs. 160 and 161

Introduction

The first half of the decade of the '60s presented me with the greatest experience of my episcopal life, indeed, the greatest experience of my whole life: the Second Vatican Council.

Providentially, the good Lord had provided me with an unforeseen yet quite remarkably apt preparation for this experience in the form of the reading that came my way during the decade of the '50s. As an experience of adult education and spiritual growth I look back on that decade with fond and appreciative memories.

Among the authors that contributed to my intellectual and spiritual growth were Aubert, the historian; Hofinger, the specialist in catechetics; Maritain, Rahner, Jungmann, Congar, Chenu, Clifford Howell, Vauyer, John Courtney Murray and, of course, the greatest of them all, Pierre Teilhard de Chardin, though in my case de Chardin belonged more to the early '60s than to the '50s.

Two fairly small volumes created quite an extraordinary impact: Father Clifford Howell's *The Work of Our Redemption* and Jacques Maritain's *Christian Humanism,* translated from the French *Humanisme Integral.* Clifford Howell's impact came from his emphasis on the central role of Christ in the liturgy. Father Albert Danker OMI lent the little volume to me just after a Mass and confirmation service in the parish of Machibisa, near Pietermaritzburg. I had meant to enjoy a short siesta but Howell hijacked the siesta. Something similar happened in regard to Jacques Maritain. His *Christian Humanism* robbed me of a Sunday afternoon rest as he brilliantly outlined the modern view of Church-state relations.

In the matter of spirituality, I look upon three authors as my special mentors: Emile Mersch SJ, Francois Xavier Durwell CSsR and the great Pierre Teilhard de Chardin SJ.

Emil Mersch's contribution was to give me a deeply personal realisation and appreciation of the presence of Jesus in the Church and in each member of it with special reference to myself. This was achieved through his book *The Whole Christ.* I took it on a retreat and my reading of it and meditating on it gave new depth, vividness and feeling to a conviction that I had been cultivating during the last year or two of my studies in Rome, the conviction associated with St Paul's great image of the Body of Christ.

It is quite amazing to remember how the Body of Christ had faded from theological memory in the Catholic Church for, I would guess, a number of centuries. If my memory is correct, the revival began in the first decade of the 20th century and the great image of St Paul actively became the inspiration of several aspects of the Catholic revival of the first half of that century, particularly in regard to liturgy and Catholic action. By 1946 I was preaching a complete retreat to religious sisters on the theme of the Body of Christ but it was *The Whole Christ* that made it an integral part of my life. I believe Father Emile Mersch was killed in an aerial bombardment in May or June 1940. May he have experienced immediately the glorious Body of Christ.

It was several years later that I came across F.X. Durwell's book on the resurrection. This was another deep, vitalising experience. I could not put the book down. I devoured it. It filled me with the exciting revelation that Jesus present in his Church and therefore in me was the risen and glorious Christ, the conqueror of death and sin, devil and hell. It was a strange experience; I felt that I had not really believed in the resurrection before and it became impossible for me not to talk about the resurrection. It became the dominant theme of all my homilies and instructions. My Vicar General at the time, Father Eric Boulle OMI, as we travelled together in a car one day, asked me: "Why are you always talking about the resurrection?" I think I gave a confused reply, something along these lines: "What else is there to talk about?"

The third great contributor to the central role of Christ in my faith was Pierre Teilhard de Chardin SJ. He had died in New York on Easter Sunday 1956 and the pent-up volume of his writings had begun to flood the world, first in French and then in a great number of translations. I first made meaningful acquaintance with him through a magazine article but his name had been familiar to me from my second to last year of study in Rome. He was listed in the manual on Creation Theology among those who held, for that time, daring views on evolution. In 1951 he passed through South Africa on his way to the United States. It had been indicated to him that he might be better off outside of France during the turbulent theological years after the Second World War. It was agreed that he reside in the

United States, specifically in New York. He was given permission to take in South Africa in the course of his journey to the United States in order to respond to the invitation of the palaeontological establishment in South Africa that knew of his work in China, particularly in regard to the renowned fossil of Peking Man. After his visit to what was then known as the Transvaal he came to Durban to embark on the ship that was to take him across the Atlantic. He spent a night or two at the Caister Hotel where, though I tried to make contact with him, my effort failed. Later I was to complain to Professor Phillip Tobias, South Africa's leading palaeontologist after the Australian, Raymond Dart, that I had failed to meet the great Teilhard whereas he, Phillip, as a graduate student, saw a lot of him while conducting him around some of the South African palaeontological sites. This was at the time when, before the Leakeys in East Africa, South Africa was the world's leader in palaeontology.

It was not precisely the palaeontology of Teilhard that meant so much to me though I was deeply impressed by it. What contributed to my personal growth was Teilhard's vision of the cosmic Christ. Teilhard had had the good fortune to become acquainted with the early development of the revival of the Body of Christ theology promoted by the Jesuits in France in the early years of the 20th century. That vision of Christ, coupled with Teilhard's scientific picture, blossomed out into the magnificent totality of the cosmic Christ – the risen Jesus present not only in his Church but present too, as the word of God, in the physical universe in all its immeasurable dimensions.

After that somewhat superficial introduction to Teilhard through a magazine article, somehow I contrived to get my hands on several volumes of his essays and when *The Phenomenon of Man* burst on the scene in its English version, I think I read it about five times to fully grasp the flow of Teilhard's argument: the argument tracing the great stages of evolution through the biosphere to the noosphere, the human collectivity representing the most exciting stage of evolution through the interplay of human thought and feelings, requiring love as the binding force to prevent disaster and hold the process on course. At the end of this breathtaking description, Teilhard emphasises the irrefutable conclusion that such systematic and consistent development must have a target, an object for which it is all intended. This Teilhard calls the omega point. You turn the page to the Epilogue where you find that for Teilhard the omega point is Christ; the aim, the object, the purpose of the evolving universe, the cosmic Christ who is at the same time the Christ of the Church, the ecclesial Christ.

Teilhard has been accused by some of confusing science and faith, the science of evolution and faith in the Christ of the Gospel. There are no grounds for this accusation. *The Phenomenon of Man* makes that very clear. The scientific consideration ends with the need for an omega point but does not define what it is. The reflection of faith identifies this omega point as Christ, an identification which is an act of Christian faith.

It was against this background that I found myself ready for the Second Vatican Council.

Chapter One

Pope John Calls the Council

Despite what I have written about being prepared for the Second Vatican Council I must confess that I showed no great excitement about it when news was received that Pope John XXIII, on the occasion of a celebration in St Paul's Basilica on 25 January 1959, Feast of the Conversion of St Paul, announced to the group of cardinals gathered there that he intended to call a general council of the Church. Somehow the idea of a general council seemed remote from my own concerns and preoccupations of the time. Like many others I felt that a council would be called only to deal with a crisis in the Church or to formulate or define some teaching of the Church that needed special emphasis. In 1959 it did not appear to me that there was any particular crisis or theme of Catholic teaching that required special treatment in a general council. Towards the end of June 1959 or early in July a circular letter arrived from Cardinal Tardini announcing that an antepreparatory commission had been set up by the Holy Father with himself as president and calling for suggestions, comments and proposals concerning an agenda for the council.

I was in Europe at the time the circular letter arrived, attending a catechetical study week at Eichstatt in Germany and an international Eucharistic Congress in Munich. I had travelled with Bishop van Velsen OP of Kroonstad and we had had the privilege of an audience with Pope John XXIII. (See photo on page 33) Can I ever forget that audience? When the door of the papal library opened to admit us, the Holy Father came towards us with his arms extended in a hearty welcome. "Come in" he said "and tell me your joys. We all have problems and I have far more than you, so let us talk about joys". There followed 20 minutes of joyful and encouraging conversation, at the end of which the Holy Father looked at his watch and said: "There are other people wanting to see me so I am sorry that I must bring this conversation to an end. Kneel down and I will give you my blessing". We knelt and heard the Holy Father say in a combination of Latin and Italian: "May almighty God bless us (I need this more than you), Father, Son and Holy Spirit".

On returning to South Africa I plunged into the usual backlog of matters that accumulate during a fairly lengthy absence from home and I failed to respond to the circular of Cardinal Tardini before the cut-off date of 1 September 1959. Having missed that date I came to the conclusion that I should resign myself to making no positive contribution to the agenda of the council. My attitude was probably something like this: If the Holy Father wants a council he surely knows what the agenda should be.

There must have been quite a few other bishops in other parts of the world who had failed to meet the cut-off date. Towards the end of March 1960 we received a letter dated 21 March from the secretary of the antepreparatory commission, Archbishop Pericle Felici, politely pointing out our failure and requesting that we do our best to send in responses before the end of April that year.

This jerked me into a sense of urgency about the council. If the matter of suggestions for the council was so important that it elicited a reminder to the negligent, obviously the matter was being looked upon in a very serious light at headquarters.

Twenty years after I had completed my studies in Rome, all through the medium of Latin, my grasp of the language had obviously slid downhill quite a lot. Nevertheless, I still had a Latin dictionary and a Latin grammar so I dusted them off and got to work.

The following are the points I submitted, divided into two broad categories: theological and practical considerations. The theological considerations included:

1. Concerning the Church as the Mystical Body of Christ and the Holy People of God, including its liturgical and apostolic activity under the influence of its Head and Spirit;

2. Concerning the hierarchy as a college of bishops united to the Supreme Pontiff offering due submission in relation to the government and teaching office of the Church;

3. The joint ministerial responsibility of priests and bishops, expressed in their teaching office and care of souls;

4. Concerning the laity and its participation in the priesthood and mission of Christ, with special attention to Catholic action;

5. Concerning relations between Church and state and concerning human freedom in relation to the requirements of the Church of Christ and the authority of the state.

The practical considerations included:

1. Concerning a method of uniting the bishops of the world in closer union with the Holy Father in the government of the Church. It is proposed that there should be fairly frequent consultations concerning questions of greater importance affecting the apostolate of the Church in order that through the sharing of views of the whole hierarchy solutions be found and put into practice.

   Consideration might be given to the possibility of establishing episcopal conferences in all areas of the world. The outcome of such consultation would be a better comprehension by the Holy See of the concrete conditions in which the life and labour of the universal Church take place, a better understanding among bishops of the mind of the Holy See and greater speed in the acceptance of policies and putting them into practice. Often the best programmes of the Holy See have little effect as bishops lack concrete and practical knowledge of an issue and do not know how to go about its practical application. It is useful to remember the slow progress in understanding and putting into effect the social doctrine of the Church. Issues dealt with in common achieve results more easily.

2. In regard to the liturgy of the Church, in the matter of pursuing these highly desirable aims, namely, instruction of the faithful on their participation in the Christian Mystery, these can hardly be achieved without fairly frequent use of vernacular languages.

3. Catholic action.

4. Catechesis of the faithful, both adults and children, with due regard for the necessity of providing the whole catechetical formation as a vision of the Mystery of Christ, inspiring mind and heart and drawing clarity and fervour from scripture and the liturgy of the Church.

5. Education of seminarians, with a view to adapting this education better to pastoral requirements. Present-day education appears too theoretical. It does not convey a true vision of the Mystery of Christ (of the Whole Christ, Head and Body) and a full understanding of the liturgical and apostolic activity of the Church. Nor are the seminarians sufficiently instructed in the art of proclaiming the mystery in words or in writing. It might be better if, in the first year before the study of philosophy, the Mystery of Christ in all its fullness were conveyed to the seminarians to the degree in which they are able to absorb it. And if they were carefully educated to write and speak well so that from the beginning of their formation the priestly apostolate might appear as practical service of the Divine Master; and so that with this vision and aim before their eyes they might derive more abundant fruit from their study of philosophy, theology and other ecclesiastical disciplines.

I posted off these proposals for the council agenda on 15 April 1960 with a humble letter of apology for my neglect and delay. I received a very friendly and fraternal acknowledgement dated 22 April 1960.

Then to my utter surprise and delight, on my return from a trip to Europe in July 1960, I found waiting for me a letter from Cardinal Tardini informing me that the Holy Father had approved of my membership of the Central Preparatory Commission. The designation had obviously been changed from the cumbersome *Antepreparatory*. The catechetical study week had been organised by Father Johannes Hofinger SJ. It also gave me the opportunity of participating in the Eucharistic Congress in Munich, seeing the Passion Play at Oberammergau and paying a flying visit to Berlin under the auspices of members of one of the papal knighthoods, before the building of the wall, but already marred by the huge difference between the opulent West and poverty-stricken East.

The Central Preparatory Commission consisted of 101 members: 58 cardinals, five patriarchs, 28 archbishops, five bishops and four superiors general of religious orders, one of whom, Father Michael Browne OP, had in 1937 been my teacher at the Angelicum in Rome, now St Thomas Aquinas University.

In due course an organogram of the Central Preparatory Commission was supplied to members. It indicated that 14 specialised committees would be submitting material to the Central Preparatory Commission. The Holy Father was to be considered President of the Central Preparatory Commission and, in addition to the members already referred to, it was to have a Secretary General and consultors. There were to be plenary sessions for the examination of the position papers submitted by the specialised commissions. These position papers were termed *schemas,* a word of Greek origin accepted into Latin which we took over in all our vernacular languages as being the most convenient one for ordinary and regular use in the Council.

There were to be three sub-commissions, one on procedure, one on inter-commission matters called *Mixed Matters,* and the third on amendments. Each was to be presided over by a cardinal and to have four members and a secretary. There was also to be a special section of the Central Preparatory Commission dealing with the organisation of the Council and consisting of a cardinal president, six members and technical experts.

We received an invitation dated 1 October 1960 from the Secretary of the Central Preparatory Commission, Archbishop Pericle Felici, to an audience with the Holy Father to be held on 14 November. The invitation indicated that it might not be possible for all members to attend. I do not know how many actually attended but I was not one of them. I had submitted my excuses.

Our Secretary, Archbishop Pericle Felici, was later to be the Secretary General of the Council. It has always intrigued me to note how many Italian ecclesiastics have ancient classical pagan names like Pericle Felici, Anibale (Hannibal) Bugnini and Amleto (Hamlet) Cicognani.

The invitation to the first meeting of the Central Preparatory Commission was sent out on 1 May 1961 and summoned us to gather in Rome for the period 12 to 22 June of that year. In the matter of dress we were instructed to wear the *habitus planus:* that is, for all bishops apart from a few belonging to special religious orders, black cassock with attached cape and purple trimmings and buttons and a purple cincture or waistband.

We duly assembled in Rome for the opening day of the first session on 13 June 1961. Our meeting place was a magnificent hall in the Vatican known as the Hall of Congregations, adorned with some magnificent tapestries.

The agenda for the first meeting consisted in drawing up replies to seven questions:

> ➤ Who besides those attending by right, should also be invited?
> ➤ What should be the criterion for choosing theologians and canonists? What should be done about establishing commissions?
> ➤ What arrangements should be made about speeches in the Council and voting procedure?
> ➤ What should the majority be for arriving at conciliar decisions?
> ➤ Granted that the language of the Council must be Latin, what means should be proposed to promote its use and understanding?
> ➤ How should Council proceedings be recorded?

In my replies to the first two questions I was all for bringing in as many as possible: Council members and consultors who came to be known by the Latin term *periti,* meaning experts. Among members this would have included titular as well as residential bishops. The term titular included auxiliary bishops, vicars apostolic in mission countries and certain prelates with episcopal rank but without territorial responsibility. Among the experts I wanted to see theologians and canonists, scripture scholars and scholars active in patrology, history, liturgy, missiology and philosophy as well as promoters of catechetics and Catholic action, including laity in that final category. The total I envisaged was 140. In dealing with the question of commissions I really took off. I could not see how a Council consisting of 3 000 members could involve itself in effective debate, so I suggested that the 3 000 should be divided into language groups, in which the tough debating would take place and from which conclusions and recommendations could be submitted to the special commissions for the finalisation of texts before being submitted to the whole assembly for voting. Obviously this suggestion implied a great use of the vernacular languages in the sub-divisions of the Council.

In making this somewhat outrageous proposal I was obviously inspired by my experience of debate according to Anglo-Saxon methods but I had no idea of the tradition of debating from which the Second Vatican Council would draw. In this tradition debating amounted to fairly long series of monologues by participants lucky enough to get their names on the list, with the responsibility falling on a commission to draw the best out of the monologues and use it in their revision of *schemas*. No doubt, this suggestion of mine was never taken seriously but I was happy to see how the procedure, more or less along the same lines, was adopted in the Episcopal Synod established by Pope Paul VI after the Second Vatican Council.

I do not know how much effect our discussions in the first session of the Central Preparatory Commission had on subsequent Council procedures. A sub-commission of the Central Preparatory Commission, under tight curial control, without further reference to the Central Preparatory Commission, produced a book of rules and regulations under the title *Order of Celebrating the Second Vatican Ecumenical Council*, promulgated by Pope John XXIII on 6 August 1962.

The Central Preparatory Commission convened again in Rome from 7 to 15 November 1961. The agenda was the cause of some misgiving to me. We did not seem to be dealing with the main issues that should be engaging our attention in so important a matter as a general council. Our agenda for the November meeting dealt with the question of inviting non-Catholic observers to the Council, with a new formula for a profession of faith, with a *schema* on the sources of revelation, with the distribution of clergy around the world and the provision of parishes and their union and division. This appeared to be quite an extraordinary collection of topics for a council called to bring new life and vigour to the Universal Church. Clearly, we in the Central Preparatory Commission were being asked to deal with certain minor matters that had been disposed of early and quickly in the labours of the special commissions.

I was very critical of the formula for a new profession of faith. I thought it far too defensive and negative, too concerned with the errors of the time. I suggested that it was inviting us to believe *against* rather than *in*.

I found it sadly lacking in the growing understanding of the Church as sharing in the mystery of the death and resurrection of Jesus and gift of the Holy Spirit.

I also found it too triumphalistic in its appreciation of how the Church appears in the eyes of people – all too often they see the warts and not the wonders. I was also critical of the *schema* on sources of revelation. At the time I did not understand the main point at issue, namely, that there are not two sources of revelation but one with two dimensions supporting each other, scripture and tradition. I regretted the lack of good scriptural quotations in the *schema*.

In dealing with the question of the distribution of clergy I maintained that the solution of this question depended on another question, namely, the participation of bishops of the whole world in the government of the universal Church. I referred with approval to a statement in the text according to which "bishops, as successors of the apostles, must remember that they should have at heart the solicitude of all the churches". I agreed with that but pointed out that there was no proper structure to promote the idea. I suggested a body of bishops drawn from the hierarchies or episcopal conferences of the world to meet with the Holy Father annually or biennially to treat with him and the Roman Curia concerning problems affecting the universal Church, among which would be the problem of the distribution of clergy. I cannot remember if this proposal was a personal inspiration or derived from some other source, but, four years later Pope Paul VI announced the establishment of the Synod of Bishops which would meet in ordinary session every three years.

I did not manage to attend the January 1962 meeting of the Commission because it clashed with the preparation of a plenary session of the Southern African Catholic Bishops' Conference. Again the agenda of the Commission appeared to lack the solidity and cohesion that one would expect to find in the preparation of such an important event as a general Council of the Church. It included, under theological questions: the model order and the preservation of the deposit of faith; under the celebration of sacraments: the sacrament of confirmation, of penance and of orders and, under questions concerning the oriental churches: references to sacraments, rites, oriental patriarchs, sacramental sharing (*communicatio in sacris*) and the use of vernacular languages in liturgies.

I attended the February meeting of the Commission, in which the agenda included questions about bishops and the government of dioceses, legislation concerning clergy and laity, aspects of the religious life, questions concerning seminaries and Catholic universities and another item concerning oriental churches.

By this time I was really getting perturbed about the way in which the Council was being prepared. To add to the consternation of many of us we were required to be in the apse of St Peter's basilica along with the Roman clergy on Thursday 22 February, Feast of the Chair of St Peter, to witness the promulgation of a measure prepared by the department of the Holy See responsible for seminaries. This measure required that teaching in seminaries be done through the medium of Latin. It was designated by the first two words of the text: *Veterum Sapientia* (Wisdom of the Ancients).

In dealing with the paper on seminaries I was very critical of what had been placed before us, contending that while philosophy and theology were very important, the most important consideration should be the pastoral training of seminarians, providing them with the ability to speak and communicate well, to relate to people, to perform liturgy well and to exercise the kind of leadership that would be required of them as priests.

Pessimism about the preparation of the Council was somewhat relieved during my flight back to South Africa on the termination of the February meeting of the Central Preparatory Commission. I had with me the *schema* on liturgy and the more I read of it the more I got excited about its contents. Finally, here was a paper very worthy of a Council of the Church. Later I learned that this was due to the fact that the commission responsible for preparing the liturgical *schema* had as its secretary Father Anibale (Hannibal!) Bugnini, a priest of the Vincentian order. Father Bugnini had been instrumental in assembling some of the best liturgical scholars in the Church to serve on the Commission preparing the draft on liturgy.

The fifth meeting of the Central Preparatory Commission was held from 26 March to 3 April 1962. There were three main topics: liturgy, missions and the means of social communication, i.e. press, radio and television. The day of telex, fax and e-mail had not yet dawned. The paper on liturgy brought some joy to the proceedings, but the other two were not so inspiring. My pessimism persisted. However, I greeted with enthusiasm the submission made by Cardinal Suenens, the new Archbishop of Brussels. The Cardinal had been appointed to the Central Preparatory

Commission at about the end of January and had attended the February meeting. Obviously he had been much concerned about the Council and had done some thinking and discussing about it. In the course of the March-April meeting he gave an excellent presentation of what he thought the agenda of the Council should be. He proposed that the topics of the Council should be grouped under two main headings: *ecclesia ad intra* and *ecclesia ad extra*, which can be roughly translated as "the Church looking inwards" and "the Church looking outwards". He gave a list of topics belonging to each of the two dimensions.

At the end of the session at which he made his proposal I moved around quickly to congratulate him and express the hope that his proposal would be accepted. I also mentioned that I had one suggestion to make and that was that under the dimension *ecclesia ad intra* he should add a special section on priests. I do not think that he heard me too well because at the end of the first period of the Council when he put his proposal to the whole Council, the section on priests was still missing. It came late onto the agenda of the Council, was first debated under the title *Priestly Life and Ministry* towards the end of the third period and was finalised only towards the end of the fourth.

I blame myself for not having made a greater fuss over the lack of a *schema* as soon as possible after the closure of the first period.

On my return home after the March-April meeting I wrote a letter to Cardinal Suenens in which my anxiety for the future of the Council was expressed in these terms: "From my own experience of the Central Preparatory Commission from last June, I really think it is time that energetic measures became evident in regard to the organisation of the Council. From the way things are going at present, I entertain the gravest fear that we shall drift into the Council with a mountain of *schemas* totally unsuitable for discussion by a huge gathering of nearly 3 000 persons, and that the procedure for discussion will be totally inadequate and impracticable. This seems to be how the First Vatican Council started and how it drifted along aimlessly for three or four months. I have just been reading Roger Aubert."

I enclosed a paper in Latin consisting of six-and-a-half foolscap pages describing how I thought discussions in the Council should be organised.

I was still promoting my idea of language groups and indicated that about 20 of them would be necessary with about 150 members in each! I also tried to describe how the findings of these various groups could be co-ordinated in a paper for presentation to a plenary session of the Council. Obviously I was still convinced of the necessity of debating in the Anglo-American style rather than in the Roman style in which there is no real confrontation of opinions but individuals make speeches collated by a person or commission charged with the task of bringing the best out of them.

In a note dated May 4 I record that "this morning Cardinal Frings made a strong remark about the tremendous amount of detail in the *schemas* and the impossibility of dealing with it all in a Council. He was warmly supported. The time seems right for a strong proposition." The note goes on to deal with meetings with Cardinal Suenens, Cardinal Frings and Cardinal König. In the discussion with Cardinal Frings he promised he was going to propose formally that the Holy Father be asked to appoint a new sub-commission to take the preparatory work firmly in hand and to give some initiative to the Central Commission. The note also records that Cardinal König promised to support Cardinal Frings.

In regard to my proposal concerning the organisation of debates in the Council, I had the nerve to send a copy of it to Cardinal Roberti, President of the sub-commission of the *Regolamento,* that is, the organisation for the running of the Council. I received a kind, fraternal response indicating that my proposals would be submitted to the Council. That is as far as they got, of course. I was obviously barging in where angels feared to tread.

I even submitted a request for an audience with the Holy Father, hoping to express my misgivings to him. On the copy of the application, two words written: "No luck!!"

In the end a proper agenda commission was set up to ensure the proper organisation of the Council, but it took the rough-and-tumble of the first period to ensure its establishment.

The May 1962 meeting of the Central Preparatory Commission had a truly massive agenda. The main item was the Church – the item with which we should have begun work at least in November 1961. Other items included matters concerning bishops, pastoral care, concern for people on the move like migrants, travellers, sailors, and care for people affected by communism. Religious life came up for consideration as well as some matrimonial problems, the censorship and prohibition of books and censures imposed on persons – all this with the opening of the Council just six months off.

The June agenda was just as crowded with a variety of topics, mostly additional dimensions of topics that had already been discussed, like the training of seminarians, Catholic schools, relations between bishops and religious, lay associations, mass stipends, ordination of persons who had been ministers in other churches, preparation for marriage, priests who had abandoned their vocations, lay apostolate, some considerations about the Blessed Virgin Mary: a beautiful, inspiring and peaceful topic of discussion; some less peaceful exchanges about Christian unity, culminating in a crashing explosion about relations between Church and state and religious liberty, the contending captains being on the right, Cardinal Ottaviani, and on the left, Cardinal Bea, scripture scholar and former rector of the Biblical Institute. On the side of Cardinal Bea I contributed what I thought was a persuasive and polished paper. My neighbour at the table did not agree. He said: "What the Archbishop of Durban has said is not Catholic doctrine"[1].

So ended our work on the Central Preparatory Commission. We were not required to have any further concern for the *schemas* that had filled our lives for a year. They came to us, as to all other Catholic bishops, as final drafts for discussion in the Second Vatican Council.

Chapter Two

The First Period

The solemn opening of the Second Vatican Council was due to take place on Thursday 11 October 1962 so I left Durban for Rome some days before that date. For reasons that I cannot now recall I travelled via Katanga, Kinshasa and Madrid.

I had made friends with a priest in Katanga called Father Pascal. He made me welcome, showed me around and introduced me to the man then in power in Katanga, Moise Tshombe. Tshombe had set up his own independent state in Katanga and the big copper mining corporation, Union Miniere du Haute Katanga seemed quite happy about this. Tshombe seemed all set to continue running his bit of the Congo but, of course, it did not last.

In Kinshasa I was the guest of the Novanium University. The rector was very kind to me and even took me on a flight in his small plane over a certain length of the great Congo River. I was deeply impressed by what was going on in regard to the university campus. Splendid buildings were going up all around and the university seemed to be flourishing with an influx of funds from the Congo itself, from Belgium and from the American government and American foundation funds. The university was looking forward to having 3 000 students in a year or two.

I went through Madrid on my way to Rome probably because there was no direct flight from Kinshasa to Rome. The last stage of my journey to the Eternal City was in the company of a great number of Spanish bishops also on their way to the Council.

After arriving in Rome "I was milling around" as I described in a letter, with about 50 or 60 French and Spanish bishops in the special hall set aside for the "inconvenience" (as I described it) of Council fathers at the airport, when a smiling little Dominican Friar put his hand out and said: "Congar". So I shot mine out and said: "Hurley". We fell on each other's necks – he had to fall upwards for this purpose. He told me that he was working hard on a book on tradition. It would probably land him in the Holy Office again. Poor Congar. He had suffered severely at the hands of the Holy Office for daring to write the kind of theology that was to influence the Council so profoundly.

The great day dawned, 11 October, and the Council fathers duly gathered in various assembly points in the Vatican at 7.30 a.m. The assembly point for the group of archbishops to which I belonged was in a hall of the Vatican Museum. The procession began to move off on its journey through St Peter's Piazza shortly after 8.30 a.m. People subsequently remarked to me that they thought they had noticed me in the procession on cinema newsreels. There was no television in South Africa at that time. Nor did I make an appearance in the Piazza. The group of archbishops to which I belonged seemed to have been overlooked by an assistant master of ceremonies. We remained in our museum assembly point (a galling situation for someone who considered himself to be a progressive), until awareness dawned about our predicament and we were hastened down a staircase of the Vatican, along the portico of St Peter's and duly injected into the procession at the main door of the Basilica. What a scene greeted our eyes. In a letter I described it as "a canyon of white mitres". The canyon was suggested by the fact that the nave of St Peter's had been transformed into a council hall (*aula* in Latin) by the construction of ascending rows of seats at the sides with a wide passage between them leading up to the high altar surmounted by Bernini's magnificent Baldachino. Despite missing out on the lap through the Piazza, archbishops had been assigned to places very near the high altar, just after the cardinals. When I reached my place I looked with some misgiving at a television camera close to me. Knowing the length of Vatican liturgical celebrations I had the awful presentiment of falling asleep under the eye of that television camera and having my liturgical snooze recorded for posterity. Thank God that did not happen.

It could not possibly have happened during the final allocution of the Holy Father, Pope John XXIII. He said that the agenda of the Council should aim at emphasising Christ as the centre of history and life and should, where necessary, bring the methods of the Church up to date (in Italian, *aggiornamento*). There were people, he said, that saw everything modern only as ruin and prevarication. He looked upon these as prophets of doom and called upon the Council to enable the Church to take a leap towards a doctrinal penetration in the formation of consciences in the light of the Gospel and of the mystery of the Church. Listening to the Holy Father I experienced no tendency for the eyes to close and the head to nod. The Holy Father was clearly favouring the progressive camp, but the Curia still had its hands on the controls.

The drama of the first period of the Council was to consist in sorting out that situation.

In a letter I wrote concerning the celebration in St Peter's I indulged in a little criticism. Firstly, I complained that "as usual, nobody told us when to stand, to sit, to cover and uncover; so there was a fair amount of mitre-fluttering in that vast canyon". Secondly, I found it unfortunate that when the ceremony ended somewhere after 1.00 p.m., it was a battle to get back to the Vatican and recover one's belongings. Nobody had thought of organising this and of keeping the traffic flowing, with the result that at one stage 1 250 bishops were trying to go westwards through one door while 1 250 were trying to proceed eastwards through the same.

Apart from these little hitches, it was a memorable day.

Saturday 13 October was the first working day of the Council and the first item on the agenda was the election of the Council commissions. These commissions were to be vitally important, a matter of life or death, in fact. The reason for this was the way in which Council discussions were to be conducted. This way was not to follow Anglo-American give and take, pro and con, exchange of views ending in proposals, seconding and voting. The Council procedure was to consist of a series of monologues on the paper under consideration and referring all these contributions to a commission that would revise the paper in the light of submissions made. Obviously in the composition of a commission a majority of progressives would produce a very different result from a majority of conservatives. Hence the importance of persons elected to conciliar commissions.

Mass was said each morning at the beginning of the Council's daily programme. After Mass on 13 October the Secretary General of the Council, Archbishop Pericle Felici, informed us that our first task would be the election of the commissions. Booklets were handed out with spaces to propose names for 16 commissions as well as the names of those who had served on the preparatory commissions, which seemed to convey the idea that bishops might like to copy those names as their candidates for the conciliar commissions. Bishops all around me got down to the task of writing. I sat motionless waiting for something to happen. I had been informed through the progressive network that a plan had been organised to ensure a fresh approach to this election of commission members. It was an agonising wait of about two minutes. Those of us who knew what was brewing thought we had been sold out. But in due course the voice of Cardinal Liénart of Lille in France came over the public address system, protesting that we hadn't had enough time to know who to vote for. Cardinal Frings of Cologne in Germany supported him and the rest of the meeting was adjourned while bishops poured out of St Peter's as if the Second Vatican Council had lasted only about two hours.

Over the rest of that weekend, Saturday afternoon and Sunday, Rome fairly steamed with activity as the hierarchies from all the countries of the world held meetings, selected candidates, exchanged information and made hundreds of alterations and adjustments. This organisation was put together by the Central Europeans: France, Germany, Austria, Holland and Belgium. In due course they were joined by Switzerland, Scandinavia, Poland, Yugoslavia and the Iron Curtain countries. The Latin Americans were also well organised. They had about 600 votes. The United States had its own tight organisation with about 240 votes, but didn't seem to be doing much horse trading with the others. The English, Irish, Australians and New Zealanders published their own lists of candidates. Africa was quickly into the field with continent-wide consultations controlling about 300 votes and Asia was split between India and Sri Lanka on one side and the Far East on the other.

Procedural rules laid down that elections must be held in terms of Canon 101, which requires an absolute majority and, failing that, a relative majority in the first two ballots. If this is not achieved a relative majority in the third ballot suffices. Each of us had to write 160 names for the ten commissions – 16 for each. So there were about 400 000 names to be counted. The results were published on Monday 22 October and to my surprise I found that I had come in as number eleven on the Commission for Catholic Schools and Seminaries. It appears that my name had become known in connection with seminaries because of an article I had written for *The Furrow*, an Irish theology publication which had been copied in periodicals of other countries. An account of the work of this Commission is contained in Chapter Six.

What filled our time between Tuesday 16 October and Saturday 22 October I cannot recall, except that under French inspiration, led by Father M D Chenu OP the idea came before the Council of sending a message to the world. The idea did not excite me very much. In due course a text was placed before the Council, was subjected to debate and duly published. As far as I can make out the world did not get unduly excited about it. I intervened briefly in the debate, criticising the formula referring to the fathers of the Council as "successors of the apostles who form one apostolic body headed by the successor of Peter". I felt that this formula was not designed to win the hearts and minds of those persons in the world who were not Catholics.

If the world had not got excited about the message from the Council, something occurred on 22 October that did not lack for excitement – an excitement of dismay. President Kennedy addressed the American nation on the Cuban missile crisis arising out of the transfer of missiles from Russia to Cuba. The world held its breath as the United States and Soviet Russia almost blundered into a nuclear war. The Council could have been over within two weeks.

I finally got to grips with the first *schema*, namely the one on the liturgy. As I have mentioned earlier, this was the best of all *schemas* prepared for the Council, in fact, apart from what Cardinal Bea's secretariat compiled, the only one of any real value.

Unfortunately, its value brought me no consolation as we moved into a method of discussion that proved painfully disconcerting to me. Possibly there is no other way of conducting discussion in a council of the Church. Any member of the Council who wished to contribute had to make application for the right to speak. A list of successful applicants was drawn up day after day, with due observance of hierarchical rank: cardinals, archbishops and bishops. Cardinals always had preference: despite the fact that they were five percent or less of the membership they had far more opportunity for speaking than other members. Contribution to discussion was called an 'intervention', a term adopted into English from languages of Latin origin. The time allowed for an intervention was ten minutes with a warning bell being sounded after eight minutes. Members caught out with far too much material to cram into the last two minutes made a desperate attempt to vocalise all they had prepared with the consequence that they often ended up wasting their sweetness on the desert air.

Sessions began every morning at 9.00 a.m. and went on till 1.00 p.m. Each began with the celebration of Mass, normally what we then called low Mass with, possibly once a week, a more solemn Mass in another Catholic rite as practised in Eastern Mediterranean areas. In most cases only the celebrant received communion.

In regard to working days, we observed the Roman ecclesiastical and academic programme of sessions on Monday, Tuesday, Wednesday, Friday and Saturday with a day off on Thursday.

As day after day went by and intervention followed intervention, with many repetitions and an occasional display of disagreement, I found myself getting more and more critical of the procedure. However, I did prepare a brief comment full of praise for the *schema* on liturgy, emphasising the close bond between liturgy and apostolate, but, when given the opportunity to present it I decided not to on the grounds that it was just a repetition of what had already been frequently said. The speaker after me did the same. It happened to be Archbishop Guildford Young of Hobart in Tasmania, with whom I was to become very friendly in the course of the Council and of Commission meetings that followed it.

Many of us suffered quite a shock on Wednesday 24 October, when it was announced that Archbishop Chichester SJ of Salisbury, Rhodesia (now Harare, Zimbabwe) had collapsed and died on his way to St Peter's that morning. He had attended a meeting of African bishops the afternoon before.

The African bishops had not wasted any time in getting themselves organised. South Africa had taken the lead in regard to the English-speaking African bishops and secured the use of a very convenient hall in a street off the Via della Conciliazione, the broad street that runs from the Tiber to

St Peter's Piazza. The African bishops got together in two groups, the Anglophone (i.e. English-speaking) and Francophone (French-speaking). There was nothing unusual about this. Council fathers of various languages and nationalities quickly formed themselves into collectivities for the purpose of consultation and study. Theologians and scripture scholars and other experts were kept busy lecturing to these groups. I referred to the phenomenon as an extraordinary example of adult education. A great deal of the drive that inspired the Second Vatican Council, under the inspiration of the Holy Spirit, of course, was generated in those educational groups.

Going back to Archbishop Chichester, his requiem was celebrated on Friday afternoon, 26 October with Archbishop Markall, the then incumbent of Salisbury (Harare), as celebrant. God rest the warm-hearted and beloved Archbishop Chicks. I remember him well for his British public school manner of addressing men by their surnames.

The Requiem took place in the magnificent Jesuit baroque church called the Gesù, not far from the Piazza Venezia and the Victor Emmanuel monument.

In regard to the interventions in the *aula* which rolled on and on, I commented in a letter: "Some of us wonder if the Curia isn't maintaining this procedure to induce the collapse of the Council. Horrible suspicion, but after a week of verbal deluge no man can be quite sane! Thank God for the coffee-bars, there is one on each side of St Peter's and hundreds of Council fathers make their little pilgrimage each morning. You meet very interesting people there and sometimes learn far more than you do inside the Council". The coffee-bars were named Bar Jona and Bar Abbas respectively: reflections of Council humour that helped to counteract the boredom.

During the nine working days that we had in October we managed to get through the introduction and two chapters of the *schema* on the liturgy. There were several more chapters to come. We began November with four days off: All Saints' Day, All Souls' Day, followed by Saturday and Sunday. I took this opportunity to visit friends in Genoa and Pax Romana in Fribourg, Switzerland. Pax Romana (Latin for Roman Peace) is a Catholic international organisation of academics and students. In the 1960s its Director was a Spanish gentleman called Sogranye de France. Once, discussing Franco, I ventured the opinion that possibly Franco was necessary in 1936, referring to the outbreak of the civil war in Spain when Franco led the conservative right against the Spanish government and its Marxist and anarchist allies. Two fists hit the table as de France exclaimed, "Franco was *never* necessary".

Council business seems to have speeded up somewhat after the four days' break. On 12 November I was writing in a letter: "We have got through the breviary since last I wrote and are now on the calendar and sacred furnishings, art and music. We should finish tomorrow." The letter continues:

> The Commission (that is, the Commission on Liturgy) is busy trying to sort the wheat from the chaff in all that has been said. From all accounts things are bogged down pretty badly in the Commission. Cardinal Larraona is the President. He is Spanish. He is a canonist and he talks interminably and in a heavy Spanish accent. Furthermore he is said to be unsympathetic to liturgical reform. The one thing few people outside of English-speakers understand is how to preside at a meeting. So with Cardinal Larraona presiding and trading punches at one and the same time, the Liturgical Commission is apparently doing its purgatory. It is wonderful how the Lord works. He always wants to make it clear that if any good results are achieved, they are achieved through Him and not through human ingenuity. This Council is a perfect confirmation of 1 Cor. 1,17-31.[2]
>
> He decides on the most wonderful objectives and chooses those least likely to achieve them. Back to prayer for charity, forbearance and patience!
>
> It was announced today that the second session would last from 12 May to 29 June. In the meantime the commissions will have to do some work. I don't think this will concern me, as we are not likely to get to Schools and Seminaries until 1965! The Liturgical Commission is going to have to sweat it out and possibly the Theological Commission. Revolution is still simmering over the theological *schemas*. The Secretariat for Extraordinary Affairs has voted to ask the Holy Father that immediately after the introduction of the *schema* a vote be taken as to whether the *schema* should be discussed or rejected out of hand. I don't think the Holy Father will allow it. It will be too severe a blow against Cardinal Ottaviani to have his *schemas* rejected without detailed discussion. Already the Italian press has got hold of a rumour that he is very sore at having

been "belled" (told his time was up) by Cardinal Alfrink at one of the early discussions. Unfortunately, as far as can be ascertained, he has been absent from the Council most of the time since then. This creates impressions. It is a pity that it had to be Cardinal Alfrink who "belled" him because as you remember, it was at the instigation of the Holy Office that the Italian translation of the Dutch hierarchy's pastoral letter was withdrawn in June. The worst of that "belling" was that it was greeted by applause from the junior bishops. We archbishops observed the proprieties! All this stuff that is supposed to be a Council secret is splashed in one of the two Italian papers.

On a cheerier note I referred to the fact that the free afternoons gave us the opportunity of attending excellent lectures from prominent theologians and scripture scholars and mentioned in particular Cardinal Suenens and Father Daniélou who both spoke fairly good English. I also mentioned that we were looking forward to lectures in scripture to bring us up to date on recent developments and indicated that part of the theological heat is generated from the tussle in Rome between the Lateran Seminary, conservative, backed by Ottaviani and Ruffini, and the Biblical Institute, moderately progressive. I ended this section of my letter indicating that "I am to dash off to the Latin American College where Yves Congar is giving a lecture in French on the theological *schema* – more subversion."

Tuesday 13 November was marked by two events: the conclusion of the discussion on the liturgical *schema* and the announcement by Cardinal Cicognani, Secretary of State, that the name of St Joseph would be introduced into the Canon of the Mass, now the first Eucharistic Prayer. It was indicated that the discussion on the Sources of Revelation would begin on Wednesday 14 November.

The point at issue here was whether there are two sources of revelation, namely scripture and tradition. Protestantism had introduced the idea that the bible was the only source of revelation, but the Catholic Church had continued to maintain the importance of tradition. In the resultant polemics, Catholic theologians tended to place bible and tradition side by side as two sources of revelation. However, the more recent renewal of theology and possibly the influence of ecumenism brought a later generation of theologians to maintain that there is only one source of revelation, God's word entrusted to the apostles and coming down from them in two streams, scripture and tradition, supporting and complementing one another.

This was the first theological issue to be debated and it brought into the full light of day the great cleavage between those who wanted biblically-inspired pastoral directives from the Council and those who preferred the old dogmatic definitions and decisions.

In a letter I wrote on 19 November I described the situation as follows.

> We began on Wednesday with some heavy artillery fire from the Transalpines. The counter-barrage was organised on Thursday and laid down on Friday. Since then the commandos from both sides have been at it toe to toe. My name was called as a speaker on Friday but, with more and more cardinals piling into the fray, I didn't get my turn until 11.35 this morning. By this time most of the Council fathers were grimly holding on to the bar and weakly gasping for coffee. On the left they have Bar Abbas and our side (the right of the presidents) the Bar Jona. Bishop van Velsen spends his time circling from one to another and calling for a one-day strike.
>
> In the course of the debate Bishop de Smedt of Bruges in Belgium gave a magnificent intervention on ecumenism. He is emerging as one of the great orators of the Council.
>
> I made use of my speaking time to call for a clarification of what was meant by 'pastoral' in the aim and methods of the Council. I was taking up the point that I had already made in the Central Preparatory Commission six months before.[3]

The debate on the sources of revelation continued for the rest of that Monday morning into Tuesday 20 November. After five or six interventions the Secretary General announced that there would be a vote on the question: Should the discussion about the *schema* on the dogmatic constitution concerning the sources of revelation be interrupted? Those who wanted an interruption should vote *placet* (in favour). Those who wanted a continuation of the debate should vote *non placet* (against). Hurried consultations here and there in the *aula* seemed to indicate that there was some ambiguity about the formulation of the matter to be voted on.

However, the voting went ahead and resulted in the following announcement by the Secretary General at the end of the session:

Total voting 2 209	*Placet:*	1 368
	Non placet	822
	Spoilt votes	19
	Majority required:	1 473

As a two-thirds majority for interruption had not been achieved, technically speaking the vote for interruption had failed. But quite clearly the *schema* was doomed.

As we were leaving the *aula* I found myself walking next to Cardinal Ottaviani and he seemed to be muttering under his breath something like *"Latrocinium Vaticanum"* meaning "Vatican robbery". He could have been echoing *"Latrocinium Ephesinum"* – "Ephesian robbery", the designation given by Pope Leo I to a rebel council held at Ephesus by supporters of monophysitism (one nature in Christ) and subsequently condemned by the Council of Chalcedon in AD 451.

Though technically the motion to interrupt the debate was lost we had the advantage of monarchical papal government. The Holy Father stepped in, upheld the interruption and subsequently set up a joint commission of representatives from the Theological Commission and the Secretariat for Christian Unity to revise the *schema*. It was placed under the joint chairmanship of Cardinals Ottaviani and Bea, not the easiest of partnerships.

Anyhow, with that decision Pope John XXIII brought the Tridentine Era to a conclusion.[4]

Because the papal decision was not made known until Wednesday morning, 21 November, discussion continued all that day on the first chapter of the *schema* on the sources of revelation. Obviously it was a discussion without much purpose or interest.

After the usual break on Thursday we began with the *schema* on the means of social communication on Friday morning 23 November. The means of communication referred to were press, cinema, radio and television. Unfortunately the debate did not excite much interest, a sad reflection on the Council which was struggling to give itself a truly pastoral identity. After two and a half days of discussion a vote of closure brought the debate to a conclusion.

The next *schema* that came up for consideration was a rather curious one. Its title was "That All May Be One" but it dealt only with Catholics of Eastern Rites united to Rome so it wasn't really concerned with ecumenism which was the theme of the Secretariat for Christian Unity under the leadership of Cardinal Bea. However, it did give an opportunity for Patriarch Maximus IV Saigh to address the Council. His contributions were always lively and interesting and usually very critical. A special feature of them was that he always spoke in French, and got away with it. It was a kind of protest on behalf of Eastern Catholics against the domination of Latin and the authoritative attitude of the Holy See, so foreign to the Eastern synodical tradition. The introduction of this *schema* resulted in the production by the Council of a document entitled Decree on the Eastern Catholic Churches.

On Tuesday 27 November the General Secretary gave the information that the next period of the Council would begin on 8 September 1963 and not in May as had been previously announced. He also made it known, on Friday 30 November, that despite objections from the President of the Theological Commission, Cardinal Ottaviani, discussion on the *schema* on the Church would begin on Saturday 1 December because the *schema* on the Church was one of the most important of the Council and it would be useful for the bishops to become acquainted with it before the termination of the first period.

So all was ready for the great confrontation over the most important *schema* of the Council.

Cardinal Ottaviani, President of the Theological Commission, introduced it on Saturday morning with his delightful command of Latin, including a dash of humour and a touch of sarcasm and the battle was on.

Cardinal Liénart opened for the progressives and Cardinal Ruffini for the conservatives. The conservatives favoured retention of a somewhat dogmatic theological style in the matter of words and propositions. The progressives favoured a style marked by more scriptural and patristic vocabulary, with images and descriptions calculated to appeal to the heart as well as to the mind. Bishop de Smedt of Bruges, Belgium, developed a magnificent intervention. In listing the defects of the *schema* he put together a memorable trilogy, maintaining that the *schema* was characterised by triumphalism, clericalism and legalism. Later he was reputed to have regretted that he ever invented that phrase because of the way it became his identification tag or trademark.

I had put my name down for an intervention and, as I described the situation in a letter that evening, invoking cricketing images, "I was called as eighteenth on the list this morning but stumps were drawn with four wickets still to fall so I'll have my pads on again on Monday morning. So far the artillery fire has been pretty heavy. We expect the counter-barrage on Monday morning – and I wouldn't be surprised if my name has slipped a little further down the list."

On Monday morning, 3 December, we reassembled in the *aula*. My name had slipped down to number 26 on the list, eight cardinals having indicated their intention to speak.

It was 11.30 when my turn came. I once again dealt with the issue of how to make the Council truly pastoral. I had sought the help of Father Yves Congar OP, who was only too willing to be of assistance.[5]

Tuesday 4 December, was noteworthy for three important interventions. The first was that of Cardinal Suenens, who communicated to the Council a programme that he had first presented to the Central Preparatory Commission eight months earlier: *Ecclesia ad intra* (the Church looking inwards) and *Ecclesia ad extra* (the Church looking outwards). Within the Church is Christ in his mystical body, evangelising, catechising, sanctifying through sacraments and praying. The outward concern of the Church would be with the human person, justice, the poor, peace and war.

This intervention received great applause as it seemed to provide a recognisable structure for discussing the reality and role of the Church at the present time.

Cardinal Montini gave support to the presentation of Cardinal Suenens. This was significant because Cardinal Montini was to become Pope Paul VI seven months later.

Another remarkable intervention was that of Cardinal Lercaro, Archbishop of Bologna. Later I was to be closely associated with him in the Concilium Liturgicum, the body set up by Pope Paul VI to work out how the liturgy would be renewed. Cardinal Lercaro referred to me as "my twin", as, despite our disparity in age, we were ordained bishop on the same day.

Cardinal Lercaro's intervention dealt with the poverty of the Church, in which he brought to the fore a concern that was being deeply and fervently discussed by a group of bishops, mainly French. Cardinal Lercaro called for limitation on the material acquisitions of the Church, simplification of episcopal appearance, fidelity to poverty in the individual lives of religious and in their community undertakings, and the elimination of what he referred to as patrimonial structures of the Church.

There was no applause for this intervention, it sounded like too strong an invitation to self-denial.

Immediately after the intervention of Cardinal Lercaro the Secretary General rose to communicate six points contained in a directive approved by the Holy Father and entrusted to the Secretary of State, Cardinal Cicognani, as follows:

1. *Schemas* must be re-examined and perfected by the respective conciliar commissions.

2. This work must be done in the light of the allocution of 11 October.

3. It is necessary to concentrate on principal *schemas*, especially the one on the Church, emphasising principles but not descending into details. Canonical matters should be left to the commissions.

4. A new commission is created to co-ordinate and direct future work. Its President will be the Cardinal Secretary of State.

5. Revised *schemas* must be sent to the bishops.

6. Conciliar commissions will work on the revision of *schemas* in the light of bishops' observations in the *aula*.

In my notes taken during the Council I find in capital letters this comment on the announcement: "MARVELLOUS, WE'RE ON THE WAY".

The debate continued for the rest of that period on Thursday 6 December.

We also completed the voting on chapters of the *schema* on the liturgy. All went well.

On Friday 7 December, the session began with announcements by the Secretary General concerning the closing ceremony later that morning, a canonisation on Sunday 9 December, the fact that there were still 54 names on the list of speakers and an invitation to send written observations, if Council members so wished, before 24 February 1963.

I spent some time outside the *aula* discussing English liturgical translations with Archbishop Grimshaw of Birmingham, England and Archbishop Hallinan of Atlanta, United States and Father Fred McManus of the Catholic University of Washington, a liturgical *peritus*; later, with Father Augustin Mayer OSB, Secretary of the Commission for Catholic Education and Seminaries. Then at 11.45 we were summoned to return to our places.

The Holy Father arrived, led us in the recitation of the *angelus* and gave a short allocution to mark the closing of the first period of the Council.

In my last letter of the period to Fathers Eric Boulle (Vicar General) and Geoff de Gersigny (Bursar) I asked them to organise a meeting in Durban at which I could speak of my experiences at the Council. This became a regular practice of mine as I endeavoured to share the great revolution that was taking place in the Catholic Church. Members of the Grail were great supporters of this undertaking and had me speaking in Johannesburg as well as in the Archdiocese of Durban.

Left:
Archbishop Denis Hurley OMI with Pope John XXIII and Bishop Gerard van Velsen OP in 1959 after the Pope had announced his intention to call the Second Vatican Council.

Below:
Archbishop Hurley outside St Peter's with Bernhard Moosbrugger (who took most of the photos included in this book) and Fr Tom Stransky (Paulist) in 1960.

Pope Paul VI

*Moderators of the Council, from left,
Cardinals Leo Suenens, Giacomo Lercaro, Julius Döpfner*

Cardinal Alfredo Ottaviani

Cardinal Laurean Rugambwa, first African cardinal and the most active African speechmaker in the Council.

Cardinal Franz König

Cardinal Joseph Cardijn

Yves Congar OP

Archbishop Pericle Felici,
Secretary General of the Council.

Edward Schillebeeckz OP

Cardinal Augustin Bea SJ

John Courtney Murray SJ

Paola Dezza SJ

Bernard Häring CSsR

Hans Küng

Archbishop Hurley in the Council

Pierre Teilhard de Chardin SJ at Sterkfontein Caves, 1951

Left:
A bishop consults the
theologian Marie-
Dominique Chenu OP.
"To a very large extent
theologians made
Vatican II." cf. pg. 122.

Below:
The Second Vatican
Council in session in
St. Peter's

Chapter Three

The Second Period

At the end of the first period we had been notified that the second would begin on 8 September 1963. A later notification indicated that the session would begin only on 29 September. Between the First and Second Periods Pope John XXIII had died on 3 June 1963 and Pope Paul VI had been elected on 21 June.

In due course special arrangements were made for bishops from South and East Africa to fly by a chartered Scandinavian plane during the last week of September. Bishops from Southern Africa and Rhodesia (now Zimbabwe) boarded the plane in Johannesburg, those from East Africa and Madagascar at Nairobi, others in Khartoum and duly arrived at the old airport in Rome.

Once again, missionary bishops of the Congregation of the Oblates of Mary Immaculate were welcomed into the wonderful hospitality of the Oblate General House.

The solemn opening of the second session took place on Sunday 29 September. Mass was celebrated by Cardinal Tisserant in the presence of the new Holy Father, Pope Paul VI, who gave an allocution that lasted the best part of an hour. His Holiness indicated clearly that he wanted the Council to proceed along the lines of *aggiornamento*, launched by his predecessor, Pope John XXIII. A few days previously he had given an address to the Curia calling on it to align itself wholeheartedly with this policy. The Pope included in his address to the Council some very heartfelt and touching words of sorrow and regret for offences committed by Catholics against members of other churches. This made a profound impact on observers from other churches present in the *aula*.

Next morning, Monday 30 September, the second period of the Council got under way but not before there had been some milling around on the part of Council fathers, looking for the new seats allocated to them. During the first period I had been in seat D78, the D standing for *dextera,* on the right hand side looking down from the sanctuary. My new seat was S66, the S standing for *senestra* meaning left. So it seemed that the number of archbishops senior to me had been reduced by at least 23 since the first period. Had they died or gone into retirement or found it just too difficult to come to the Council?

The Monday morning session began with several announcements from the Secretary General, Archbishop Pericle Felici. Among the topics were a message from the Council to the new pope, slight changes in the organisation and procedure of plenary sessions in the *aula,* and points about the proposing and accepting of *schemas,* the co-ordination of interventions and admission of new Council *periti* (consultors).

In regard to organisation and procedure, 12 presidents would remain but only four, designated in Latin *moderators,* would conduct meetings. The four were Cardinals Agagianian, Lercaro, Döpfner and Suenens.

The first *schema* on the agenda for the second period was on the Church. We were resuming the debate on this topic after the first *schema* had been rejected at the end of the first period.

A somewhat altered Commission to which quite a few progressive theologians had been added as consultors had been working on the new *schema* since December 1962. They had assisted appreciably in moving the text away from what had been a too scholastic and defensive mentality to a more scriptural and pastoral emphasis. "Scholastic" relates to the scholars or "schoolmen" who were the university professors of the middle ages. The greatest of them had been the Dominican, St Thomas Aquinas, who had taken over the philosophy of Aristotle, once it had entered Western Europe through the Arab philosophers of Spain. Aquinas found the thought patterns of Aristotle a suitable medium for clarifying and synthesising the revelation that Jesus had entrusted to his Church, and this form of theology gradually moved into the most prominent position in the Church. The result might have been subject to change as a consequence of the Renaissance but at the height of the Renaissance the Reformation broke out, marked by theological polemic and religious warfare. For the next 400 years after the Reformation the Church seemed continually on the defensive: against Protestantism, the consequences of the Scientific

Revolution and later the Industrial Revolution, the Enlightenment (a philosophy of human culture, development and rights that threatened to replace Christian faith in Western Europe), political revolution and the ideological revolution involving capitalism, socialism (particularly in its extreme form of Marxism), and fascism. It was a Church on the defensive: a fortress Church.

It could not go on living like that, so in due course a great revival began to emerge taking several forms: theological, liturgical, social and catechetical. The theological revival drew a great deal of its inspiration from the renewed study of scripture and of tradition enshrined in the writings of the so-called Fathers of the Church, like Basil and the Gregories of Cappadocia (now Turkey), Athanasius and Origen of Egypt, Jerome of Rome and the Holy Land, Augustine of North Africa, Ambrose of Milan and Popes Leo I and Gregory I.

Being a leader in the theological revival had not been easy or comfortable and several of the great theologians, who later served in the development of the Second Vatican Council, like the Dominicans Yves Congar and Marie-Dominique Chenu, and Jesuits Henri de Lubac, Karl Rahner and John Courtney Murray had been disciplined by the Holy Office, a Department of the Holy See charged with the duty of protecting the integrity of the Catholic faith. It was poetic justice when some of these theologians found themselves consultors to the bishops charged with the duty of giving expression to that faith more in keeping with the requirements of the times.

The debate on the acceptability of the new *schema* took up most of the morning of the first day of the new period of the Council. The vote in its favour accumulated 1 231 votes out of 2 301. We were on our way. Then began discussion of the *schema* chapter by chapter. The first chapter created no difficulty. It was entitled The Mystery of the Church. Mysteries are dealt with better by images than by concepts. To understand what is meant by this, one must remember that the human mind operates on two levels: the level of concept deals with abstract ideas like philosophical, mathematical and scientific formulas, and the level of image which is more strongly represented in the narrative and poetic. The two levels, of course, always function together but according to the field of operation there is more emphasis on one than on the other. If you want to present a truth firmly and clearly you concentrate on the concept. If you want to present it warmly and winningly you favour the image.

That first chapter fairly revelled in images and gave ample opportunity to each speaker in the *aula* to emphasise his preferred image: the People of God, the Kingdom of God, Kingdom of Christ, Body of Christ, Family of God, Bride of Christ. Over and above image preference, some called for greater emphasis on the future glory of the Church, some on the missionary dynamism of the Church, some on the poverty that should characterise the Church, some on the Mass as the sign and constitutive sacrament of the Church.

Bishop van Velsen OP of Kroonstad in South Africa got in just before the end of the debate to emphasise an ecumenical aspect: the appreciation of divine elements in non-Catholic Christian communities. His tone was in contrast with that of Archbishop Heenan of Westminster in England who laid it on the line that the big objective of the Catholic Church was to convert all non-Catholics – rather undiplomatic from a member of the Secretariat for Christian Unity – but apparently that is what the English hierarchy felt should be said.

Halfway through Friday morning the debate began on the second chapter of the *schema*: the hierarchy. The word, of Greek origin, means "sacred government". In the Catholic Church the hierarchy consists of three ranks: bishops, priests and deacons. The main issue under debate in the chapter on the hierarchy was the significance of bishops and the collegial character of their ministry. The debate lasted eight working days, from Friday 4 October to Tuesday 15 October, and dealt mainly with the issue of bishops. Some time was given to deacons because of the desire to revive their active role and, with that in mind, to allow married men to be promoted to the diaconal order. The order of the presbyterate, i.e. non-episcopal priests, was mentioned in only three interventions.

According to *aggiornamento* theologians, the image of the bishop needed reconditioning owing to historical circumstances and theological corrosion. The historical circumstances included, in the late 18th century, Gallicanism in France and Josephism in the Austro-Hungarian Empire. The reaction from Rome was obviously to re-affirm vigorously papal authority. Theological corrosion had the effect of insisting strongly on the distinction between the incremental power of a bishop and his power of jurisdiction. There was also a theological slide towards accepting that empowerment came not from the sacrament of episcopal orders but by delegation from the pope. This left very little episcopal power for auxiliary and titular bishops not in charge of dioceses.

The *aggiornamento* theologians looking very thoroughly into this situation had come up with conclusions like these: that by episcopal ordination a person became a member of a corporate body known as the College of Bishops and received his powers directly from Christ, not from the pope, though the pope, as head of the College, had the right to indicate where and how the powers could be exercised. Furthermore, having joined the College of Bishops and become successors of the apostles, all bishops were corporately responsible for evangelisation throughout the whole world. This was quite a shake-up to the image of bishops. No wonder it took eight working days to thrash it out. Missionary bishops were delighted at this new view that Archbishops of Milan and Madrid, New York, Westminster, Paris and Cologne had direct responsibility for missionary work in their territories. The financial implications sounded interesting.

All these considerations and several others came up for debate in the discussion on the hierarchy. In my capacity as Council correspondent for *The Southern Cross* I wrote as follows:

> The debate on collegiality opened dramatically with a fighting speech by the doughty conservative warrior of Palermo, Sicily, Cardinal Ruffini. He is a Scripture scholar and lets nobody get away with loose play around the Scriptural quotations. He maintained that he found no clear proof in the New Testament for collegiality. His speech was actually delivered on the Friday of the previous week[6]. He gave the *aggiornamento* theologians a busy weekend. They had to work overtime to assemble texts and arguments for the counterattack. This opened on Monday 7 with eight cardinals firing over open sites. After them came the irrepressible Patriarch of the Melchites, Maximus IV Saigh, who pointed out that too much emphasis on papal primacy made it difficult to promote reunion with the Orthodox Churches.

The Transalpines (cardinals and bishops from north of the Alps), as was to be expected, carried the main burden of the collegiality case. The

Italians and Spaniards were strongly represented among those who, with conservative caution, pointed out the uncertainties and pitfalls.

My article in *The Southern Cross* continued as follows:

> The week ended with another powerful Italian contribution, this time on the progressive side. The speaker was a young, newly-consecrated (five days previously) auxiliary of Bologna, Bishop Bettazzi. He charged into the fray spraying a torrent of eloquent Latin, gesticulating magnificently. In fifteen hectic minutes that galvanised a weary, end-of-the-week[7] assembly he poured out an imposing array of theological witnesses to prove that the Italian tradition was as surely behind collegiality as any other. Fifteen minutes! The comment was that Cardinal Lercaro, presiding that day, was so personally involved in this display of his young auxiliary that he forgot to be neutral and to ring the warning bell after the eighth minute, as the rules prescribed. (The warning bell is a very discreet tinkle on a telephone that hardly anybody other than the speaker hears.) Another speaker had been allowed extra time that day, Archbishop Slipyj, the man released recently from Siberia after 18 years.
>
> One weakness of the chapter on the hierarchy is that buried among its ten sections on pope and bishops is one solitary section devoted to priests and deacons. The deacon issue received treatment right from the beginning, as it involves some innovations in the modern Church, but the poor priests seemed destined for eternal oblivion. However, their day of salvation dawned on Wednesday, when three speakers emphasised their sorry plight: Bishop Anoveros, Coadjutor of Cadiz, Archbishop Conway of Armagh and Archbishop Hurley of Durban[8].
>
> The following day, Bishop Renard of Versailles rounded out the case for the priests with a splendid exposé of how, just as the bishops constitute a *collegium* around the Pope, so the priests constitute a *presbyterium* around the bishop.

My intervention was that, though by the very nature of episcopal ministry it belongs to the bishop to teach, to sanctify and to rule, ministries of teaching and sanctifying in their daily actuality and in nearly all their aspects, are fulfilled not by the bishop but by priests. I went on to say:

> To 99 out of 100 of his flock the bishop appears as an unfamiliar and remote figure, a complete unknown at the personal and human level. It is up to him to establish general directives, to arrange and organise diocesan business, to co-ordinate the various projects and

undertakings. But he most often has no direct hierarchic influence upon his flock; this is left to the priests, through whom the bishop does almost everything in the diocese. They are the bishop's hands and feet, his eyes and ears and voice. Just as no-one can act except through bodily organs, so too all the things that the bishop wishes to accomplish, all that he may hope to be done, depend completely on his priests to be put into effect. We all know that in the reading of pastoral letters, whether the bishop's words sound like the trumpet of an archangel or like a list from a telephone directory depends completely on the priest.

The conclusion of this intervention reads as follows:

> In order therefore that the priesthood may be dealt with as it deserves, I propose that chapter two be divided into three articles, so that it treats clearly and distinctly each level of the hierarchy – episcopacy, priesthood and diaconate.

A glance at the chapter on the hierarchy in the Dogmatic Constitution on the Church (*Lumen Gentium*), now Chapter 3, indicates that this proposal was not accepted.

Throughout the debate on the hierarchy, fairly frequent reference was made to the diaconate. Those who pleaded most powerfully for the permanent diaconate seemed to envisage the conferring of the order on men who had already proved themselves as laymen in the service of the Church. The order would give them sacramental status and grace and entitle them to perform a few sacred functions, like baptising, distributing communion and burying the dead, besides attending to instruction, visitation and parochial organisation. The strongest advocates of the idea did not want the obligation of celibacy imposed, as it would rule out too many deserving and capable candidates.

Opposition to the permanent diaconate hinged mainly on the question of celibacy. Some hair-raising pictures were painted of the conjugal misery to which married deacons could be reduced – unfaithful and garrulous wives, delinquent sons and fashion-conscious, beauty-queen daughters. Married deacons were also seen as the thin end of the wedge that would one day wreck the celibacy of the western clergy in general.

From certain mission territories, from South America (horribly short of priests) and from certain European countries, eloquent pleas were addressed to opponents of the permanent diaconate not to close the door but to leave open the possibility for those who thought they could use it. But those who were wary were not convinced that the permanent diaconate without celibacy should be permitted on a take-it-or-leave-it basis. The question was still wide open after eight days of debate.

At 11.45 on Tuesday 15 October, the closure vote was put by the day's moderator, Cardinal Suenens, and the shuffle and rustle of figures rising to signify the percent was like a great sigh of relief. But the relief was shortlived, for next morning it was announced that eight or nine speakers had claimed the right, enshrined in the new rules, to speak on behalf of groups of more than five after a vote of closure.

About halfway through Wednesday morning, 16 October, the debate on the hierarchy finally petered out and discussion began on Chapter Three of the *schema* on the Church: The People of God and the Laity in Particular. Already it had been generally accepted that the "People of God" would become a chapter on its own, preceding "The Hierarchy" (as the hierarchy also belongs to the people of God!) and "The Laity" would become Chapter Four.

I do not know if the slow pace of the Council was reminiscent of cricket in keeping with the story that the English, because of their low capacity for religion had to invent cricket to remind them of eternity, but in my report to *The Southern Cross* on the beginning of the debate on the laity I wrote that "Cardinal Ruffini played his usual role of opening batsman and, with the keen eye and built-in caution of a born opening bat, he dealt firmly with any swing he detected in theological terminology and biblical quotations." A Sicilian archbishop at the wicket!

Good speeches were made on the need for more emphasis on the Christian family, on the lay calling to life and work in the world, on the consecration of the world through Christian laity. But there was a problem on how to reflect on the laity without using negatives. It is hard to define lay people without saying that they are not clerics and not religious. Several suggestions were made but in practically every case the would-be definer of the laity was almost the whole way down the track with positive elements until, to the undisguised amusement of his audience, he fell at the last ditch with a jolting negative.

Bishop Menager of Meaux in France, applying some French logic and theology, suggested that we should term the people of God in all its theological fullness distinguishing between clergy, religious and laity by way of "enumeration" and not "negation".

Another thorny issue was that of the priesthood of the laity. Progressives pointed out that the laity, as part of the body of Christ, shared in his priesthood and shared too in his teaching ministry and kingship. Bishop Arneric of Sibernik, Yugoslavia, spoke movingly of the prophetic role of the family in lands where almost no other form of Christian teaching is possible and also of the liturgical role of family prayers. There were some in the ranks of the bishops who feared that their special priesthood was threatened by too much emphasis on the priesthood of the laity. They seemed to have visions of the laity invading the sanctuary – possibly crowding in behind the married deacons. Despite these misgivings the accent throughout the week was generally positive and it would have warmed the hearts of the laity the world over to hear what their bishops thought of them, how highly they were regarded, what trust and faith the bishops felt must be placed in them, what freedom, responsibility and initiative they must be given.

Some contributors to the debate called for a clarification of the word "charism". Some ventured into the field of Church-State relations and Bishop R. Tracy of Baton Rouge, Louisiana in the United States took occasion in reference to the universality of the Church to make a powerful speech against racial discrimination.

Cardinal Suenens spoke on Tuesday 22 October, about the need to have women among the lay observers in the Council. Observers were referred to as listeners by the Latin term *auditores* and Bishop Hakim of Palestine, who had Nazareth in his diocese, paid a powerful tribute to women for their magnificent share in the lay apostolate. He was applauded as he sat down. Cardinal Suenens, moderator of the day, proposed the closure vote. The alacrity with which the Council fathers rose to their feet seemed to indicate that they felt that the debate could not close on a better note. So the ladies had the last word – or nearly so. The next day a few unchivalrous speakers claimed the right to continue with the debate, speaking in the name of groups. However, before they had their say and as the closing act on Thursday, the question was debated as to whether a declaration on the Blessed Mother should be included in the *schema* on the Church or should be dealt with in a separate *schema*. Cardinal Santos of Manila, Philippines, presented the case for a separate *schema* and Cardinal König of Vienna spoke for inclusion in the *schema* on the Church. The vote was postponed until the following week.

The debate on the fourth chapter of the *schema* on the Church was begun during the last hour on Friday 25 October: Vocation to Sanctity in the Church. A special reference to the religious life was included in this chapter. The chapter emphasised that all members of the Church are called to sanctity and that there is a particular form of Christian life which gives special witness to this: the religious life.

Many speakers expressed satisfaction that the universal vocation to holiness and the religious life were treated together. This would help, they maintained, to dispel the illusion that the religious life had a sort of monopoly on holiness and that others were not expected to compete with them. Some, however, pointed out that it was illogical to combine the universal vocation to holiness with one particular form of Christian life in the same chapter. The call to holiness should have been treated, they argued, in the first or second chapter of the *schema* on the Church, because it concerned the whole mystery of the Church. The entire people of God and the religious deserved a chapter to themselves as much as the hierarchy and the laity because they constituted a very powerful influence in the Church.

Some speakers regretted that the holiness of the secular clergy had not been sufficiently emphasised, others that the bishops were somewhat overlooked in the general sharing out of holiness, and still others that the laity had not come in for their fair share. The Theological Commission would obviously have its work cut out trying to be just to all.

There appeared to be a certain lack of enthusiasm about the debate, possibly because many of the Council fathers were conscious of the fact that they were not such conspicuous examples of holiness themselves. However, some excitement was engendered with the announcement that the question concerning the Blessed Virgin would be decided by vote on Tuesday 29 October and that finally the four questions, now grown to five, that were to serve as a guide to the Theological Commission in its revision of the *schema* on the Church would also be put to the vote.

The question concerning Our Lady was whether she should have a special *schema* to herself or a chapter in the *schema* on the Church. Cardinal Santos of Manila and Cardinal König of Vienna presented arguments for the conflicting opinions on Thursday 24 October and the voting to choose between the two was held on Tuesday 29 October as previously announced. This left a little over four days for the canvassing of the two opinions. Many Italian and Spanish bishops and their theologians and some South American ones looked upon anything short of a special *schema* for Our Lady as an insult to her. Several tracts on Our Lady were hastily drawn up and circulated to the Council fathers. Those who did not share this opinion were equally convinced that Our Lady enjoyed being associated as intimately as possible with the Church. Besides, the presentation of Mary in the context of the Church and the whole mystery of salvation seemed more in keeping with the ecumenical spirit of the age. The *aggiornamento* theologians were mainly of this opinion and were kept very busy over the weekend addressing various groups of bishops. The French Catholic paper *La Croix* reported that Karl Rahner had addressed five groups himself in one day but that was probably a pious exaggeration. Anyhow, Karl Rahner and company were determined to keep Our Lady in the Church.

They only just succeeded. The vote, taken on Tuesday 29 October, was the closest yet recorded: 1 114 to 1 074.

On the same Tuesday the text of the five questions arising out of the debate on the hierarchy was distributed and the vote on them was taken on Wednesday. This did not leave much time for meetings, tracts and pamphlets. The purpose of the questions was to give the Theological Commission an idea of what the Council fathers felt in regard to the more hotly debated points. The substance of the questions is given below together with the voting results in this order: votes for, votes against, invalid votes.

1. Should the *schema* indicate that episcopal consecration constitutes the supreme degree of the sacrament of orders? 2 123 - 34 - 1

2. Should the *schema* indicate that every bishop, lawfully consecrated in communion with the other bishops and with the Roman Pontiff, is a member of the body of bishops? 2 049 - 104 - 1

3. Should the *schema* indicate that the body or college of bishops succeeds the college of apostles in preaching, sanctifying and pastoral functions and that, together with the Roman Pontiff and never without him and without detriment to the primacy, enjoys full and sovereign power in the universal Church? 1 808 - 366 - 4

4. Should the *schema* indicate that the episcopal college, united to its head, enjoys power by divine right? 1 717 - 408 - 13

5. Should the *schema* make provision for the restoration of the diaconate as a distinct and permanent degree of the sacred ministry for use according to local requirements? 1 588 - 525 - 7

There was no reference to the thorny question of celibacy in the question on the diaconate.

The overwhelming favourable response to the five questions gave the Council a psychological lift. The *aggiornamento* theologians were overjoyed. For them the collegial responsibility of the bishops was the hinge of the whole Council. They saw all the seeds of future reform in its acceptance. The long debates of October were forgotten in the joy of the bright dawn of collegial collaboration.

The answers to the five questions did not settle them once and for all. These answers were only a guide to the Theological Commission in its revision of the *schema* on the Church.

The week embracing the last few days of October and the first two of November was a very short working week, consisting of three days only. Monday 28 October was taken up with the celebration of the anniversary of the election of Pope John XXIII. The Church in Rome has a strong feeling for occasions and lets nothing interfere with the celebration of them. We owe the Council to Pope John so this was an excellent opportunity of saying thank you. Mass was celebrated by Pope Paul VI, his successor, and was followed by a magnificent and inspiring sermon preached in French by Cardinal Suenens, a sermon that went a long way towards capturing the spirit of the great pope of the *aggiornamento*.

Friday of the same week was to be All Saints' Day and Saturday All Souls' Day. So the week's work had to be crowded into three days. This was a pity because it cut down the time given to the treatment of sanctity in the Church, an important aspect of Church life if ever there was one.

Thursday 31 October was really a bad day for speakers. The closure vote had been passed the previous day but by now the Council, though suffering from long drawn-out debates, seemed unable to get them out of its system. The malaise arising out of the rushed closure showed itself in the number of speakers who applied to have their say on behalf of groups. Twenty-five were named and that apparently did not exhaust the list. Cardinal Döpfner, moderator for the day, was determined to push them along. Speaking time was reduced. Deviations from the point were mercilessly called to order. Repetitions were cut short. It couldn't have been pleasant to be a speaker that day. No wonder it was suggested that Cardinal Döpfner should be referred to as His Vehemence.

After the four days' break consisting of All Saints' Day, All Souls' Day, Sunday and the celebration on Monday of the fourth centenary of the decree of the Council of Trent concerning seminaries, Vatican II finally got back to work again on Tuesday 5 November. A new *schema* was presented for debate. Its title was "Bishops and the Government of Dioceses". It was introduced by the president of the Commission responsible for it, Cardinal Marella, and was presented by Bishop Carli of Segni, one of the toughest of the hard core of conservatives in the Council. He had to explain that, owing to pressure of work and a somewhat complicated interchange between the coordinating commission and the commission responsible for the *schema*, this commission had never had a full meeting of its members to finalise the *schema* before its publication. Obviously, behind that difficulty of holding meetings lay a problem of communication.

In the debate on acceptability the French hierarchy was particularly to the fore, having, so it appeared, come back from the All Saints' break full of fight. Of the 13 speakers who managed to get in a word on Tuesday, six belonged to the French *force de frappe*. The vote in favour of acceptability went through by 1 610 votes to 477, registering a more than 20 % attitude of opposition. On Thursday and Friday the first chapter of the *schema* was discussed: relations between bishops and the Curia, and, wonder of wonders, it died a natural death without the intervention of the guillotine. Perhaps the guillotine was unnecessary after the fireworks of Friday morning. About which more later.

The question occupying centre stage was how to give practical expression to the newly-emphasised collegiality of the bishops and their participation with the Holy Father in the government of the Church. There was strong support for the establishment of a council of bishops representing the hierarchies of the world and meeting with the Pope from time to time to deal with major issues concerning the Church. The Holy Father had himself invited discussion on this possibility in his speech to the Curia on 21 September. There were naturally differences of opinion in regard to the details of organisation and operation.

Excellent speeches in favour of the idea were made by Cardinals König, Alfrink and Bea, but one of the best presentations of the subject came from an outstanding member of the Italian hierarchy, Archbishop Florit of Florence, though he made the reservation that he could not accept juridical collegiality as the theological foundation of the idea. Archbishop Florit looked and spoke, to some extent, like an enlarged slightly more theological edition of Pope John XXIII. African support for the idea of the "episcopal synod" came from Cardinal Rugambwa and Archbishop McCann who spoke on behalf of the bishops of South Africa and Southern Rhodesia (now Zimbabwe).

The French, running true to form, complained that the *schema* was sadly deficient in theology. Archbishop Veuillot, Coadjutor of Paris, maintained that the *schema* could not be properly discussed until the theological question of collegiality had been more thoroughly dealt with.

The Anglo-Americans wondered when they would be given a little respite from theology in order to get on with the job of organising the Church. They had already given an example of practical collegiality by forming a nine-nation liturgical "common market" to work towards uniform liturgical texts in English. This was later given the name "International Commission on English in the Liturgy."

Theology, however, would not lie down. The theological misgivings of the conservative wing concerning collegiality came to the surface continually. Cardinal Ruffini of Palermo and Cardinal Browne, a Dominican and formerly Professor of Theology at the Angelicum (now the University of St Thomas) whose lectures I attended during my first year of theology, pointed out that the answers to the test questions of the week before had by no means settled the issue. Cardinal Browne spoke with emphasis and feeling as he hammered out the point that acceptance of episcopal collegiality with the inherent right to share in the government of the Church must inevitably detract from papal primacy. He came back on this point in a second speech during the week – a short, powerful, prophetic warning that culminated in a resounding *caveamus* (let us beware). Even the calmest of Irishmen become great orators in moments of stress.

The collegialists pointed out that they had no intention of limiting papal primacy. They just wanted the fact recognised that the episcopate is of divine origin and received a divine and corporate mandate to preach the gospel and govern the Church *with and under* Peter. The stumbling block of the pure primacists seemed to lie in the expression "fullness of power" in regard to the papacy. If the bishops share in his power, they asked, how can the pope have the fullness of power? He has fullness of power, replied the collegialists, within the limit of the divine constitution of the Church, which constitution provides for the existence of an episcopate, which cannot be abolished by the pope. If there must be bishops there must be some reason for them, namely, participation under the pope in the government of the Church.

That is how theology kept intruding into practical discussions of the episcopal office.

The Melkite Patriarch, Maximos IV Saigh, rose to his greatest height. He specialised in cutting the Curia down to size and putting cardinals in their place. The present College of Cardinals, he complained, had its historical origin in the organisation of the clergy of Rome. Born with this original sin, it could never be truly representative of the universal Church. The new sacred college should include patriarchs (in first place!), cardinals who are residential bishops and heads of bishops' conferences. Such a college would contribute substantially to universalising the Church and promoting its adaptation to varying conditions in the world, with special reference to the emerging Catholic communities of Asia and Africa.

There always seemed to be an Oriental willing to trade punches with His Beatitude of Antioch. This time it was the Patriarch of Armenia, Ignatius Peter XVI Batanian. He put the sacred college back in perspective by pointing out that after all, the pope is the pope and he has the right to constitute his advisory council the way he wants to. For this spirited defence of the Curia he received great praise from Cardinal Ruffini – praise that lost some of its impact when His Eminence mentioned that the Patriarch was a beloved past pupil of his.

In the free and easy general discussion of Tuesday and Wednesday, comment ranged far and wide over the contents of the *schema*. Bishops' conferences were discussed. True to form the French called for a theological foundation for bishops' conferences. Bishop Browne of Galway (also a Michael Browne, but not to be confused with Cardinal Michael Browne) made a great speech. Bishops, he said, should be left to run their dioceses without too much interference from bishops' conferences or other sources. The Irish hierarchy had been holding regular meetings for 100 years without ever hearing of collegiality and without getting involved in too much red tape. "Collegiality for the Irish", came an unkind comment, "means living in the same island". Bishop Browne's misgivings about bishops' conferences had already found earlier expression in speeches by Cardinal Ruffini and Cardinal McIntyre of Los Angeles.

The general discussion had also brought to the fore the idea that residential bishops should not be given a list of special powers or "faculties" by the Holy See, as if these powers did not belong to the office and had to be specially delegated. It would be better, it was maintained, to consider a bishop as having all powers to rule his diocese except in regard to special matters reserved to the Holy Father. The list should include reservations and not powers.

Throughout the week there was the odd outburst of sniping against the Curia, answered from time to time by those who found it difficult to see in the Curia the heartless machine that was being painted for them. The Curia's defenders remembered kind and courteous officials who helped them with their problems and administered the law humanely.

These exchanges were mere skirmishes in comparison with what was to come at the end of the week.

On Friday Cardinal Frings was speaking in his carefully thought out, clearly enunciated, graceful Germanic Latin. As he was nearly totally blind he had difficulty with notes but spoke far better than most of the others. Suddenly the assembly was rigid with attention: His Eminence, on the Holy Office. Quietly, affectionately, the kindly old professor delivering a lecture, he voiced a complaint that had been general in Catholic intellectual circles for some time. His Eminence complained that the methods of the Holy Office were not up to date: it reproved and condemned authors without hearing them in their own defence. To many of the *aggiornamento* theologians it must have sounded like something out of a fairy tale: that here in St Peter's before the Catholic hierarchy of the whole world a great cardinal was saying what so many of them had experienced and suffered. They had been trying to do what theologians must do in every age: restate the faith in the contemporary idiom and in relation to contemporary problems. The Holy Office had not always understood, for, like all ancient institutions it was tied to ancient vocabulary and outdated methods. There was applause for Cardinal Frings.

The Council fathers noticed that the name of Cardinal Ottaviani was on the speakers' list two or three positions after that of Cardinal Frings. When the time came for Cardinal Ottaviani to speak there was not an empty seat in the *aula*. He was the highest official of the Holy Office, of which the Holy Father himself was the head. His sight was not too good but he had no need of notes to speak his eloquent and elegant Latin. He said that before coming to the speech he had prepared he had a few remarks to make. One could have heard a pin drop in St Peter's. The passionate outburst of His Eminence reverberated over the hushed assembly. What had been said about the Holy Office, he asserted, could only have proceeded from ignorance, if nothing worse. The Pope was the head of the Holy Office so any criticism of the Holy Office was a reflection on the Pope. It was a protest, but not an answer, for it merely transferred to the Pope the blame for whatever was wrong with the manner and methods of the Holy Office.

Cardinal Ottaviani then turned to the speech he had prepared, a complaint about the way in which the five questions had been put the week before. The formulation was bad, he maintained, and could have been vastly improved had the questions come under the scrutiny of the Theological Commission. Though His Eminence had only a minority of support in the assembly, its sporting instinct rose to the occasion and expressed itself in a great burst of applause (applause was prohibited but it broke out from time to time). This time the applause was hardly for the content but rather for the style. It reminded me of a Macaulay poem we had learnt in school about how Horatius kept the bridge against Tuscan invaders of Rome so that "even the ranks of Tuscany could scare forbear to cheer". On this occasion the progressives were the Tuscans. It looked as if those five famous questions and the answers to them were in for a torrid time. Both the President of the Theological Commission, Cardinal Ottaviani, and the Vice President, Cardinal Browne, disagreed with the answers so overwhelmingly given to them. Were they going to consider it their duty to be guided by the replies or to oppose them with every means in their power?

Further to this situation, at this time about halfway through the second period of the Council the chief item of concern seemed to be the Theological Commission. As I wrote to a friend,

> The Commission has a mountain of work as a result of the five weeks of debate on the *schema* on the Church. The President, Cardinal Ottaviani, and the Secretary, Father Tromp, seemed quite happy to let things drift along with one two-hour meeting a week; until somebody went to the pope. The outcome was a directive from the Holy Father to get on with the washing. The Commission now meets every afternoon in seven or eight sub-commissions. They are the galley-slaves of the Council. The curial tactic seems to be either play for time with the delaying game or kill off the *aggiornamento* theologians with overwork. The underground is still simmering restlessly. The general feeling is that the President and Secretary of the Theological Commission can control progress on the revision of the *schemas* to their heart's content; so a strong petition has been sent forward for a new election of commissions and according to the commissions the right to elect their own chairmen and secretaries. One wonders whether anything will come of it in this session. It took two whole weeks to get a decision on four or five guide questions that the moderators wanted put to the general assembly to serve as indications to the Commission of what it should say about the sacramentality and collegiality of the episcopate. Council morale

was at a low ebb at the end of October. Wild proposals were beginning
to fly around again for a change of procedure. The trouble is everybody
has his own plan. However, the overwhelmingly favourable answers
to the five guide questions have restored morale to some extent.

The next working week of the Council began on Monday 11 November.
The agenda for this week included discussion of coadjutor and auxiliary
bishops, retirement and removal of a bishop from one diocese to another.

A coadjutor bishop is one appointed to succeed another with right of
succession if the latter dies or retires. An auxiliary bishop is one appointed
as an assistant without right of succession. His position often has very
little ecclesiastical stature, but the debate in the Council had shown that
anybody ordained a bishop belonged to the College of Bishops and was a
successor of the apostles.

Much was said about retirement, but no conclusion was reached about
a statutory age for retirement. That had to be decided later by the Holy
Father. Concerning the removal of bishops from one diocese to another,
the negative aspect of this phenomenon was pointed out by Cardinal
Suenens when he mentioned that if there were any value in the image of
mystical nuptials between a bishop and his diocese, a great number of
bishops in the Council were divorcees.

There was also some discussion on the problem of dioceses. Some had
become such enormous metropolitan complexes that it was difficult for
them to retain the traditional image of dioceses.

The opposite problem was also found in Italy where there was a
multiplicity of small dioceses.

The discussion died a natural death at 11.45 on Friday 15 November
and the moderator kindly allowed the adjournment half an hour before the
usual time. The Council fathers streamed out into the bright autumn sunlight
of St Peter's Piazza like scholars who had been granted a long weekend
without homework.

Not all, however, would be without homework. A very important
meeting was to be held that evening involving the Council of Presidents,
the Coordinating Commission and the Moderators. The pope himself was
to preside. Had the famous five test questions on the *schema* concerning
the Church brought matters to a head? Who had authority to do what?

What was the mandate of the moderators? What were the powers of presidents of commissions? Outside of those queries were people in powerful positions who could not accept the majority view of the Council. This was blocking the work of certain commissions, in particular the Theological Commission.

In the end some decisions might depend on the man holding the primacy. He needed much prayer to enable him to hold the Council firmly on course and to render certain commissions more workable.

The eighth week of the second period of the Council opened on Monday 18 November. It was a relief to have come to the end of all questions involving the identity and activity of bishops. Ecumenism was to be the topic of the week's discussions. But we got off to a slow start owing to the fact that so many other concerns had to be dealt with, like final voting on the last chapters of the *schema* on the liturgy, discussed in the previous period, and announcements about alterations to the Council commissions. From now on the membership of most commissions was to be increased from 25 to 30 and each was to have an additional vice-president and secretary. Lists of candidates were to be prepared over the weekend and voting was to take place the following week.

The *schema* on Ecumenism presented to the Council consisted now of five chapters:

1. The Principles of Catholic Ecumenism

2. The Practice of Ecumenism

3. Christians Separated from the Catholic Church

4. The Jews

5. Religious Liberty

Cardinal Amleto Cicognani gave a general introduction. Archbishop Martin of Rouen, speaking Latin with a French accent strong enough to defend Gaul against Julius Caesar, gave a report on the first two chapters of the *schema*. He spoke with warmth and enthusiasm and received a good round of applause. A further three reports were given on Tuesday morning, 19 November: the first on the Oriental Churches by Bishop Bukatko, Coadjutor of Beograd, Yugoslavia; the second on the Jews by

Cardinal Bea and the third on Religious Liberty by Bishop de Smedt of Bruges, Belgium.

The debate on the acceptability of the *schema* in general ran from Monday 18 until Thursday 21 November with the multiplicity of interruptions referred to earlier. The main objections to it bore on the inclusion of the chapter on the Jews, on the treatment of Orthodox and Protestant Christians in the same chapter and on the issue of religious liberty.

Some speakers felt that the great difference between Orthodox and Protestant Christians should be reflected more fully in the treatment accorded to the two groups.

The chapter on the Jews came under heavy fire from the Orientals who live in an Arab and Muslim culture. They could not see why the Jews should receive special treatment in a *schema* devoted to a specifically Christian issue. Other speakers pointed out how invidious it could appear to deal with Jews and not with other non-Christian bodies. It is certainly a delicate issue and much as one can see the point of referring to the Jews because of Christianity's deep roots in Israel and the *amende honorable* we owe the Jews for so much unchristian anti-semitism, obviously the problems involved had to be carefully weighed.

The objection against the chapter on Religious Liberty was that it was not a specifically ecumenical question. It belonged to the discussion of human rights which pertained to the future S*chema XIII* on *The Effective Presence of the Church in the World.* Along with this procedural argument a few of the old chestnuts were trotted out: about error having no rights and people having no right to be wrong. The affable Archbishop Florit of Florence was responsible for one of those "unfreedom" speeches. It did not seem to suit his character but he belonged to the Italian tradition in this matter. In speaking, however, he very graciously quoted the French author and "lay auditor", Jean Guitton, who once commented that in the Council there are no victors and no vanquished, for to be vanquished by the truth is to be in truth a victor.

In the Anglo-American world it may appear a little surprising that the Catholic Church still had difficulties about religious liberty. The issue looks clear enough: who can prevent a person from worshipping God the way he or she wants to? The Church cannot. It has no means of coercion. The Swiss guards would not be particularly keen on the job. The State cannot. It has no right to interfere in matters of religion, unless religious exuberance upsets the public order.

This is how simple it looked in some parts of the world. But there was a much more complicated background of history and tradition. In the Middle Ages a Catholic culture prevailed, a culture in which religious and civil interests were inextricably entangled and the stage was reached where heresy in religion constituted rebellion against the civil society. The pope became a sort of president of a federation of Christian states and he got involved directly or indirectly in the violent suppression of heresy from which the Inquisition emerged. From where we stand now it all looks cruel and unchristian, but at the time it looked fairly normal and necessary.

Add to this the theological and philosophical problems. The scholars wrestled with the right to obey one's conscience against the law of God and of the Church, with the rights of error as against truth and the right of a person to be wrong. Those who accepted that the Reformation and the era of revolution rejected the authority of the Church had no theoretical difficulty about admitting freedom of conscience and freedom to err, but it was not so easy for the Catholic theologians who had an authoritative Church with a divine mandate and guarantee to uphold. The situation got very confused in the 19th century when those on the side of freedom were there mainly because they denied God and those against freedom were there because they believed in God. Besides, too much political freedom would have been bad for the pope's hold on the Papal States of which he remained the sovereign until 1870. Some rather sticky papal statements came out in the course of the 19th century about freedom of conscience and freedom generally. In their historical context they are understandable but taken absolutely they need some subtle interpretation.

In Italy and Spain, where society had remained officially Catholic, the 19th century outlook still seemed valid in the 1960s. The rest of the Catholic world was moving on rapidly to other views. The moving on had been occasioned mainly by direct experience of freedom from state entanglement or the lack of it. But the experience had made the theologians think and a new theology of freedom was in rapid progress of formation – with its roots, of course, in solid Catholic doctrine and the duty of a person to be obedient to conscience.

The question of religious liberty had obviously much to do with ecumenism. Some Protestant scholars were saying: "We cannot really begin to talk to you until you come out unequivocally on the side of freedom, for we are not interested in promoting any sort of Christian unity in which the old Catholic restrictions on freedom have some say." One prominent American observer said that he would be happy if, as far as ecumenism was concerned, the Council managed nothing more than an all-out declaration on religious liberty.

About halfway through the session of Thursday 21 November, the question of closure was put and strongly supported. In regard to voting on acceptability it was announced that because there had been so much difference of opinion on the last two chapters of the *schema* the vote of acceptability would not apply to them but only to the first three chapters, the genuinely ecumenical ones. The vote in favour was 1 966 to 86.

The discussion in detail of chapters 1, 2 and 3 of the *schema* on ecumenism began immediately that Thursday morning, 21 November. The chapters dealt with the unity of the Church and its links with separated brothers and sisters and what ecumenism intends in regard to self-criticism, self-improvement, the recognition of the Christian heritage in other churches and the action of the Holy Spirit in those churches. Reservations were expressed by those who had had little experience of mixing with non-Catholic Christians. Spanish cardinals and bishops were anxious about what could happen in Spain if Protestants were given full freedom to proselytise. Cardinal Ruffini and Bishop Carli of Segni were the main exponents of Italian misgivings.

In a different vein the assembly heard strong support for the *schema* from Cardinal Ritter of St Louis, USA, and an impassioned plea from Cardinal Quintero of Caracas, Venezuela for an addition to the *schema* expressing Catholic confession of guilt for our share in the sundering quarrels of the past.

Two of the most memorable speeches were made by Bishop Elchinger, Auxiliary of Strasbourg, and the new Archbishop of Westminster, Dr. Heenan.

Bishop Elchinger maintained that ecumenism required the honest presentation of historical facts. It must be admitted that at first those who separated from us had no intention of breaking with the Church. Their first concern was to reaffirm basic doctrines or traditions. In the case of the Orthodox, it was the question of the rites of the ancient apostolic churches. In the case of the reformers it was the question of justification by faith in Christ as defined in the Council of Jerusalem, of personal responsibility, of the importance of scripture and the freedom of the children of God. Ecumenism, according to Bishop Elchinger, also required that along with insistence on unity of faith in sacraments, a certain freedom should be allowed in matters of church institutions and rites. He had another stinging point about the separated brethren having more confidence in their scripture experts than the Catholics.

Archbishop Heenan spoke on behalf of the bishops of England and Wales and it did not take long to realise that what he was saying had been thoroughly discussed and prepared. He expressed joyful acceptance of the *schema* and maintained that it could no longer be held that English Catholics were indifferent to ecumenism. He gently chided those who felt that they must leave England for ecumenical dialogue. The dialogue, he said, must take place in the home country and under the conditions in which the participants normally live. He pointed out a deficiency in the *schema* arising out of the failure to distinguish carefully between the ultimate aim of ecumenism and its proximate object. The proximate object was a conversation between communities with a view to understanding one another's faith. The ultimate aim was the visible union of Christians, but this must be left to God.

In making this distinction Archbishop Heenan went a long way towards clearing up the unfortunate impression created on separated Christians by his earlier proclamation of the Church's firm determination to convert them all. Such conversion belongs to the ultimate aim, as Catholics see it, but ecumenism is impossible if the ultimate aim is nailed to the masthead. Catholics and Protestants see the ultimate aim differently, but that does not mean to say that they must keep emphasising the difference nor that the difference must prevent them from collaborating on the immediate objective: understanding.

Having appeased the separated brethren, Archbishop Heenan turned to allaying the suspicions of the Catholic camp by saying that the *schema* must affirm the obligation to preach the whole truth. He concluded a very moving address by declaring that the hierarchy of England and Wales was prepared to do everything short of denying the faith to promote the union of Christians.

So, taking it all round, it was a good week. The work on the liturgy was completed and the debate on ecumenism well launched.

Then on Friday evening came the thunderbolt of the assassination of President Kennedy. As it appeared from Rome the whole free world mourned the gallant leader and wept with the stricken Jacqueline and her children.

There was something of an anticlimax about the ninth and last week of the second period of the Council. So much had been said about the Council being a Council of ecumenism but in the end, after the promise of the eighth week, ecumenism did not set St Peter's on fire. There were several reasons. The American tragedy certainly had something to do with it. People who had seen the full television portrayal could not find it easy to banish from their minds the image of a stunned and mourning nation and the memory of the incredibly brave widow and her little ones.

Then there were the interruptions: announcements of one kind and another, especially those dealing with the election of the new commission members. This election had been very well prepared through the collaboration of a great number of bishops' conferences. The common list of candidates they had drawn up swept the board.

The procedure was that the names had to be written in spaces provided on an 11-page ballot form. These forms were given out on Wednesday 27 November and had to be handed in the next day. The results were announced on Friday 29 November and Southern Africa was gratified to hear that Archbishop McCann was among the four elected to the Commission on Bishops and the Government of Dioceses and that Bishop Lamont of what was then Umtali in Rhodesia was among the eight new members of the Secretariat for Christian Unity.

Almost the totality of the new commission members reflected in greater or lesser degree the majority view of the Council so that it swung the commissions more to the side of the *aggiornamento*. In due course additional vice presidents and secretaries were to be elected.

One other interruption was the vote on the *schema* concerning instruments of social communication which was taken on Monday 5 November and resulted in the *schema* being approved for promulgation by 1 598 to 503. One of the 503 votes was mine.

There seemed to be something unusual about the way this *schema* had got where it was. It dealt with press, radio, television and cinema, on which it purported to set out the Church's attitude. The *schema* had been debated for two and a half days in November 1962, approved in substance and sent back to the Commission to be amended and shortened. It had suddenly reappeared in November this year in its new form and had been submitted to vote in two chapters on 14 November. Both chapters had got through with very substantial majorities. This was surprising as there had been no debate on the revised *schema* and in itself it did not seem to contain the sort of declarations that Councils are called for.

When it was realised that the *schema* was coming up for a final vote there was a sudden eruption of concern. Fathers of the Council began to express their dismay to one another and in due course a petition was drawn up addressed to the Council of Presidents asking them to declare it illegal to proceed to a general vote at this stage. Two articles of the Order of Celebrating the Council were invoked: Article 33.2 which requires that on any *schema* there should first be a general debate and subsequently a debate on particular issues, and Article 60.3 requiring that the General Secretary read every amendment and that there be a vote by *placet* or *non placet* on each amendment.

On the copy of this petition that I received I wrote the following note: "Submitted to meeting of African Presidents of Conferences, Saturday November 23, reply: *schema* will probably be rejected in the final vote".

On Monday morning, 25 November, there was something of a scene in the Piazza of St Peter which I did not witness. Apparently some Council fathers were handing out a paper to others and in one case there appears to have been a bit of pulling-and-pushing between two otherwise dignified ecclesiastics, with an embarrassed policeman wondering what to do.

On the paper was an urgent appeal to Council fathers to vote *non placet* in regard to the *schema* on the Instruments of Social Communication.

The names included Bishop Volk of Mainz, Bishop Reuss, Auxiliary Bishop of Mainz, Bishop Schmidt of Metz, Bishop Carboy of Monze, Northern Rhodesia, and Bishop Bogarin from Paraguay. The name that caused me most surprise was that of Bishop Hugh Boyle of Johannesburg, who was the last person I would expect to get involved in matters of this kind. Why my name was not on the list I cannot imagine. Possibly the promoters of it failed to contact me over the weekend.

Later, in the course of the morning, Cardinal Tisserant issued a stern rebuke to those involved in the scuffle in the piazza, saying that the Council of Presidents and the moderators deplored behaviour unworthy of the Council.

There still seemed to be one way of opposing the promulgation of this *schema* as a decree of the Council and that was by trying to have it annulled on the grounds that the procedure leading to its adoption had been illegal, that is, not in conformity with the requirements of the Order of the Celebration of the Council. I tried this procedure, presenting my argument to the body known as the Administrative Tribunal, claiming that in regard to the *schema* on the Instruments of Social Communication, the non-compliance with the Order of Celebration of the Council, could give rise to doubts concerning its value as a Council document. My submission was based on the same two articles of the Order, namely, 33.2 and 60.3. The submission was made with the help of Bishop Reuss, Auxiliary Bishop of Mainz in Germany, on 28 November. The reply from His Eminence was dated 17 December 1963 and reached me some days later together with a copy of a report from the Administrative Tribunal, which was couched in the calm, courteous and canonical Latin of the Curia.

The report indicated that, because there were only three days remaining before the public session of the Council on 4 December 1963, the issue had been treated as a matter of urgency. The decision of the Tribunal amounted to this: that, before the discussions began on the *schema* on 23 November 1962, the Secretary General had announced that the *schema* would be treated both in general and in its particular parts, to which no difficulty or opposition was raised by the assembly. Consequently there was no offence against the requirements of the Order.

Some time later I wrote to thank His Eminence, Cardinal Roberti, for his reply. I cannot understand now why I left it at that and did not raise the question as to what person or body had the right to allow exceptions to the rules. Perhaps the promulgation by Pope and College of Bishops wiped out any lingering stains of original sin.

Reverting to Monday 25 November, the final vote on the *schema* was held and resulted in the score mentioned earlier. The *schema* was now ready to go ahead for promulgation on 4 December.

All this contributed to drawing attention away from the main topic of the week, ecumenism. The end-of-term feeling also contributed. After two long, tiring months with up to 15 speeches a day, even the toughest fathers were beginning to wilt. The coffee bars were no help. You couldn't get in. And once in, it was almost impossible to get out. It was concentrated collegiality and solidarity. Just thinking of the break-up due the following week took minds off the debate. It was a pity, because ecumenism was to be one of the great topics of the Council.

As the week drew to an end there were few memorable speeches but a number of sensitive issues were touched upon. The use of the word "churches" for non-Catholic communions without inhibition was recommended by one speaker. Another advocated the revision of textbooks with a view to eliminating slanted Church history. Cardinal Frings mentioned religious schools and mixed marriages.

The obligation, he said, must remain for the Catholic party to insist on the Catholic upbringing of the children, though he favoured the recognition of the validity of mixed marriages contracted outside the Catholic Church. Reference was also made to the painful problem of Protestant proselytism in Latin America. Archbishop Blanchet, Rector of the Institut Catholique of Paris spoke well on the intellectual approach to the ecumenical problem and referred to Cardinal Newman's great contribution in his Essay on the Development of Dogma.

Cardinal Bea as usual spoke well, but he was merely answering criticism and repeating in different words what the *schema* said already about common (though not officially liturgical) prayer with the separated brethren, revision of Catholic attitudes, presentation of doctrine and collaboration in the solution of social problems. Many Council fathers who had scarcely ever met a Protestant or Orthodox Christian took off on theory and mysticism.

Those unacquainted with conditions in the Middle East did, however, learn something of the situation there – of the tenacious traditions and prejudices and how often in the past ill-informed Latins had blundered into tramping on sensitive Oriental corns.

The drawback about the discussion was that the theology of ecumenism had been exhausted in a day or two (even the French ran out of theological clues) and very few speakers had had any real experience of ecumenical dialogue on which to talk. Three Anglophone contributors injected the spice of reality into the debate. Bishop Leven, Auxiliary of San Antonio, Texas, had been bottling up some strong feelings about the way he thought certain Latin hierarchies imagined that they had the monopoly of Catholic tradition. He let go in a speech that drew some rather unfortunate comparisons between where the faith is known and where it is not known, where the pope is respected and where he is not respected, where Catholics vote communist and where they do not. Bishop Dwyer of Leeds, England, also spoke realistically of his experience of what some of the separated brethren believe about Christ, the virgin birth and the resurrection. In the sense that it was not flattering it was scarcely ecumenical. Bishop Goody of Bunbury, Australia, also gave some valuable reflections from personal experience.

But in reality ecumenism had been talked out three or four days before the end. Cardinal Döpfner tried to convey this idea when, in calling for a closure vote at one stage, he referred to the meditations and pious exhortations into which the debate had resolved itself.

The last "general congregation" or plenary debating assembly of the second period of the Council took place on Monday 3 December. Twelve speakers battled manfully with the distractions caused by secretarial announcements and the last-day-of-term atmosphere.

Cardinal Ruffini was the first to speak, making a final addition to his already impressive batting average. He enumerated carefully the foundations of the Catholic faith that must in no way be affected by the ecumenical spirit.

Bishop Green of Port Elizabeth made an excellent contribution. He spoke on two aspects of Anglican orders. He asked whether it would be possible for the Council to take up again the question of validity and raised the practical issue of making arrangements for convert married Anglican clergy in the Catholic priesthood.

Bishop Muldoon, Auxiliary of Sydney, Australia, was in a fighting mood. He had listened too long to praises of the separated brethren and exhortations to Catholics to apologise for their share of the guilt in the clashes of the past. He asked the assembly not to imagine that there was nothing but goodwill on the side of the Protestants and urged those who felt in a penitential mood to find a good confessor but, in the name of God, *"parcite nobis"* – Latin for "spare us". Abbot Butler of Downside subsequently took him gently but firmly to task. He wondered if the news of the Reformation had reached Australia and suggested that Catholics could not very well repent in private and in public act the pharisee while leaving the publican's role to the separated brethren. It was top class Oxford Union debating. A little more of it would have made St Peter's a livelier place.

Cardinal Bea wound up the debate later in the morning and expressed his regret that it had been impossible to deal with the chapters on the Jews and religious liberty for lack of time. He emphasised lack of time as the reason. This meant that the directing powers had not been ready without further debate about whether the two chapters were acceptable as the basis of discussion.

Why not? The consequences could be far-reaching in several countries. Those who live in the Arab world and in countries where other important non-Christian faiths prevail are nervous about the chapter on the Jews, and in regard to religious liberty it is considered dynamite in Italy and Spain. The issue is complicated by political considerations. In Spain the state supports the Church. Will too much talk of liberty in religion constitute an invitation to ask for more political liberty? In Italy will the communists derive profit from a loosening up of the establishment as they are supposed to have derived profit from the attitude of good Pope John?

These are very real problems in the countries they concern. It is hard for English-speakers to imagine a social situation in which the Catholic

Church belongs to the establishment and is supported for political and economic reasons by people who have little interest in religion as such. One must try to picture the role of the Anglican Church in England, and how it belongs still to the social and political fabric of the nation. The Catholic Church has a comparable role in Spain and Italy so new religious attitudes can have political consequences. There is much nervousness about religious liberty which amounts to a declaration of disestablishment in principle.

Despite the misgivings on these two aspects of ecumenism the Secretariat for Christian Unity was highly pleased with the discussion. Its members expressed gratified surprise at the solid and enthusiastic support given to the ecumenical ideal by the great majority of speakers. They felt that in amending the *schema* they could go further than they had dared to go previously. It was pleasing to hear this from the Secretariat because the debate on the *schema* had suffered the inevitable drawbacks of coming at the end of a period of the Council.

All through this period there was an almost limitless series of interruptions for voting, which was quite a complicated process but essential in order that the Council could reach unanimity on the texts submitted, or arrive as closely as possible to it. In voting, the terms we used to indicate choices were the Latin words: *Placet* meaning "it pleases"; *Non Placet* meaning "it does not please" and *Placet juxta modum*, meaning "it pleases but with a reservation", amounting therefore to an amendment. *Modum* is the accusative case of *modus*, which became part of our conciliar vocabulary. The diagram set out below indicates the process of debating and voting in the Council. The three possible votes are indicated by the capitals: P NP PJM.

Diagram of Debating and Voting in the Council

1. Debate and vote on acceptance of *schema*.　　　P or NP

2. If accepted the *schema* is debated chapter
   by chapter or paragraph by paragraph. If
   amendments are proposed they must be submitted
   in writing.

3. Amended *schema* is presented and voted on.　　　P or NP

4. Amended *schema* is presented in totality and
   voted on.　　　P or NP or PJM

5. Final amendments are voted on until all are
   dealt with.　　　P or NP

All that remained after this was the formal or ritual vote before promulgation.

Besides what had been taking place in plenary sessions of the Council, a fair amount of work had been going forward too in Council commissions, finalising texts after debate and voting or preparing texts for presentation to the Council. The Commission on Seminaries and Catholic Schools and Universities had held its first meeting in March 1963 and had continued to meet at regular intervals during the second period in the months of October and November. I shall deal with this topic when I come to report on the presentation of the Seminaries' Commission's text to the Plenary Session in November 1964.

Possibly the busiest people during the second period of the Council were the theologians advising the bishops from France, Switzerland, Germany, Austria, Belgium and Holland. Names that come to mind are the Dominicans Yves Congar, Marie-Dominique Chenu and Edward Schillebeeckx, Jesuits Henri de Lubac and Karl Rahner, Mgr. Gerard Philips of Louvain and the brilliant young rising theological star, Hans Küng.

The characteristic of the great debates of the Second Vatican Council was that the bishops of the Western European bloc had the advantage of this magnificent pool of theologians and also of Scripture scholars, historians, liturgical experts and prominent promoters of lay apostolate, social concern and catechetics. It was this combination that brought the theological and other revivals forcefully into the consciousness of the Council and neutralised and almost extinguished the traditional grip of the Roman Curia on the Catholic outlook. The struggle between these two tendencies was the drama of Vatican II.

The second period of the Council came to a conclusion on Wednesday 4 December, when amid the renaissance splendour of a pontifical ceremony in St Peter's, Pope Paul VI "in union with the Council fathers" as he himself formulated it in a mood of collegiality, promulgated the Constitution on the Liturgy and the Decree on the Instruments of Social Communication.

The Constitution on the Liturgy was, in the very near future, to reduce considerably the renaissance splendour of ceremonies carried out in St Peter's but, please God, to intensify the liturgical significance and participation.

We packed our bags and went home for Christmas.

Chapter Four

The Third Period

We were duly informed in the course of 1964 that the third period of the Council would begin on Monday 14 September, the Feast of the Exaltation of the Cross. It had occurred to Father Johannes Hofinger SJ that the time, just before the start of the session, would be a good opportunity for holding a catechetical study week for Africa. This was duly held at Katigondo Seminary in Uganda. Four representatives of the catechetical scene in South Africa were designated to attend: Father Paul Nadal; Sister Theodula of the Congregation of the Precious Blood, based at Mariannhill; Frances Broekhoven, a member of the Grail and Secretary to the Catechetical Commission of the Southern African Catholic Bishops' Conference; and myself in my capacity as Chairperson of that Commission. We flew to Entebbe. From there we were driven by car to Katigondo, crossing on the way a concrete strip across the tarred road with a capital 'N' on one side and a capital 'S' on the other. We had some photographs taken on this designation of the equator.

At Katigondo we participated vigorously concerning catechetical renewal. Various methods of catechesis were being promoted in various parts of the Church and a favourite designation for one of them was "kerygmatic", indicating that the teaching of catechism should be based less on memory work and more on a cheerful announcement of the good news of the Gospel.

Among the personalities who participated in the study week I remember Bishop Laurian Rugambwa, later Cardinal Archbishop of Dar-es-Salaam, Father Clifford Howell SJ and Father Adrian Hastings, the third of whom was later to achieve scholarly and literary fame and a certain mild notoriety for his advocacy and practice of "constructive disobedience".

Father Clifford Howell had become known as a vigorous promoter of liturgical and catechetical reform, having got involved in this development through study as a Jesuit on the continent of Europe. One had the impression that he was not too popular among the Church authorities in England. Possibly he was rocking the boat in a fairly conservative area of the Church. He had also a somewhat outspoken manner characteristic of his county of origin in England. I experienced something of his tendency not to pull his punches when, towards the end of the study week, several of us were trying to draft sections of the "findings" of the study week. I showed Father Clifford a brief draft of a section that I had been asked to report on. His comment was: "Awful". Bishops are more used to compliments than comments of that nature. Later, when we were flying out of Uganda and had to pass through Nairobi, Father Clifford had quite a showdown with a Kenyan airport official who was insisting that he fill in two forms, one for immigration, the other for emigration. This in no way appealed to Father Clifford who insisted in a loud and strong voice that all he wanted to do was "to borrow your runway".

A year or so later there was the occasion when a few bishops, including myself, held a celebratory dinner in honour of Father Clifford after the acceptance by the Council of the *schema* on Liturgy. One bishop raised his glass and said: "Father Clifford, you now go home to England in triumph". "No, no, no," said Father Clifford, "people will always forgive you for being wrong, but never for being right." He was certainly an unforgettable character and I, for one, remained ever grateful to him for his wonderful little book on the liturgy entitled *The Work of Our Redemption*. By a curious coincidence, on a Sunday when he visited Durban, shortly before the beginning of the Council, the prayer over the gifts (in those days known as "the secret prayer") carried a reference to the work of our redemption. It was, in the manner of designating Sundays at that time, the Ninth Sunday after Pentecost. May Father Clifford be now participating in the joyful liturgies of heaven.

After the catechetical study week at Katigondo, there were a few days remaining before the opening of the Council so I travelled to Bordeaux in France to visit the General House of the Congregation of the Holy Family of Bordeaux where a good friend was fulfilling the role of Assistant General. She was known at that time as Sister Margaret Mary and had taught for several years at the Convent High School in Durban before becoming Superior of the Holy Family Community at Parktown in Johannesburg and later Provincial Superior in South Africa. Subsequently she reverted to her baptismal name, Brigid.

My previous visit to Bordeaux had been in May 1940 when a group of Oblate scholastics, including myself, having been ordained the previous year, spent a few days hoping to find a ship to get away from France after we had left Rome in a hurry to avoid being caught in Italy which at that time was threatening to enter the war on the side of Germany. As it turned out there was no possibility of getting a ship at Bordeaux, so we moved to Paris where we spent a week of incredibly beautiful late spring weather visiting the overpowering scenes and monuments that Paris had to offer. It was hard to imagine that not a great distance away the horror of war was in full spate. We left for England, many of us on our first air journey, on an Imperial Airways flight. The lovely weather held for Dunkirk.

Twenty-three years later, as I left Bordeaux I headed for Geneva to call on friends at Pax Romana, a Catholic institution catering for academics and students. A former resident of Johannesburg, Maire Pompe, was very much involved in this. Council fathers, as may be well imagined, were in great demand at this time so I was called upon to give talks to students of the Marianist Congregation, whose hospitality I was enjoying, and to some Marist Brothers on a refresher course. I also got involved in long discussions with Maire's father-in-law who had been a professor of criminal law in a Dutch university. In a letter concerning the situation I wrote: "He is a typically intelligent and enquiring Dutch Catholic so we had a full day on the Pill and natural law and all the rest of it. It is a difficult job explaining the natural law today."

I got to Rome shortly before the opening of the third period of the Council on Monday 14 September. Describing this opening I wrote as follows in an article for *The Southern Cross*:

> The way in which the opening Mass was celebrated was significant. It showed the influence of the Constitution on the Sacred Liturgy, discussed in the first session and promulgated in the second.... the contrast between the opening Mass in 1962 and the opening Mass in 1964 was striking. In 1962 renaissance pageantry was still piled high over the divine mystery. The emphasis was very much on the outward show designed to impress the uncritical eye. In 1964 a great deal of that has disappeared, though by no means all. The

emphasis was on the participation of the community. The community, it is true, was largely a community of bishops. Participation was emphasised in two ways. Firstly, by concelebration. Three cardinals and 21 other dignitaries concelebrated with the Holy Father. Secondly, by ritual designed to encourage the participation of the assembly. The sung parts of the ordinary of the Mass were chanted to simple Gregorian melodies, in which even the most inexpert of bishops could join, provided he felt carried along by the crowd. The sung parts of the proper were chanted *recto tono* to a responsorial arrangement. The lesson and gospel were proclaimed in a high, solemn tone by two of the concelebrants, and the Holy Father recited the collect, secret, preface and post-communion in the same way. He also shared the canon with three of the concelebrants, each taking a turn to say part aloud. All joined in the words of consecration, and the whole assembly joined in the Our Father as in a dialogue Mass.

This arrangement went smoothly, swiftly and reverently up to the breaking of the hosts, but at that stage and during the communion by the concelebrants there was a distinct slowing down and the usual signs of tiredness and boredom became apparent in the assembly.

Most of what has been described here would cause no surprise today, but in September 1964 they were obvious signs of innovation and promise of what was to come.

In my article for the *Southern Cross* I went on as follows:

The Holy Father's allocution (I was speaking of Pope Paul VI) was a follow-up to his recent encyclical. He dealt with the Church's need to explore more and more her innermost reality in order to present herself to the world with as much impact as possible. The characteristic of Pope Paul is balance. In his allocution he balanced the external organization of the Church against the indwelling Spirit, the papal primacy defined by Vatican I against the episcopal collegiality to be formulated in Vatican II, in a lyrical and warm-hearted address to the separated churches against the sober realism of his treatment of them in his encyclical. He called them the "churches" over and over again, a term that so far had been applied with the utmost reserve in official Roman statements to Christian communities separated from Rome – O churches far from us and yet so near!... O churches that we long for... O churches that we cherish... O churches of our tears...

Work began on Tuesday September 15. There were quite a few announcements to introduce the new period of the Council. One of these was to the effect that anyone wishing to make an intervention, that is, speak in the debate, had to hand in a summary of what he intended to say at least five days before the estimated start of the debate. This would enable the Secretariat to ask prospective speakers with practically the same message to join forces and to appoint one of their number as spokesman. Unfortunately, this would also make it practically impossible to take up a point emphasised in an intervention.

Council *periti*, that is, consultors, were warned as they had been earlier not to write articles critical of the Council or to discuss confidential matters. But, as I wrote in an article for the *Southern Cross*, "one wonders if there is really any halfway between total secrecy and total openness".

The first topic of debate was Chapter VII of the *schema* on The Church. It rejoiced in the breathtaking title of The Eschatological Nature of our Vocation and our Union with the Church in Heaven. The term "eschatological" comes from the Greek *eschatos* meaning "last". As children we had learnt in our catechism about the Last Things: death, judgment, hell and heaven. Only 17 speakers dealt with this mixture of threat and promise. Some felt that the *schema* had no mention of hell and very little of purgatory. They felt that this was leaning over backwards to be optimistic and ecumenical. While appreciating the emphasis on the mercy of God they were of the opinion that a little hell-fire and damnation are not out of place in keeping wayward Christians on the straight and narrow.

Cardinal Suenens called for reform of the process of canonisation. He found the present method too long, too expensive and too centralised. He also complained that it resulted in one-sided representation of the Church among the canonised. Since the eighth century, he maintained, 85% of the canonised had been religious and 90% from three countries. He suggested that beatification should be within the competence of bishops' conferences and canonisation reserved to the Holy See and accorded only in cases of world-wide reputation for sanctity.

The debate on eschatology came to an end on Wednesday September 16, and the Council immediately moved on to the next topic: Chapter VIII of the *schema* on the Church, the Blessed Virgin Mary.

Concurrently voting began on the chapters of the *schema* on the Church debated in the previous year. A vote was taken on Chapter I: The Mystery of the Church, and the result was to be published later. Another mystery concerned the identity and whereabouts of the women "auditors" (listeners). They had been referred to quite frequently and even addressed, but no-one knew who or where they were – another dimension to the eternal enigma.

In the course of Wednesday morning, September 16, discussion began on Chapter VIII of the *schema* on the Church, on the Blessed Virgin Mary. To clarify the picture it is necessary to recall that most of the great central *schema* of Vatican II, the one on the Church, was debated in 1963, during the second session. As a result of that debate, the part already dealt with had been arranged as six chapters, namely:

I   The Mystery of the Church

II   The People of God

III   The Church is Hierarchical

IV   The Laity

V   The Universal Call to Holiness, and

VI   Religious

Chapter VII, about the Last Things was to receive the name The Pilgrim Church and Chapter VIII was to be on Our Lady.

Originally there had been a proposal that a special *schema* should be devoted to Our Lady but in the second session by the narrow majority of 2% it was decided that in place of a separate *schema* Our Lady would have a chapter in the *schema* on the Church.

In the original *schema* too, the expression "Mother of the Church" had appeared in the title. In the debate on the revised text many deplored the dropping of the expression. In fact, most of the speeches at the beginning of the discussion were in the nature of complaints that the titles attributed to Our Lady and the praise accorded her had been toned down too much. In fact, I got the impression that the lion's share of the talking was done by participants expressing dissatisfaction with the text. However, there were speakers who defended the text. They pointed out that a Council *schema* was concerned with theology and not with devotion, that terms should be used in their strict sense and should not give rise to misunderstanding. Bishop Mendez Arceo of Cuernavaca (Mexico) jokingly pointed out that if Mary is called the Mother of the Church, and we are the children of Mother Church, Mary ends up as our grandmother. He was severely taken to task next day by a very upset Spanish bishop.

The idea of Mary's mediation was brought up several times. Those who wanted it emphasised quoted papal expressions in abundance. The more moderate pointed out how difficult it was to explain the exact meaning of the term and how easily it causes confusion in the minds of the separated brethren who think we are claiming a share for Mary in the unique mediatorship of the Son. The term does occur once in the chapter as it now stands but without great emphasis.

On the final day of the debate Cardinal Frings of Cologne and Cardinal Alfrink of Utrecht (Holland) pleaded that the chapter be accepted as it stood and that no pressure be brought to bear to have it include theological opinions still under discussion. Cardinal Alfrink would have preferred to see the word "mediator" dropped entirely. As against this moderation a more enthusiastic attitude to Mary had been advocated by other cardinals such as Wyszynski of Warsaw, Ruffini of Palermo and Suenens of Malines-Brussels. But it was that redoubtable conservative, Bishop Carli of Segni (Italy) who really turned the argument of Cardinal Frings and Alfrink against them when, in the course of the next debate on the Pastoral Role of Bishops in the Church, he dragged in the collegiality issue and maintained, if theological opinions on Our Lady were not to be admitted, neither should theological opinions on collegiality be accepted.

Among those who spoke in the debate on Our Lady was Archbishop Gawlina, the Prelate in charge of the Poles in exile. He died suddenly three days later and no doubt received a loving welcome from the Mother he had so fervently honoured.

The debate on Our Lady closed shortly after 10.00 a.m. on Friday September 18.

The next topic was the *schema* on the Pastoral Role of Bishops in the Church. A great deal of this had already been dealt with in the previous session, so speakers had to be very circumspect about keeping strictly to the points that were new. They were scattered throughout the *schema*. Many speakers found themselves in trouble with the stern chairmanship of Cardinal Döpfner, living up to his title of "His Vehemence".

The question of men in religious institutes came up from time to time with special reference to religious exemption (that is, the non-application of certain aspects of Church law to them) and the problem of harmonising the duties of religious personnel with their obligations to the bishop of the diocese in which they served.

Archbishop Eugene D'Souza of Bhopal (India), well-known already for several outstanding speeches in the Council, made his comments on this subject, calling, as he had done on a previous occasion, for the inclusion of representatives of religious institutes in bishops' conferences.

The French hierarchy was out in force on Tuesday morning, September 22, with six of the first eight speeches. Most of them dealt with the relations between bishops and priests, episcopal leadership, contact and so on, searching always as the French are wont to do for the deep theological foundations. Bets were laid as to whether a French bishop can avoid the use of the word *"dialogus"* in an intervention. Inspired by my Episcopal motto: *Ubi Spiritus, ibi libertas* (Where the Spirit is, there is freedom), I suggested a jingle: *Ubi Gallus, ibi dialogus* (where there is a Frenchman, there is dialogue).

On Monday September 21, the debate was held up as the voting got under way on the crucial Chapter III of the *schema* on The Church. Chapter I (The Mystery of the Church) and Chapter II (The People of God) had successfully come through the test of the vote the week before. Chapter III dealt with the hierarchy of bishops, priests and deacons and included two issues that had been hotly debated in the second session: the collegiality of the bishops and the acceptability of married deacons. There were 39 amendments to be voted on. Most of Monday morning was taken up with reports on these amendments. Normally reports were straightforward presentations explaining how the commission dealing with the topic reached its conclusions. But, in the case of this critical chapter there was a departure from the standard procedure and one report was allowed to cover arguments against the views expressed in the amended texts. Another unusual phenomenon was that the key issue of collegiality, normally associated with the progressive view in the Council, was presented by Archbishop Parente, Assessor of the Holy Office, an institution not often identified with the progressive wing.

Collegiality is a real nightmare to some Council fathers as they fear that it will derogate from papal supremacy. Collegialists, however, see great value in the affirmation of their view, maintaining that it will provide in the episcopate of the whole world that corporate and community sense, that joint responsibility which is the proper hierarchical reflection of the corporate sense growing generally throughout the Church today.

Wednesday September 23, began with a function inaugurating the return of St Andrew's head to the Orthodox Church in the Greek town of Patras. Apparently the relic had been entrusted to Rome by the Greeks in 1462 to prevent its falling into the hands of the all-conquering Turks. Rome kept it for 502 years, a little longer, apparently, than the Greeks had expected. But what are 500 years in Rome? Anyhow, we were giving it back now and the solemn restitution began with the Pope entering St Peter's carrying a reliquary which was made of silver in the shape of a man's head. Mass was celebrated by Cardinal Marella, Archpriest of St Peter's and the relic took the place of the Gospel book as a symbolic focus during the rest of the day's proceedings.

After the final speeches on the pastoral function of bishops, the important topic of religious liberty was introduced by Bishop de Smedt of Bruges (Belgium), a member of the Secretariat for Christian Unity and famous for his criticism of a *schema* during the first session of the Council as being too loaded with "legalism, clericalism and triumphalism". It will be remembered that there was much talk about religious liberty at the end of the second session. At that time it constituted Chapter IV of the Decree on Ecumenism. Chapter V was on the Jews, and the impression current at the end of the second session was that the controlling powers were playing for time and avoiding a discussion on these two contentious subjects. Both topics were now squarely before the Council – no longer as fully-fledged chapters in the *schema* on Ecumenism but as appendices. Whatever the implications of this change of status, the searchlight of the Council was now on them for better or for worse.

Religious liberty has been a real problem in Catholic theology both because of the inherent difficulty of the subject and because of its historical entanglements. Briefly, the theological problem is how to reconcile the demands of a divinely revealed religion entrusted to an authoritative Church, with the great human values of conscience and freedom. Historically the problem got horribly involved in the titanic clash between the mentality produced by a thousand years of Catholic culture in Western Europe and the mentality of the French Revolution. The Catholics defended too much – what was specifically mediaeval along with what was of the essence of the faith. The revolutionaries attacked too much – what was of God as well as what was of a transitory human situation. Now that the revolutionaries are dead and the Catholics have had time to let their tempers cool we can look at the subject of religious liberty with conciliar calm and objectivity – almost!

The importance of the debate can be judged by the number of cardinals who fire the opening salvoes. This time there were nine – five for liberty and four, if not against, at least suspicious and reserved. The reserve and suspicion came, as was to be expected, from the representatives of Italy and Spain, Cardinals Ruffini, Ottaviani, Quiroga y Palacios and Bueno y Monreal.

Those who spoke for freedom were all from the Americas: Cardinals Cushing, Ritter and Mayer of the United States, Léger of Canada and Silva Henríquez of Chile.

One can understand the hesitations of Italy and Spain. Their society is still, in many ways, a traditional Catholic one that has known no other influential religion and whose only experience of "liberalism" has been the clash between clericalism and anti-clericalism. And this clash has not created the best environment for a calm reassessment of theological arguments against freedom of religion and conscience.

The New World entered the debate with a mighty roar. The stentorian voice of Cardinal Cushing rolled and thundered under the dome of St Peter's. It was his first speech in the Council. After a few more like it St Peter's may need a new dome. He ended with a rousing peroration showing how religious freedom stands or falls with the four great pillars of society proclaimed by Pope John XXIII in *Pacem in Terris*: truth and justice, love and liberty. The assembly could not help disregarding the rules and indulging in a rousing round of applause.

All things considered, freedom got the better of the exchanges on the first day of the debate, but tradition came back strongly on the second day when, of the 16 who spoke, 11 were representatives of the old school, mainly Italians and Spaniards, but including one Irishman, Cardinal Browne OP and one Frenchman. They produced variations on the old theme that the right to liberty in religion depended on possessing the true religion and that conscience was not the ultimate norm of moral behaviour. These considerations are fine but they fail to take into account that the only way a person applies the ultimate norm (God's law) is by conscience, and that, if all human rights are dependent upon the possession of the truth, no-one can ever be sure of a human right, certainly not at birth and for quite a long time thereafter.

On the final day of the debate the balance was somewhat redressed when, of the 11 speakers, seven, including myself, spoke up for liberty.

At midday on Friday September 25, the question was put as to whether the assembly wanted the debate closed and the answer was in the affirmative.

Cardinal Bea, who was due to leave for Patras over the weekend to lead the delegation taking back the relic of St Andrew, was then called upon to introduce the second appendix to the *schema* on Ecumenism, the Declaration on the Jews and Non-Christian Religions.

The discussion that followed on Monday and Tuesday September 28 and 29 was an excellent one. Over 30 speakers took part and every aspect of the issue was covered. If the degree of cardinalatial interest is a true criterion, it was an important issue, for the first ten speakers on Monday were cardinals and another joined in on the following day. On Monday 28 September, after religious liberty had been dealt with by four additional speakers who had mustered 70 names to support their application, most of the interest was concentrated on the Jewish question. Nearly every speaker advocated a heartier approach than that contained in the text. This text had been much reduced from the original version of 1963. Somehow, both versions had become known in Jewish circles and there had been much criticism of the shrinkage with reference especially to the issue of deicide. The original text had been much more explicit in exculpating the Jewish people as such of this crime, that is, the murder of Christ. The new text explicitly excused only their descendents. Many speakers dealt with the issue and favoured total exculpation. The whole nation was not guilty and, if it was, so in a certain sense was the rest of humanity.

Speakers called for a strong condemnation of all references to reprobation and of all hatred and persecution of the Jews. These condemnations had to be clear and uncompromising so that no occasion could be left in Catholic culture for antipathy towards Jews.

Many mentioned Christianity's debt to the Jews, as emphasised by St Paul, for their part in the history of salvation and the great religious heritage shared in common. Others disapproved of a passage that seemed to advocate an all-out effort to convert the Jews. Bishop Elchinger, Auxiliary of Strasbourg, spoke movingly of experience in dialogue (being French he could not avoid that issue) with the Jews, whose consciousness of God he had learnt to love and respect. He quoted a French description of the Jews as "pilgrims of the absolute".

The United States hierarchy showed itself as keen to be in this debate as in that on religious liberty and again the thundering voice of Cardinal Cushing rocked St Peter's to its foundations.

Archbishop Heenan of Westminster spoke for England. He managed two speeches in two days: on Monday as one of the additional speakers on religious liberty and on Tuesday as a speaker on the Jewish issue. He was rather caustic about what had happened to the Declaration on the Jews without the full knowledge of the full Secretariat for Christian Unity to which he belonged. There had obviously been some disorganisation.

Not everyone sang in the chorus of fraternal love. There were inevitably some reservations. Cardinal Ruffini referred to Jewish association with Freemasons in opposition to the Catholic Church and asserted that, if we decided that we were going to be nice to the Jews in the future, they should do the same in regard to us. His quotation from the Talmud (collection of rabbinical sayings) about all gentiles being "beasts" was particularly unhappy. We did call one another names in the past. This was not the time to refresh memories on the subject.

Then there was the powerful statement from Cardinal Tappouni of the Syrian Rite, with which most of the Eastern patriarchs associated themselves. This statement called for the entire declaration to be suppressed as it was going to lead to political trouble between Jews and Arabs and to disruption of the Church's apostolate in the Near East.

Other critics of the Declaration dealt with its lack of balance. It paid too much attention to the Jews and not enough to Muslims and faithful of other great religions. Several speakers mentioned the proximity of Muslims to the Christian faith, their participation in descent from Abraham through Ishmael and their tenacious belief in the one true personal God. Speakers from the Far East laid emphasis on Hinduism and Buddhism and the other religions with which they were acquainted.

Proposals were made about changing the order of treatment; so that from a more general view at the beginning the Declaration would move on to mention specific religious faiths, including the Jewish and the Muslim. Cardinal Bueno y Monreal of Seville and Bishop Lamont of Umtali (Rhodesia, now Zimbabwe) were associated with these proposals.

By the time the adjournment was reached at 12.30 on Tuesday September 29, the topic had been well and truly covered and the Secretariat for Christian Unity had plenty of material on hand for the revision of the two declarations.

In the meantime the voting on Chapter III of the *schema* on The Church continued. On Wednesday September 23, the climax of collegiality was reached with proposition 13 which read:

> the order of bishops, which is successor to the college of the apostles in teaching function and pastoral government, in which indeed the apostolic body is continued, holds in union with its head, the Roman Pontiff, and never without this head, supreme and full power in the whole Church, which power, however, it cannot exercise independently of the Roman Pontiff.

Again the vote was overwhelmingly in favour: 1 927 to 292, with five spoilt ballots.

On Tuesday September 29, the Council reached another vital issue in its voting: the re-establishment of the permanent diaconate. This was a complicated vote as a number of alternatives had to be provided for, such as, should local hierarchies have a say or should the matter rest entirely with the pope. The decision was that local hierarchies should have a say in the re-establishment of the diaconate (68% to 32%); that the Supreme

Authority (pope alone or pope and council?) could decide that the diaconate could be conferred on "more mature married men" (71% to 29%) but not on young men not bound by celibacy (62% to 38%). The decision was not taken to re-establish the permanent diaconate and to confer it on married men. It was just decided that this can be decided!

So much for the vote, clause by clause, on the hotly-debated Chapter III. There would follow now the general vote in which qualifications could be expressed. This was to be taken in two stages: 1. Primacy and Collegiality and 2. Episcopal Functions, Priests and Deacons. There could be a great number of qualifications or *modi* as they were called in Latin. These could delay the approval of the chapter as a whole and could necessitate much revision work on the part of the Doctrinal Commission. But in principle collegiality and deacons were in.

There is no little irony in the fact that a topic that led to a dramatic showdown in 1962 became somewhat boring in 1964. In 1962 this topic was discussed under the title The Two Sources of Revelation and culminated in an almost two-to-one vote of rejection, manifesting for the first time the strength of the reform movement in the Council. The formulation of the *schema* then was criticised for being everything that a Vatican II *schema* should not be: abstract, juridical, polemical and unecumenical. The very expression "two sources" was questioned, the "two sources" being scripture and tradition.

The matter came back again for discussion in 1964, very much altered and its title was now simply Revelation. It was presented towards the end of the session on Wednesday 30 November. There was no further talk of two sources. But by many it was felt that the *schema* had swung too far in the opposite direction. The 1962 *schema* had separated tradition and scripture too much, in the line of the Catholic polemical stand against Protestants. Protestants had proclaimed the principle of *sola scriptura*, scripture alone. Catholics had retorted by pointing out that tradition played its part in the transmission of revelation and, as is nearly always the case in controversy, had so played up tradition that they appeared to have played down scripture.

The 1964 *schema* laid great stress on scripture to the extent even of not mentioning that there may be real truth transmitted by tradition that is not in some way contained in scripture. This was bound to cause controversy and it did. Thursday October 1 and Friday October 2 were spent in a ding-dong battle between those who wanted it explicitly stated that tradition contains truth not mentioned in scripture (such as the list of inspired books of the Bible and the dogmas of Our Lady's perpetual virginity, immaculate conception and assumption) and those who preferred to leave the question undecided, on the grounds that in some implicit and roundabout way even the list of biblical books and the dogmas concerning Our Lady may be referred to in scripture.

For all but the experts and the combatants themselves it was a monotonous discussion. Each of those who took part probably thought he was saying something new and exciting but the listeners were not impressed. Grumbled one bishop on his way to the coffee bar: "There should be a limit to a man's right to bore people". Nevertheless, from time to time a few words were said that shed some light on the very delicate and obscure question of the relation between the written word of God and the living tradition of the Church.

To Anglican and Protestant observers it was no doubt satisfying to note the intense interest in biblical matters that had grown up in Catholic circles and the desire not to ascribe to tradition or the teaching authority of the Catholic Church anything that would derogate from the value of God's written word.

One of the most interesting and moving speeches was made by Archbishop Edelby of the Melkite Rite, counsellor to the redoubtable Patriarch Maximos IV Saigh. He pointed out that much of the trouble in the West is due to the unfortunate concern with painstaking analysis of ideas and juridical hair-splitting. The East, he claimed, escaped this plague by retaining the sense of mystery, of the wholeness of God's approach to the human family. In the East scripture is a liturgical and prophetic reality. Before being a book it is a proclamation, a witness of the Spirit. And tradition is that too, the living voice of the Spirit in the Church. Had this conviction prevailed in the West, concluded Archbishop Edelby, there would never have been that fatal clash at the time of the Reformation, setting Church and scripture in opposition to each other. Well, maybe ... It is interesting to get an outside view of what split Europe religiously in half.

On Monday October 5, and Thursday October 6, the debate moved on to other issues connected with scripture: inspiration, inerrancy, historicity and the use of the bible in the Church.

Inspiration and inerrancy are not easy questions. Inerrancy means that the bible, as the inspired Word of God, cannot contain falsehood. The question is: how do you explain the minor inaccuracies that occur? Do you say that the sacred writer was merely quoting and not asserting, or that God used him with his human shortcomings or, despite God's inspiration, he was permitted to write according to the custom of the times, that is, not intending to be precise in every detail? All these possibilities were mentioned by those who were anxious to explore as fully as possible how much of the human element is allowed to assert itself when a person writes under divine inspiration.

In dealing with the practice of biblical interpretation the *schema* followed the recent trend of making liberal allowance for the literary forms and conventions used by the sacred writers in keeping with the custom of their time. Some of the Council fathers sensed danger and wanted a stricter rein kept on biblical scholars but, on the whole, the tone of the discussion was one of confidence and trust.

Cardinal Meyer of Chicago spoke well on the need for a fuller understanding of what inspiration means. For too long, he said, we have been concentrating on the conceptual content of God's word. There is more to a word than its conceptual content. There is the revelation that the speaker makes of himself and the response he endeavours to elicit from his hearers. All this should be taken into account when we talk of inspiration in scripture. Archbishop Edelby and others from the East would no doubt agree with that.

The last chapter of the *schema* deals with Sacred Scripture in the Life of the Church. This gave an opportunity for the more pastorally inclined to enter the debate and to say a few words about the promotion of biblical knowledge and biblical piety in the Church. Even on this point there was a discordant note, a warning against the indiscriminate placing of the bible in the hands of the unprepared. It sounded like something out of the 16th century. Bishop Volk of Mainz (Germany) referred to the British and Foreign Bible Society and wondered why there wasn't something similar in the Catholic world. He was not too enthusiastic however in regard to an idea mentioned in the *schema* on ecumenism concerning collaboration with non-Catholic churches in the production of up-to-date translations. But his lack of enthusiasm was hardly likely to arrest a movement already well into its stride.

The Council had shown that it wished to place the seal of its approval and encouragement on the momentous biblical revival that had been taking place in the Church. We can look forward to a magnificent future in this regard.

On Monday 5 October voting began on the *schema* on Ecumenism and by Tuesday morning the first chapter had come through successfully and all the amendments to Chapter II had been approved, not however, without a significant number of *non placets* against a reference to opening the door to *communicatio in sacris*, participation in official liturgical functions by Catholics and non-Catholics together. There would have to be some clarification of the text concerning this.

The fast pace of the Council was being maintained. It looked more than ever likely now that all the discussions would be completed by November 20, the day fixed for the closing of the session. But the problem remained for the commissions to revise their texts for voting before that date. The suggestion was being mooted that the Council should reassemble for a week or two after the Bombay (now Mumbai) Eucharistic Congress (November 28 to December 6) to attend to the voting and to make a fourth session unnecessary. But it would be a miracle if all the revised texts could be ready by that time, especially the *schemas* on The Lay Apostolate and The Presence of the Church in The Modern World which looked like being in for a severe mauling during the following week.

A good deal of time was taken up on Wednesday October 7, with reports that introduced the voting on Chapter III of Ecumenism. As a result there were only seven speakers that morning, a slow start to the debate on The Lay Apostolate. However, the debate went on for three days after that, so the subject had been fairly well covered when the vote of closure was taken at midday on Monday October 12. The debate was supposed to have proceeded in two stages: firstly in general and after that with reference to particular points. The dividing line turned out to be imperceptible. From start to finish it was a free-for-all.

As had been expected, the *schema* came under heavy fire. It was accused of being vague, disorderly, confused, repetitious, superficial and clerical. The *schema* also had its defenders, but the adverse critics were more numerous and aggressive.

The chief accusation was of clericalism. There had been quite a history behind this.

Up till quite recently the theological treatises on the Church dealt almost exclusively with its hierarchical structure and the exercise of authority. This was the reaction to the Protestant Reformation which had belittled Church authority, denied papal supremacy and, in several cases, got rid of bishops. As a consequence, when one thought of the Church in Catholic circles, one thought principally of what had to be defended, namely the hierarchical organisation. It was only after the new emphasis on the mystical body and the people of God and the development of the lay apostolate in the previous 50 years, and more specifically in the past 25 years, that we began to consider the laity as an important element in the Church.

The lay apostolate first came up for consideration as Catholic Action, and Catholic Action was defined by Pope Pius XI as "the participation of the laity in the apostolate of the hierarchy". This was the situation in the late 1920s and in the 1930s. In this concentration on helping the clergy with their task, there was obviously no clear understanding yet of the proper role of the laity in the Church.

The 25 years from the end of World War II to the calling of the Council had seen rapid evolution in this regard and no-one would dream at the end of that period of applying to the lay apostolate the 1920 designation of Catholic Action. It was clear now that the laity constituted 99% and more of the Church, that most of the Christian witness was given by the laity and most of the Christian impact on the world made by them – not because they were doing the clergy's job, not because there were not priests enough to do the work, but because this was the inherent and inescapable role of the laity. It flowed from the sacraments of baptism and confirmation. It was becoming clearer by the day that an apostolic attitude, a readiness to radiate Christ, was part and parcel of one's identity as a Christian.

Yet this general apostolic attitude did need, in certain cases, definition, organisation and concentration. So the basic apostolic obligation that went with belonging to the Catholic laity had been sharpened and channelled in the organised forms of the lay apostolate.

This brief historical survey, superficial and inadequate though it is, reveals an interesting fact: that the understanding of the lay apostolate grew down instead of up. It grew down from the form of lay apostolate (helping the clergy with their specific task) to a deeper and more general understanding of what the lay apostolate truly is in all its profound significance. It hadn't stopped growing at the time of the Council. We were right in the middle of a theological effort to try to understand and evaluate the role of the laity in all its fullness. This was no small problem, because we had been living in a clerical Church, dominated by a monastic view of sanctity, suspicious of marriage and suspicious too, rather than appreciative, of the rest of God's creation. Looking back now it seems as if we feared that interest in creation might lead to a loss of interest in redemption.

Those who sought a vision to inspire the lay apostolate realised instinctively that there was something wrong and began probing the true Christian significance of work and the human role in the world and, as if in answer to their prayers there arose in the Church some towering figures like Father Joseph Cardijn (later Cardinal) with his brilliant see, judge, act method of training the Young Christian Workers (YCW); and the Jesuit Father Teilhard de Chardin with his exciting vision of Christ in the universe which gave a tremendous impulse towards a proper evaluation of the natural order and its essential role in God's plan for the human family. Exciting years lay ahead of us in which to unravel the fantastic consequences of the new understanding that had dawned. In its unravelling we should see more and more clearly the vocation and role of Christian laity.

In such a rapidly evolving situation it was not easy for the Commission to prepare a *schema* that would receive anything like a unanimous welcome. Inevitably the concepts, the images and the language of the past weighed heavily on the presentation.

So the cry of clericalism arose on all sides, meaning that the *schema* had not really emancipated the laity and launched them boldly into their true vocation, but had, albeit unintentionally, shackled them with clerical objectives and clerical controls.

Cardinal Ritter of St Louis (USA) raised a hue and cry on the opening day of the debate. It was taken up with tremendous relish by Archbishop D'Souza of Bopal (India) who was all for a strong lay representation in the Vatican Curia and diplomatic service, though in this he was veering away a bit from the laity's true role in the world. The outcry reached its apogee when Bishop Alexander Carter of Sault Ste. Marie (Canada) denounced the *schema* as being "conceived in sin": the sin of clericalism.

Many speeches, and among them one of mine, called for more clarity, logic and order. Others wanted a more precise distinction between the apostolate of the hierarchy and that of the laity. Still others wanted definitions and indications of how lay apostolate differed, if it did, from the laity's share in consecrating the world. Cardinal Suenens set the cat among the pigeons by raising the Catholic Action issue. It amounted to this. In the '20s and '30s Catholic Action was vigorously promoted in the Latin countries. In these areas like Italy, Spain and South America it came to mean a particular organisation established by the bishops on parochial, diocesan and national levels for "the participation of the laity in the apostolate of the hierarchy" in every way in which this was possible. It was a particular organisation with a particular constitution and object. In France it appeared to have included all forms of "specialised lay apostolate", the apostolate of like to like, of the social environment, as for instance, the Young Christian Workers, Young Christian Students, Young Christian Farmers and so on. Outside of the Latin countries the term was never clearly understood and was used as a synonym for lay apostolate and designated any sort of corporate Catholic activity, and now in many places seemed to be disappearing out of circulation.

Cardinal Suenens went on to say that an association that ranked as Catholic Action in Latin countries had a certain standing. It had arrived. One that was not designated as Catholic Action was somewhat on the sidelines officially, though it might be doing an excellent job in the lay apostolate. His Eminence went on to say that the term Catholic Action should be broadened to have a generic meaning, applicable to any association doing apostolic work under the bishop. He was thinking particularly of the Legion of Mary.

Those who had grown up in the old Catholic Action tradition could not see any sense in this. On Wednesday 12 October, it was strongly opposed by five or six speakers. One protested that if we opposed the use of the term Catholic Action in the narrow sense we should also oppose the use of such terms as the Society of Jesus, the Holy Office and the Apostolate of Prayer. This speaker spent most of his ten minutes explaining that the Council should not waste its time on words.

Many speeches dealt with the corporate nature of the lay apostolate and the need for organisation. Many also dealt with the even more fundamental need for thorough spiritual and practical formation related to the life and role of the laity.

Much insistence was laid on the family. As Archbishop Šeper of Zagreb (Yugoslavia) pointed out, in Iron Curtain countries the family was often the one and only instrument of Christian and apostolic training. He asked that as much attention should be given to Christian family training as to preaching and the sacraments.

Archbishop McCann of Cape Town emphasised the importance of proper training of the clergy to make them capable promoters of the lay apostolate.

Bishop De Smedt of Bruges (Belgium) warned against over-zealous lay apostles who infringe the religious liberty of their victims.

Several, notably Archbishop Heenan of Westminster, called for strong lay representation in any post-conciliar organisation set up to promote the lay apostolate.

The vote of closure was taken on Monday October 12, at midday. There were three more speeches the next morning by speakers who had mustered 70 signatures each in support of their applications. Pat Keegan of England, well-known for his work in the YCW and now at the highest and broadest levels of international co-ordination in the lay apostolate, addressed the Council in English on behalf of the laity of the world, and the debate was wound up with the reply of Bishop Hengsbach of Essen (Germany), *rapporteur* for the Commission on the Lay Apostolate who promised on behalf of his Commission to amend the *schema* inasfar as this was humanly possible in the light of the debate.

Over the weekend, interest in the lay apostolate was somewhat eclipsed by a minor crisis in Council affairs. From what was noised around and about, letters purporting to come from high up, but how high nobody seemed to know, were read in the Secretariat for Christian Unity on Friday evening, October 9, directing:

1. the withdrawal of the Declaration on the Jews and its substitution by a passage in the *schema* on the Church which could have no possible political repercussions;

2. the complete revision of the Declaration on Religious Liberty by a special sub-committee consisting of four members of the Secretariat for Christian Unity and four non-members, three of them vigorous opponents of the Declaration.

Speculation, interpretation and lamentation rose to great heights and the direst consequences were foreseen. The opinion was advanced that the Holy Father himself had not originated the action, though it was accepted that he was under almost unendurable pressure from the Arab states, either directly or through the Eastern Churches, Catholic and Orthodox; under heavy pressure too in regard to religious liberty from the hard core of conservatives who saw in the Declaration a denial of accepted Catholic doctrine.

It appeared that on Sunday evening, under the leadership of Cardinal Frings of Cologne a group of cardinals assembled and made a strong protest to the Holy Father against the way things had been done.

And there, for the time being, the matter rested.

The original agenda of the third period had provided for the discussion of the *schema* on The Church in the Modern World immediately after the Lay Apostolate. However, it was announced on Monday October 12 that the introductory report was not yet ready and that the discussion would have to be postponed. Various interpretations were placed upon this. The prophets of doom, stunned by the news about the Declarations on Religious Liberty and the Jews that had come out two days before, suspected that a sinister move was afoot to withdraw the *schema* entirely. Others suspected that a revision of the *schema* was under way, for it had already been severely criticised. Possibly compilation of the report had been delayed pending a decision in this regard, but from the way the General Secretary of the Council spoke of it, it was about to make its appearance.

In the meantime two shorter *schemas* were dealt with. On Tuesday October 13 the first of these, Priestly Life and Ministry, came before the Council. There were several reduced *schemas* that owed their new shape to a decision of the co-ordinating commission at the beginning of the year to speed things up after the slow progress of the first and second periods. Those *schemas* that had not been introduced at the plenary session at the end of the second period were to be reduced to a series of propositions. It was later decided these propositions would not even be debated but merely voted on. How this decision ever came to be made was a great mystery, because it was obvious that it could never have worked. Strong protests poured in from all sides and resulted in the reversal of the decision. All the reduced *schemas* would be discussed at least briefly and the assembly would then vote on them proposition by proposition.

So the propositions on Priestly Life and Ministry came up for discussion on Tuesday 13 October. Immediately they were under heavy fire. Cardinal Meyer of Chicago was the first speaker and he proceeded in no uncertain manner to point out the deficiencies in the *schema*. Its object was not clear. What did it intend to achieve? It amounted to nothing more than a string of juridical norms and offered nothing by way of encouragement and inspiration to priests. Priests deserved a treatment as full as that accorded to bishops.

Others spoke in the same tone, especially Cardinal Ruffini, who wanted a good message in the *schema* about the splendour and nobility of the priesthood and Cardinal Alfrink, who wanted to see much more consideration of present-day conditions under which the priestly apostolate has to be exercised, and also of priestly celibacy which was coming under criticism from various sources.

Archbishop Fernando Gomes of Goiania (Brazil) speaking on behalf of his own and other countries called the *schema* a profound disappointment and proposed that it be withdrawn for radical revision, even if this meant a fourth session of the Council. It was more important to do things well than to do them hurriedly. He wanted less of the juridical and more of the theological in the *schema*.

One practical problem that constantly recurred in the speeches of the bishops from some Latin countries was that of ecclesiastical benefices. In these countries, and particularly in Italy, the old system of ecclesiastical benefices still prevailed. It was altogether unknown in most other countries. Nevertheless it was spoken of in canon law as if it was characteristic of the whole Church. A benefice was the income derived from property attached to an ecclesiastical office, like that of parish priest. For instance, the office of parish priest in an Italian village might have some land attached to it, the rent of which provided the parish priest's income. This system had serious drawbacks in later times. Where it prevailed, the people felt themselves under little or no obligation to contribute to the support of the Church and its ministers and moreover in a rapidly changing industrial society it could produce a situation in which long-established offices retained their benefices while newly-established ones had none or hardly any. And, obviously, it was not too pleasant not having a benefice in a benefice-minded society.

A proposal was made that all income should be pooled and evenly distributed. While the proposal looked simple enough on paper and abstracted from the human element, it had its complexities in countries where all income consisted of the voluntary contributions of the faithful.

The debate came to an end in the course of Thursday morning, October 15. It had been announced that voting on the individual propositions would begin forthwith, but the fierce criticisms of the *schema* had led to a reconsideration of this decision and instead it was decided that in future, in regard to all reduced *schemas*, there would be, before the voting on individual propositions, a general vote on the acceptability of the *schema* as a whole. All these changes of procedure were the inevitable result of improvising procedure to speed up discussion and decision. In a vast assembly the longest way around is usually the shortest way home. The vote on the *schema* as a whole was taken on Monday October 19, and resulted in rejection by 1 199 votes to 930. It had now to go back to the Commission for total revision and probably further discussion in the fourth session.

I found it hard to dismiss the temptation to say: "I told you so". In an intervention in the first period I had proposed, concerning the chapter on the hierarchy in the *schema* on the Church, that the chapter should consist of three sections, the first on bishops, the second on priests and the third on deacons. This appeared to me to be a much more logical and co-ordinated approach. But it was not accepted and now we had ended up floundering in the discussion on priests.

As The Church in the Modern World was not yet ready for presentation on Thursday October 15, another abbreviated *schema* came up for discussion: The Oriental Church. It had already seen the light of day for a short while during the first period in 1962 under the curious title That All may be One and had been sent back for re-drafting. Early in 1964, with other *schemas,* it had come under the axe and had been reduced to a series of propositions.

One great merit of the *schema* was that it brought Patriarch Maximos IV Saigh, who had been strangely silent, back into the fray. He was the last speaker on October 15. Usually the last speaker talks to a restive and unresponsive audience whose one great aspiration is that he should shut up and let them go home. Not so Patriarch Maximos. With all his old fire and verve, and he was well over 80, he held the audience spellbound as he launched forth into an eloquent plea for the restoration in all their pristine glory of the ancient patriarchates of Constantinople, Antioch, Alexandria and Jerusalem. They may have meant something in the days before the Arab and Turkish conquests. Then they stood for vast Christian populations presided over by bishops and metropolitans with the patriarch at the peak, enjoying full ecclesiastical autonomy with some rather vague recognition of the Roman primacy. Each patriarchate had stood for an area with a distinctive culture and political complexion and had a rite and language of its own. But history had been hard on these patriarchates. What was left of their ancient glory (and there is certainly not much left of a place like Antioch) belongs to churches separated from Rome by heresy or schism.

With the exception of the Maronite Patriarchate which has maintained its continuity, the modern uniate patriarchates of the East are all of fairly recent creation, having been established by the Holy See since the 16th century to group together under a familiar form of church organisation the Eastern Christians who re-entered the Roman communion. They are a small minority scattered among the Muslims and the Orthodox. Since creating these new patriarchates Rome has kept them under very strict control and they enjoy not even the shadow of the independence that characterised the patriarchates of ancient times. Maximos did not like this. He wanted to see those modern patriarchates enjoying something of the old status and not dictated to by subordinate officials of the Roman Curia. The idea of a Vatican official telling a patriarch what he can do made his blood boil.

He would also have liked to see the Pope re-emphasising his title of Patriarch of the West. This would prove that he understood the significance of the patriarchates and, while retaining the primacy, was willing to recognise a sort of superior college of patriarchs – superior to cardinals anyway.

For Patriarch Maximos and for many other Oriental bishops the reactivation of the patriarchates would be the "test" of what Rome could offer the Orthodox Churches. This was very clearly stated by a westerner, Abbot Hoeck of the Bavarian Benedictines.

Not all agreed with this opinion. The final speech of the debate was made by a Chaldean Bishop, Bidawid of Amadiyah. He tore into all the patriarchal aspirations as if he saw precious little sense in them. After all, he concluded, the patriarchates were not of divine origin and seemed to have had their day in the history of the Church.

Another question that was hotly debated was that of the freedom of Eastern converts to choose the rite they wished to join. At present they enjoyed this freedom. The *schema* proposed to abolish it and to restrict converts from one of the separated Eastern churches to joining the parallel rite in the Catholic Church. Those who opposed this restriction did so on the grounds of religious liberty; those who favoured it did so on the grounds of ecumenism. Apparently freedom of choice usually favoured the Latin rite and consequently upset the Orientals. There was much to be said for both sides of the question, and at the end of the debate it was not easy to decide which opinion one should favour. There was, however, a little irony in the fact that Orientals were strongly advocating a little legalism – the vice they always attributed to the Western Church.

The final paragraph in the *schema* dealt with liturgical and sacramental participation with members of the Orthodox churches and sanctioned what had already become recognised practice. Members of these churches in good faith could go to confession to a Catholic and receive Holy Communion and the anointing of the sick from him. And a Catholic could receive the same sacraments from an Orthodox priest "whenever there is need or true spiritual benefit and it is physically or morally impossible to approach a Catholic priest".

Despite the criticism and hesitations about the *schema* the consensus of opinion was that it was a good and constructive document and the vote on acceptability resulted in a majority of 1 911 to 265.

In the meantime voting had been completed on Chapter VII of the Decree on the Church, "The Eschatological Nature of the Church on Earth and its Union with the Church in Heaven". There remained one more chapter to vote on, Chapter VIII on The Blessed Mother.

Tuesday October 20, was D-Day for The Church in the Modern World. Much had been said about this *schema*. It had been built up in publicity as the crowning climax of Vatican II. It was to make the Church relevant to the world. It was to bring illumination and hope to many who were lost in uncertainty and obscurity. It was to jolt the agnostics and sceptics into the realisation that the Church was really significant. No-one directly concerned with the Council was saying these things, but they were expectations that were becoming current. That immediately made The Church in the Modern World doubly difficult. It had to say something significant on a topic that had never before been treated by a Council, and it had to say it intelligibly.

No *schema* had proved more troublesome in its compilation. It had gone through the process of total redrafting four or five times, and the joint commission (Doctrine and Lay Apostolate) engaged on it had to experience all the uncertainties, confusions and frustrations that were to be strongly reflected in the criticisms hurled against it in St Peter's.

The compilers had this basic problem, that they were not drawing up a statement dealing with the doctrine of the Church on the topics usually dealt with in such statements. They were expected to give formulation to the Church's preoccupation with the world and the manner in which the Church should contribute to the solution of the major problems of the modern world.

They were doing this at a time when the Church's theology was only just beginning to face up boldly to the relations between the Church and the world. Officially the Church had never had any other attitude to the world than that of appreciation of God's creation, but her theologians had never worked out a satisfactory relationship between the work of creation and the work of redemption. Nor had it been easy to say exactly what was meant by the "world", since the term is used with different meanings in the gospels. At times there seems to be an irreconcilable enmity between Christ and the world. At other times the world is the object of his compassion and saving mercy.

The compilers of the *schema* were also working at the end of a period in the life of the Church that had seen a profound estrangement between the Church and the prevailing culture. Like all Catholics in modern times they were only just emerging from the ghetto into which this estrangement had locked them, and inevitably a good deal of the old mentality was bound to manifest itself despite their best intentions.

For these reasons there seems to have been a general air of sympathy among those who spoke about the *schema*, sympathy with the issues it raised and sympathy for those who had attempted to deal with them. This sympathy revealed the conviction that the Council was involved in a make-or-break situation and that there was no easy way out.

After the final speeches on the Oriental Churches the Secretary General announced that the *schema* on The Church in the Modern World would be discussed first in general and, if accepted as a basis for further discussion, under eight detailed headings:

1. Prologue and Chapter I: The Human Vocation in its entirety
2. Chapters II and III: The Church at the Service of God and Humanity, and the Conduct of Christians in the World

All the remainder would fall under Chapter IV:

3. The Dignity of the Human Person
4 The Dignity of Marriage and the Family
5. The Promotion of Culture
6. Economic and Social Life

7. The Unity (solidarity) of the Human Family

8. The Preservation of Peace

The introduction was given by Cardinal Cento and the report by Bishop Guano of Leghorn, President of the Joint Commission charged with drafting the *schema* in the name of the Doctrinal Commission and the Commission on Lay Apostolate. Bishop Guano spoke with the tone of a man expecting trouble. Perhaps this attitude of expectant humility touched many hearts and produced more leniency than might have been hoped for.

There were some whose hostility to the *schema* was based on the uncomfortable feeling that its approach to the modern world was wholly wrong and that the manner of speaking was not that of the Church at all. But they were few in number. The great majority realised that somewhere, somehow, the intention was right but that there was an awful lot of confusion.

There was confusion as to who the audience was: Catholics or non-Catholics or both and, if both, how do you compile a document aimed at both? There was confusion as to whether the *schema* intended to solve problems or just formulate them. Was it a monologue or a dialogue? To many anything that wasn't a dialogue wasn't really respectable.

There was confusion between the natural and the supernatural orders.

There was confusion as to whether the world and human work in it were really significant in relation to the supernatural destiny of humankind.

There was confusion in regard to the Church's function, whether it transcended the worldly order or got too immersed in it.

There was confusion about the nature of the world.

There was confusion about the nature of the Church, whether it was the hierarchy or the people of God.

In a word, there was confusion.

And, nearly everybody had a plan for clearing it up. No two plans coincided. To the members of the Joint Commission it must have sounded strangely familiar.

The first 11 speakers were cardinals. This surpassed the previous record. The outstanding contribution was made by Cardinal Meyer of Chicago, who gave a magnificent résumé of St Paul's cosmic Christ theology, with abundant quotations from Romans, Colossians and

Ephesians. He brought out Paul's teaching on the sovereignty of Christ over the universe as a result of his death and resurrection, how the salvation that comes to people through the mystery of Christ, through them also affects the universe in which they live and work and which, in the end, will be transformed into the new heaven and the new earth.

But the most memorable speech was that of Archbishop Heenan. He had a few opening compliments for the compilers of the *schema*, but not too many. He had soon left the compliments behind and was out in the high seas firing torpedoes, rockets and depth charges. As far as he was concerned the *schema* was a tissue of empty platitudes which would make the Council the laughing stock of the world.

He maintained that on some of the vital issues the *schema* gave no clear answer. In fact, it seemed to be saying that the Church had no answer and that it was up to the conscience of individuals to decide. This was particularly the case in regard to the delicate matter of marriage morality. Here, His Grace really took off. Some of the Council *periti* had annoyed him during the previous months by their liberal criticism of traditional Catholic positions and their willingness to make statements at the drop of a hat.

Father Häring CSsR was one of these. Father Häring was the secretary of the Joint Commission responsible for the *schema*. Archbishop Heenan was a brilliant and witty speaker in this kind of free-for-all and, if anything, the Latin highlighted the pungency of his style. He almost had the Council convulsed.

His Grace's conclusion was that the *schema* should be entrusted to a new commission, comprising a good number of lay *periti* and that it should come back to the Council after four years, by which time no doubt many of the present bishops would have gone to their reward, but they would be able to help more with their prayers than with their speeches.

The *periti* found their defender the next day in the person of the Abbot of Beuron in Germany. He referred to the fact that Archbishop Heenan had berated the *periti* for wanting to solve the world's problems from the isolation of their religious houses, monasteries, seminaries and universities. The good abbot expressed his trepidation at daring to speak on the subject since he too hailed from a monastery as a member of the order whose founder was about to be declared the patron of Europe and 40 of whose members had been sent by Pope Gregory the Great to change the Angli into Angeli.

Subsequently the story circulated that Archbishop Heenan suffered somewhat from "peritinitis" as a consequence of too much Häring, and that the remedy prescribed was Benedictine.

A theme that recurred frequently on the lips of speakers was that of atheism and Marxism and how they should be dealt with. Many references were made to poverty in general and the voluntary poverty that should characterise the Church.

I was responsible for starting a minor controversy in the major debate. I had been nursing for some time no little resentment because of a *monitum* (warning) that had been issued by some official of the Roman Curia against the writings of Teilhard de Chardin. I took the occasion of the debate on the Modern World to speak up for Teilhard saying that "mention should be made of the concepts that in these recent years have begun to be publicised that owe their origin especially to the splendid vision, religious and scientific, evolutionary and eschatological of that illustrious son of the Church, Pierre Teilhard de Chardin." The Abbot of Beuron, after dealing with Archbishop Heenan, expressed his misgivings about Teilhard who had not seen enough evil in the world and tended to reflect Origen's erroneous opinion arising out of his teaching on the *apochatastasis* that there is no eternal punishment. I must admit that it was the first time that I had ever heard that Greek word referring to the restoration of all things in Christ at the end of time (see Acts of the Apostles 3:21). Bishop Spülbeck of Meissen (East Germany) later entered the lists in favour of Teilhard emphasising the influence he had exerted in scientific circles.

The discussion on the *schema* in general went on until Friday, when the closure was applied. Bishop Guano of Leghorn, President of the Joint Commission dealing with the *schema* on The Church in the Modern World, made a brief response and the vote was taken on the acceptability of the *schema* for further discussion. This went through with 1 579 in favour to 296 against.

In the course of his response, Bishop Guano announced that the Pope had reserved to himself the major marriage questions (contraception, the

Pill) pointing out that it was being studied by a special commission of scientists and theologians.

On Friday October 23, the Council got down to the work of analysing the *schema* chapter by chapter. It was an analysis that ranged far and wide: as far and wide as the relations themselves between the Church and the world, and these are well nigh infinite.

From that Friday until Tuesday October 27, the Council dealt with the first three chapters of the *schema*: the Human Vocation, the Church at the Service of God and Humanity, and the Conduct of Christians in the World.

Among the points dealt with was that of the "signs of the times". This expression has come into its own theologically and found frequent mention in this discussion. We owe the expression, of course, to Our Lord who, in warning us to be prepared for the happenings connected with our final destiny, told us to take note of the signs of the times. Modern theology maintains that, since all that we experience and do contributes to our final destiny, we are living in an "eschatological" age and should therefore be on the lookout for the signs of the times.

The signs, for want of a better description, may be identified as happenings and developments of urgent significance for the Church in her work of illuminating and sanctifying the human family. By not noticing a sign of the times the Church can miss the boat. By detecting it in time she can make use of it for the fulfilment of her mission. Signs of our times are the universalisation of culture, the rapid growth of science and technology, the intense socialisation of the human family, the emancipation of women, atheistic communism. The Church dare not disregard these signs if it wishes to remain relevant to the human situation.

Having learnt what it cost to be late with Galileo, the French Revolution and the Industrial Revolution, we are trying hard to persuade ourselves to be on time in future.

The discussion also entered into the precise role that must be played by the Church in its dealings with the world's problems. That role must always be spiritual and supernatural but must remain deeply concerned with the material and physical facts involved in these problems. It must be a role of charity, of loving compassion for all people, especially the poor. The conscious and grievance-laden poverty of so many hundreds of millions of the world's population, undernourished and degraded by their poverty, is a terrible sign of the times. The Church dare not neglect that. It must approach this problem in a spirit of poverty, of true appreciation of the world's goods and humanity's needs, and use all its influence and example to persuade people to share in a spirit of fraternity.

The topic of atheism came back time and time again. Obviously it is a sign of the times that must come under the Church's earnest consideration. How is it that so many millions can remain utterly oblivious of God and, indeed, hostile to the image they have formed of God? Why this disastrous failure?

Three speakers alluded to the legalistic spirit that characterised the attitude of the Church in recent times: Bishop La Ravoire Morrow of Krishnagar (India), author of a well-known catechism, Bishop Mendez Arceo of Cuernavaca (Mexico) and Patriarch Maximos IV Saigh, who was always available when there was any criticising to do of the legalistic spirit of the West. Bishop Morrow could not conceive of someone spending eternity in hell for eating meat on Friday. Bishop Mendez Arceo thought it a poor show that the only way to get people to the Eucharistic banquet was by threatening them with hellfire. Where was the joyous freedom of the children of God?

Chapter IV came under discussion on Wednesday morning, October 20. The first section deals with the dignity of the human person. Several speeches called for a more satisfactory theological treatment of the subject. Others dealt with particular aspects of human dignity in the modern world. Racial discrimination came under heavy criticism. A clearer condemnation was called for by Archbishops Athaide of Agra (India), O'Boyle of Washington (USA) and Malula of Leopoldville, now Kinshasa (Congo) and also by Bishop Grutka of Gary, Indiana (USA). Archbishop Malula was just as severe on tribalism. Unfortunately, on the question of racism, the South African hierarchy missed the boat. We had not thought in advance of the opportunity given by the topic of human dignity and, of course, by the time racism was mentioned it was too late for us to make application for the right to intervene on the subject.

Archbishop Malula was also one of those who ensured himself of a tumultuous welcome home from the women of his diocese for, along with

Bishops Coderre of St Jean of Quebec (Canada) and Frotz, Auxiliary of Cologne (Germany), he took up the feminist cause.

Bishop Coderre was the best of the three and spoke eloquently of woman's role of complementing and perfecting man and in regard to her work inside and outside the family. No limits should be placed on what nature and her gifts contribute to society and the Church. Bishop Frotz heartily endorsed this view and advocated that the Church should not merely recognise the emancipation of women as a sign of the times but actively promote and make the most of it.

Marriage and the family were discussed on Thursday and Friday October 29 and 30. It was an awkward and difficult discussion. The *rapporteur*, Archbishop Dearden of Detroit (USA), in introducing the subject pointed out once again that the crucial issue of birth control had been reserved by the Holy Father for study by a commission responsible to him alone. However, a number of speakers came as close as they could to the topic without actually mentioning the Pill or its antecedents. Among those who took what might be called a sympathetic attitude were Cardinals Léger, Suenens and Alfrink and Patriarch Maximos IV (more legalism to demolish!). The traditionalists were represented by Cardinals Ottaviani, Ruffini and Browne.

The former group argued that there had been in the past only a limited and partial appreciation of marriage in the Church with unbalanced insistence on the duty of procreation. Scientific advances in many fields had shown that there was much more to marriage than this and now it was essential to recognise that love and fulfilment were as important as procreation and that the parents had the right to decide, in the light of Christian conscience, how many children they should bring into the world. It was the duty of the Church to investigate the whole question thoroughly and find out with certainty what was natural and what was not, and to make use of every assistance that science could offer to solve the painful dilemma between love and procreation, the demands of procreation and those of education.

Cardinal Suenens' speech was the most forthright, but like that of Cardinal Alfrink, it was not without ambiguities. What exactly did it suggest: that scientific discovery could help to solve the problem or that the re-examination of the Church's attitude to natural law might change her attitude? Many felt that speeches like these, while manifesting the sympathy of the hierarchy with the laity in one of their most grievous problems, could create false impressions and raise premature hopes.

The more conservative speakers recalled the traditional teaching of the Church. The best among these was Bishop Hervas, Prelate Nullius of Ciudad Real (Spain), founder of one of the most successful methods of lay formation, *Cursillos de Christianidad.* He pointed out that the *schema,* in becoming too preoccupied with the problems of marriage, tended to lose sight of its supernatural dimensions and begged the Council not to forget the debt of gratitude that was owed to large families which are the finest source of vocations and a splendid manifestation of faith and trust in Divine Providence.

While these discussions rolled on, the final chapter of the *schema* on the Church was voted through, the chapter on the Blessed Virgin Mary. There were, however, 521 votes with reservations, reflecting the number of Council fathers who wanted to have more uninhibited formulation of teaching about Our Lady.

On Friday October 30, the adjournment was more light-hearted than usual. It was the All Saints break and the Monday and Tuesday of the following week would be free. Some of the sparkle was taken off the picture, however, by an announcement of the Secretary General to the effect that to compensate partially for the loss of two days, Saturday November 7, would be a working day.

The Council came back to the problems of the modern world after the long weekend that had provided a most welcome rest. But it came back to a broken week, because there had to be a lot of reporting to introduce the voting on the *schema* dealing with the pastoral role of bishops and on Friday November 6, the Modern World was interrupted to make way for the debate on The Missionary Activity of the Church.

Whatever would emerge from the discussion on The Church in the Modern World was far from clear at this stage. It was like looking into a concrete mixer: what you see there bears little resemblance to the final product.

After the discussion on marriage it had already taken up the question
of culture on Friday October 30. We came back to this question on
Wednesday November 4.

Cardinal Lercaro of Bologna opened on Wednesday with a reference
to his favourite topic, the need for the Church to embrace voluntary poverty.
He said that the Church must manifest this spirit also in regard to culture.
It must not be afraid to strip itself of the culture and glories of the past in
order to consecrate itself to the achievements of the present and the future.
To do this it must not hesitate to change its system of education, including
education of the priests. Its duty is to give prominence to the Gospel and
not to hide it under a cultural bushel.

A Mexican bishop, Talamas of Ciudad Juárez, spoke well on the need
for respecting the freedom of research, and the irrepressible Auxiliary of
Strasbourg, Bishop Elchinger, did a little examination of conscience for
the Church on the same point and also called for a solemn rehabilitation of
Galileo. If His Eminence, Cardinal Ottaviani, was called upon to do that
in the name of the Holy Office, what celebrated phrase could he mutter
under his breath to match the historically unverified, "Nevertheless, it
moves" of Galileo?

Archbishop Provenchères of Aix-en-Provence regretted the tragic
privation of culture that afflicted such a large proportion of the world's
population and was as serious a problem as physical undernourishment.

Bishop Proaño of Riobamba (Ecuador) related this to Latin America.
He described how 80 million of its inhabitants were illiterate, 15 million
children did not attend school, 25 000 schools were needed every year and
there was a shortage of 6 000 teachers.

Archbishop Zoa of Yaounde (Cameroun) spoke on the meeting of
cultures and the need for representatives of different cultures to respect
one another's values: the scientific spirit of the West, the religiosity of
Africa.

The sheer magnitude of the topic and the hopelessness of saying
anything meaningful seemed to have overwhelmed the Council fathers, so
after 15 speeches, the cultural stream dried up and the Council moved on
to social and economic problems. Under this heading there were references
to papal encyclicals, relations between capital and labour, a fairer
distribution of material goods and similar ideas.

There were four interventions on the subject on Wednesday and great was the surprise on Thursday morning when, after the announcement of the list of speakers, three of whom had asked to speak in the name of 70 to guarantee that they got a hearing, the Moderator put the question: were the Council fathers in favour of hearing only those four and no others? Relieved at the prospect of being spared a long series of unrelated monologues on social and economic problems, the great majority rose to their feet to signify assent.

So the impenetrable jungle of these problems was neatly bypassed and the whole matter dealt with in six interventions – seven minus one, this one prepared by a speaker in the name of 70 supporters, but arriving too late for the discussion on marriage. This was further proof that nobody seemed quite to know how to continue dealing with The Church in the Modern World.

Bishop Benítez of Assuncion (Paraguay) treated the Council to another statistical survey of Latin America's tragic situation and the need for a vigorous application of the Church's social teaching.

Archbishop Zoungrana of Ouagadougou (Upper Volta, now Burkina Fasso) gave the African point of view and lectured the "have" nations on their duty to the "have nots": what is superfluous belongs in justice to the poor. Donors must renounce all selfishness and the international order must be re-thought in terms of the common good.

The brevity of the treatment accorded social and economic problems was compensated for, to some extent, by the fact that the next heading of discussion was in reality a continuation of the same debate. The new chapter was The Solidarity of the Human Family. The debate on it dealt mainly with the problem of global poverty.

It was presented in quite dramatic fashion by the choice of a layman to give the introduction, Mr James Morris, an American, auditor of the Council and President of the International Catholic Migration Council. Mr Morris read his speech in Latin and read it very well. It was a model of good diction. He pointed out that 16% of humanity, constituting the North Atlantic community, enjoyed 70% of the world's riches, that the disproportion was growing by the day and that the kernel of the problem was to spread the benefits of the know-how and resources of the North

Atlantic community to the rest of the world. In great areas of the world, life expectation was about 35 and a mother gazing on her newborn child realised that there was a strong probability that the little one would die within a year. The wealthy nations were those of Christian tradition. They could not remain indifferent. The Church had to throw all its spiritual and moral resources into the solution of this problem and Mr. Morris hoped that the Council would decide to set up machinery on a global scale to mobilise the Catholic effort.

Cardinal Frings of Cologne spoke immediately afterwards and made some concrete proposals about how such machinery could be organised and operated, not just to relieve want but to help people to help themselves. Cardinal Alfrink of Utrecht (Holland) warned against the desire, often expressed in the Council, to issue a new condemnation of atheistic communism. Condemnations were useless. We needed constructive action and contact and communication with people.

Father Gerald Mahon, Superior General of the Mill Hill Missionaries, considered socio-economic activity as an integral part of the missionary function of the Church and pleaded for co-ordination in that field.

Cardinal Richaud of Bordeaux (France) supported the idea of worldwide co-ordination of the Catholic effort with special emphasis on the education of the Catholic conscience. Two speakers called attention to the right of people to seek a living through emigration and the wrongfulness of raising barriers to such emigration, since the earth belonged to the whole human family.

On Monday November 9, this topic gave way to the discussion on peace. This turned out to be disappointing. Perhaps, after 12 full days of the world's problems the Council fathers were feeling a little battered and bruised and in no shape to trade telling blows about atomic bombs.

Cardinal Alfrink called for more clarity. Two French bishops and one German advocated the encouragement of national and international conferences on ABC warfare: atomic, bacteriological and chemical. One of them, Bishop Ancel, Auxiliary of Lyons, pointed out that the only safeguard of peace would be a supranational organisation in sole possession of the weapons of war.

Two speakers called for an all-out condemnation of nuclear warfare and presumably, by implication, advocated unilateral disarmament: Bishop Guilhem of Laval (France) and Patriarch Maximos IV. His Beatitude attempted another of his prophetic utterances but this did not quite get off the launching pad.

Two English-speakers, Bishop Hannon, Auxiliary of Washington DC, and Archbishop Beck of Liverpool brought the argument back to earth where the fighting usually occurs, and pointed out the drawbacks of unilateral disarmament and vague generalisations about atomic warfare. The vagueness of the unilateral disarmament case suffered by comparison with the precision of these two speakers.

So, with no very constructive proposals to offer on the issue of peace and war, beyond of course committing the Church to an increase of effort to remove the causes, the discussion on The Church in the Modern World ended in a confused truce. A lay auditor, Dr. Juan Vasquez, said a few words of appreciation in Spanish and the *rapporteur*, Bishop Guano of Leghorn, made a suitable reply to the whole debate, expressing the usual promises on behalf of his Commission to try to draw clarity out of the confusion. It was going to be a herculean task.

The debate on The Church in the Modern World was interrupted on Friday November 6, to allow the *schema* on the missions to be brought before the assembly. The Holy Father himself presided in the opening stages and said a few words of encouragement and of guarded approval of the *schema*, which was one of those that had been reduced to a series of propositions. The guarded approval caused some uneasiness as it was generally known that a heavy onslaught on this *schema* had been prepared and that there could be a clamorous demand for a renewed and enlarged *schema*.

With the time taken up by a Mass in the Ethiopian rite, complete with drums at the enthronement of the Gospel, the pope's allocution, the introduction of the *schema* by Cardinal Agagianian, Prefect of the Congregation for the Propagation of the Faith, the speech of the *rapporteur*, Bishop Lokuang of Taiwan, and a report on part of the *schema* on the pastoral role of bishops which was being presented for voting, there was time for only four speakers that day.

It is possible that out of respect for the Holy Father's favourable view of the *schema*, these speakers toned down their criticisms. But the heavens opened and the storm burst the next day. Nearly every speaker, beginning with Cardinal Frings of Cologne, asked for a new and complete *schema* which would be a real source of inspiration to the missionary work of the Church. Various aspects of this work were dealt with: the theology of missions, adaptations to local cultures, the need for a central policy-forming body connected with the Congregation for the Propagation of the Faith and comprising representatives of the "old" churches and of the "new", catechists, lay participation and finance.

Some speakers from South America had a special axe to grind. Because South America did not fall under the Propagation of the Faith, the areas where the Church was just being established were not known as apostolic prefectures and vicariates but as *prelacies nullius* and they received no regular financial aid from Rome. Their incumbents had a legitimate grievance and they aired it forcefully.

The two memorable speeches were those of Bishop Lamont of Umtali (Rhodesia, now Mutare, Zimbabwe) and Bishop Fulton Sheen. Bishop Lamont made heavy calls on his not inconsiderable endowments in the line of histrionics and humour and produced a sidesplitting lament over the emaciated condition of the *schema*. In glowing language he described what members of the Council had been expecting and contrasted that with what they actually found in the *schema*, borrowing the image of a field of dry bones from the prophet Ezechiel. Pausing for effect, he brought out two words with devastating emphasis: *ossa arida* (dry bones). The Council was convulsed but the Bishop received an admonition from the Moderator, Cardinal Döpfner, who did not seem to appreciate the "oratory". When Bishop Lamont got back to his seat he found a note waiting for him. It read as follows: "Your mission subsidy has been cut by 50%, signed Cardinal Agagianian". The perpetrator was Bishop Ernest Green of Port Elizabeth, South Africa. Bishop Lamont later described how while he was listening to the words of commendation pronounced by the Holy Father, he had felt the text of his intervention burning a hole in his pocket.

Bishop Fulton Sheen, the well-known radio and television speaker and preacher, gave the last speech in the debate. It was lively and imaginative.

He called for the recognition of the fact that Church and mission were identical ("What God has joined together, let no *schema* put asunder") and pleaded the cause of those poor territories that received no help from the Propagation of the Faith. It was pure Fulton Sheen: dramatic, rehearsed and aimed at the emotions. It earned prolonged applause.

However, the most dramatic moment of the debate had nothing to do with the mission *schema*. It occurred when Cardinal Suenens, having completed his remarks on lay participation in mission work, added a brief reference to the comments that had been stirred up by his "birth control speech" of the week before. He explained that erroneous interpretations had been placed on his words. He had not intended to suggest that the established doctrine of the Church should be changed, but that a better synthesis of all its elements should be made, the scientific as well as the theological. Nor had he intended to tell the Holy Father how to handle the special pontifical commission that had been set up to investigate the problem. The debate on the missions ended with a vote on whether or not the *schema* should be referred back to the relevant commission for revision. The ayes had it by 1 601 to 311. While all this was going on the amended *schema* on the pastoral role of bishops was subjected to the vote. Two of its three chapters got so loaded with amendments that they had to go back to the commission for revision. They would reappear in the fourth session.

The question now was: would four sessions be enough?

The next item on the agenda was religious life, the life lived with the vows of poverty, chastity and obedience by women and men in convents, monasteries and similar houses. The debate on the relevant *schema* began late on Tuesday morning, November 10. It was concerned with the sometimes conflicting demands of religious life and apostolic work, adherence to the original vision and spirit of the institute in question and adaptation to modern conditions. No-one mentioned Cardinal Suenens' book *The Nun in the World* but there can be no doubt that many of the speeches made in St Peter's were continuing rumbles of the slight explosion it had caused.

There was only one intervention that Tuesday after the introduction of the *schema* and that was by Cardinal Spellman of New York. He did not mince matters. Quite obviously the nuns in his diocese had let him know that they had been reading *The Nun in the World.* His intervention called for a return to the true concept of religious life as a life dedicated primarily to prayer and abnegation and not to glorified lay apostolate by people with vows.

On Wednesday, Cardinal Spellman was ably abetted by Cardinal Ruffini of Palermo, who spoke with such eloquence and intensity that even the most progressive in the assembly joined in the applause. From then on, however, the *schema* got the worst of it as speaker after speaker, with Cardinal Döpfner in the van, criticised it for being too meagre (it was one of the reduced *schemas*), too juridical, and in no way calculated to inspire a renewal of religious life and to fill people with enthusiasm for it.

Later, however, the defence rallied and there were several excellent speeches pointing out the merits of the *schema*, its insistence on a revival of the authentic religious spirit, a fuller formation and deeper education, on community as well as individual poverty, ruling out houses and institutions that looked too wealthy for people dedicated to poverty.

In the course of Wednesday 10 November, Cardinal Suenens had the opportunity of defending his view: that since the Church is by its very nature apostolic the vows of religious which are a dedication to the service of the Church have an inherent apostolic dimension. This dimension must be fully explored and the proper conclusions drawn, particularly in the case of active religious, particularly too in the case of women religious whose apostolic potential is not being fully recognised and utilised. Much in the life of some religious congregations of women is archaic, reminiscent of a period when women were perpetual minors and in need of the protection of unscaleable convent walls. Obedience should be properly understood and should not be imposed to such an extent as to produce infantilism.

Other speakers followed something of a similar line, particularly Father van Kerkhoven, Superior General of the Missionaries of the Sacred Heart who, talking mainly of congregations of men, maintained that many of them had been founded for apostolic purposes but with a spiritual outlook derived from the monastery. This resulted in unresolved tension.

Bishop Huyghe of Arras (France) was a strong opponent of the *schema.* He claimed that its theology dated back to before the Council and needed to be brought up to date with emphasis on the fact that religious should be witnesses to charity and unity and therefore should not be so eager to separate themselves from the rest of the Church and from the world that needed them so much. It was not going to be easy to sort out how much withdrawal from the world a religious vocation demanded and how much apostolic and charitable involvement it required.

Father Buckley, Superior General of the Marist Fathers, wanted special mention in the *schema* of the need for fraternal understanding between diocesan and religious priests. There was more in common between diocesan priests and religious priests in ministry than between the latter and contemplatives. He also wanted the old distinction between religious orders and religious congregations abolished. It created the impression of first and second-class citizens. He pointed out the anomaly that all the superiors general of orders had the right to be at the Council no matter how few subjects they had, whereas superiors general of congregations had to have a thousand subjects to qualify.

Bishop Carroll, Auxiliary of Sydney, spoke well on the life of religious teaching brothers. So did Father Hoffer, Superior General of the Marianists.

When the vote was taken on this *schema* it got through by 1 153 to 882. In subsequent voting on separate propositions there was a heavy pile-up of amendments. So the *schema* would have to be substantially revised to command the sort of acceptance necessary in a Council.

The *schema* on priestly formation was introduced by the *rapporteur*, Bishop Carraro of Verona (Italy), late on Thursday morning, November 12. It received powerful support from Archbishop Colombo of Milan and never looked back. Archbishop Colombo pointed out that the two outstanding defects of modern seminary education were its disregard of much of the human element and its lack of co-ordination between the spiritual, intellectual and pastoral elements of formation. He indicated that the *schema*, though reduced to a set of 20 propositions, managed to achieve all that was asked of it in the line of suggesting remedies for these defects.

On Friday November 13, there was no debate as the day had been set aside for a solemn concelebration in the Byzantine (Greek) rite in the presence of the Holy Father. Patriarch Maximos IV was the chief celebrant and the Mass was multi-lingual in character: Arabic, Latin, Old Slavic and Russian were used as well as Greek. The Russian singing was magnificent. Patriarch Maximos showed that he knew and pronounced Latin well despite his record, as a protesting Oriental, of never having spoken Latin but only French in the Council.

It was at the end of this Mass that the Holy Father donated to the poor the tiara he had received for his coronation.

Saturday's meeting of the Council resolved itself into a chorus of praise for the Seminary *schema*. Members of the Commission who had prepared speeches in its defence did not have to use them or had to alter them hastily to include a few criticisms of their own to make a debate of it. It was quite a change after the torrid treatment that had been accorded the *schemas* on the Missions and on Religious.

What won many hearts in the Seminary *schema* was the reference in the opening paragraph to the liberty that was to be left to local hierarchies to make the necessary adaptations of the general norms laid down in the *schema*.

The *schema* had also been particularly fortunate in its secretary, Father Augustin Mayer OSB (later Cardinal), Prior of the Benedictine Monastery of St Anselm in Rome. He had proved an indefatigable worker and had managed to obtain enough reaction from bishops after the reduction of the *schema* in March 1964 to get the Commission to revise it entirely during the first month of the third session. The revision had resulted in the re-inclusion of a lot of the material that had been discarded in the slimming process. So there were very few of the kinds of complaints that had characterised the discussions on the Missions and Religious Life. The only real clash of opinions came over the place of St Thomas Aquinas in the seminary curriculum. The reference in the *schema* was broad and general. Some, like Cardinal Léger, wanted it still more general. Others, like Cardinal Ruffini and Archbishop Staffa, Secretary of the Congregation of Seminaries and Universities, wanted it more binding and specific.

Cardinal Suenens' speech dealt with the need for adaptation to modern conditions, giving seminarians concrete experience of the situation they would have to face as priests and the role they would have to play as "animators" of the laity. He called for the reorganisation of the curriculum, postponing the more difficult and abstract parts of philosophy until near the end of seminary training. This reflected, he said, the experiment he was carrying out at that time in Belgium.

Speaker after speaker rose to commend the balance of the *schema*, the apostolic orientation, the scriptural and realistic treatment demanded for theology, the apostolic character of the spiritual formation recommended and the insistence on practical experience of pastoral functions.

It was no surprise when the vote on the *schema* resulted in its overwhelming acceptance by 2 076 votes to 41. The members of the commission responsible for the *schema* walked tall as they left St Peter's. That included me.

On Monday November 16, a touch of drama was given to the conciliar scene when the Secretary General rose to make some announcements about the hardest fought chapter of the whole Council, Chapter III of the *schema* on The Church, the chapter dealing with primacy and collegiality.

It appeared that a last desperate effort had been made to head off this chapter. A protest had been lodged against alleged infringements and an appeal had been made to the Holy Father to intervene in regard to its doctrinal content. It appeared that about 100 Council members had been involved in this move.

The objection, on procedural grounds, had been overruled and in regard to the doctrinal question the Holy Father had issued a Prevenient Explanatory Note (*nota explicativa praevia*). The purpose of it was to give an authoritative interpretation of certain words and phrases used about collegiality in Chapter III of the Constitution on the Church. Four points were dealt with:

1. The meaning of becoming a member of the college by consecration and thereby assuming the functions associated with the office.
2. The consent of the Holy Father still remains necessary for the exercise of these functions.
3. The college enjoying supreme and full power in the Church. This is true only insofar as the pope is the head of the college.
4. The pope retains his right to exercise his power without reference to the college of bishops.

The announcement about all this was made on Monday and on Tuesday morning printed copies of the text were made available to Council members.

Obviously there was no little anger, upset, grousing and grumbling about this playing down of collegiality. The substance remained, of course, but the atmosphere around it was anything but cheerful. Clearly the Holy Father had issued the Explanatory Note to try to prevent the 100 protesters from becoming a real pain in the neck of the Council and perhaps too to ensure that there were no misunderstandings about his position as the supreme authority in the Church.

Against the background of the Explanatory Note the next *schema* that came up for discussion was the one on Catholic education. This was the responsibility of the same commission as had produced the *schema* on priestly formation. The commission had actually been divided into two sections, one dealing with priestly formation, the other with Catholic education, but both coming together in the finalisation of the documents and both taking responsibility for them.

The *schema* on Catholic education had gone through the same agonies as that on priestly formation and had been reduced to a series of propositions. Its title initially had been Catholic Schools and Universities but this was altered when commission members pointed out that this was too narrow a field in the whole broad expanse of Catholic education.

The *schema* was presented by Bishop Daem of Antwerp on Monday 16 November. He referred to the universality of educational problems, their human and social aspects and their spiritual and apostolic, political and juridical dimensions. He pointed out that according to statistics published in the International Review of Education, 1960, out of 860 million young people between the ages of five and 19 only 30% attended primary school, 7% secondary schools and 3% benefited from higher education. Inevitably in the discussion that followed, speakers expressed their regrets that not sufficient attention was paid to this or that aspect of Catholic education. But, as in the case of other *schemas* severely limited by the authorities in terms of extent and scope, there was not much more that could be realistically expected.

The vote was taken on this *schema* in five sections and all got through safely by 75% and more but with over 600 amendments to be attended to.

Late on Wednesday morning, November 19, a somewhat unexpected item took its place on the agenda not claiming to become either a constitution or a decree or a declaration but just a *votum*. This word is difficult to translate into English. The closest one can get is recommendation. So it was a recommendation about marriage in four paragraphs. The first three dealt with the dignity of marriage and the duty of the Church to insist on the necessary safeguards. The fourth paragraph called for a simplification of the Church legislation about impediments to marriage and the fifth about mixed marriages concerning which suggestions were made for changes in legislation in the light of ecumenism and religious liberty.

In the meantime, religious liberty was again causing quite a rumble in the Council.

On Tuesday 17 November, it was announced among other items that the amended *schema* on religious freedom would be suggested for a vote on Thursday 19 November. On Wednesday 18 November, it was announced that in response to misgivings expressed by certain Council fathers who held that the topic had not been sufficiently examined and debated, the President and Moderators had determined that there should be a preliminary vote the following day to decide whether the regular voting should be proceeded with.

The next day Cardinal Tisserant announced in the name of the Presidential Council that voting on the *schema* would not take place in that period of the Council and invited all members who so wished to submit written observations before 31 January 1965. Cardinal Meyer of Chicago, one of the Presidents, reacted like a bomb. He was out of his place in a flash, protesting vehemently against the countermanding announcement. Council fathers, Americans particularly, came streaming out of their seats and gathered in the open spaces around the high altar of St Peter's. In an incredibly short time the text of a petition was accumulating signatures. The petition wanted the Holy Father to override the decision of the Presidential Council. Three cardinals, Meyer of Chicago, Ritter of St Louis and Léger of Montreal took the petition to the Holy Father. He could not see his way clear to overruling the Presidents' decision.

The petitioners obviously had felt that delaying the vote would have a disastrous effect on public opinion. The Americans were particularly sensitive. They felt that the promotion of religious liberty was their greatest contribution to the Council and they wanted to show that they could get results and not allow a small minority to outmanoeuvre 2 000 bishops, including 300 Americans.

Along with all the other activity of the final week there had to be voting on several *schemas* in different stages of finalisation. We reached finality on the Church, the Oriental churches and ecumenism and voted to refer the recommendations on marriage to the Holy Father to be finalised by agencies at his disposal.

A final announcement from the Secretary General was in respect of letters he had received from bishops prevented by the oppressive governments of their countries from attending the Council. A paragraph from one such letter read: "I embrace you all with fraternal love and I express our respects associated with an unshaken faith in Christ and an indestructible fidelity towards the Church, associated too with tears and sufferings rendered more bitter by the fact that I am not allowed to do anything else".

On Saturday 21 November a so-called public session was held during which three completed documents of the Council were promulgated: The Dogmatic Constitution on the Church, The Decree on Ecumenism and The Decree on the Catholic Eastern Churches.

Before returning to South Africa I went eastwards to enjoy two very pleasant experiences: a visit to the Holy Land and participation in the Eucharistic Congress in Bombay (now Mumbai).

Chapter Five

The Fourth Period

The fourth period of the Council began on Tuesday 14 September, 1965 with the celebration of Mass by the Holy Father in St Peter's. After Mass the Holy Father gave an address emphasising the importance of the Council, the role of the Holy Spirit, the cultivation of a three-fold love: love of God, of the Church, of all people throughout the world and in particular of those who are persecuted. He made another appeal for peace and went on to refer to the Synod of Bishops about to be inaugurated and spoke about his acceptance of an invitation to visit the United Nations. The day closed with a penitential pilgrimage to which all fathers of the Council were invited.

The pilgrimage consisted of a walk from the Basilica of the Holy Cross to the Basilica of St John Lateran. As far as I was concerned, the walk was easy enough but the long wait before the beginning of the walk and at the end of it was truly penitential, as was the homily.

The next day, Wednesday 15 September, was the first working day of the fourth period of the Council. The Holy Father came in and occupied a position between the altar and the table of the presidential council.

Mass was celebrated as usual, but there was this improvement: that to facilitate the participation of the congregation – bishops mainly – books were made available with the chant of the introit, gradual, offertory and communion. The first two items retained their old designations. All the bishops needed now was a little rehearsing and some direction from the conductor. As it was, they were expected to sing some fairly difficult antiphons off the cuff. The absence of leadership in this sphere indicated that, though the means for participation were beginning to be provided, there was still in many quarters a lack of instinctive understanding of all that was required to make it succeed. It was not yet second nature.

Nevertheless we had come a long way. It was probably good for the bishops to find themselves like sheep without a shepherd. It made them appreciate what the laity goes through not infrequently.

After Mass the Secretary General announced a decree from the Holy Father known by the Latin title *motu proprio,* meaning "my personal decision". This was to the effect that a Synod of Bishops was being established. After the announcement a cardinal indicated its main points and later on copies of the text were distributed to the bishops. The first impression created by the announcement was that a big step had been taken in regard to episcopal collegiality, but an even cursory reading of the text revealed that this was not the case. For only the pope is authorised:

1. to convoke the Synod whenever this would seem appropriate and to indicate the place where it will be held;

2. to approve the election of members in keeping with the prescriptions of Sections V and VIII;

3. to decide the agenda at least six months before the Synod is held;

4. to decide the programme;

5. to preside over the Synod himself or through others.

The Synod is a permanent body and all its meetings have conformed to these prescriptions.

It fell to me to represent the Southern African Catholic Bishops' Conference in some of the early meetings. I deplored the absence of theologians. To a very large extent theologians made Vatican II.

As had been promised at the end of the third period of the Council when, under dramatic circumstances, no vote had been taken on the *schema* on Religious Liberty, that topic was the first on the agenda of the fourth period. Most of the arguments for or against that had been advanced in the third period, came up again. To the conservatives it seemed clear that since the Catholic Church had been established by God and given to his human children, there was no choice in the matter. How could one choose to refuse such a gift from God? The progressives saw it differently. Religious differences and religious clashes had helped them to realise that, along with the gift of the Church and even prior to that gift, God had given his human family the gift of conscience which played a very important part in the exercise of that other great gift of God, freedom. Freedom of conscience implied religious liberty. Some of the great moments of the debate came more from the pathos of personalities than the force of argument – as when men spoke who knew what freedom was from having suffered a lack of it, men like Cardinals Slipyj of the Ukraine, Beran of Czechoslovakia, Wyszynski of Poland. Cardinal Beran said that he felt the Church in his country was expiating the tyrannies that it had committed in the past in the name of the Catholic faith, as when it burned John Huss and imposed forced "conversions" in the 17th century.

On Tuesday 21 September, the debate was guillotined and the moderators put a question which amounted to asking for a vote on the principle of the declaration, while leaving it open for further amendment by the Secretariat for Christian Unity in the light of the debate. The result was 1 997 to 224 in favour.

The Holy Father could now go to the United Nations confident that the Church he represented stood for the highest and noblest values of human freedom.

On Tuesday 21 September, after the closure of the debate on Religious Liberty, discussion was begun on the revised text of the *schema* on The Church in the Modern World. In the absence through illness of Bishop Guano of Leghorn (Italy), Archbishop Garrone of Toulouse presented the revised text. It consisted of a preface, an introductory explanation and two parts. Part I dealt with the Church and the human situation and consisted of another introduction and four chapters. Part II consisted of another introduction and five chapters on certain more urgent problems.

It was obvious that the Joint Commission (Doctrine and Lay Apostolate) had been working extremely hard to compile a new text taking into account the heavy criticism of the previous text during the third period of the Council. Nevertheless the Joint Commission had not succeeded in warding off a further heavy bombardment of criticisms. One had to entertain great sympathy in their regard because they were providing a text for the first ever discussion in the history of the Church on the Church's view of the world and some of its principal problems. Speakers in the debate were critical not only of the contents but also of the Latin style of the *schema*. Cardinal Bea said that he had been teaching in Latin for 50 years but he had been unable to decipher the Latin text without the help of the French version. One critic was of the opinion that whoever was responsible for the Latin had tried too hard to give it a classical expression whereas the Church in its long history had built up a different kind of Latin style. Other speakers found that references to the world were too optimistic. It was true, of course, that St Paul had emphasised that the whole universe would be restored in Christ (Romans 8:21) but there was no scarcity of sin. Others pointed out that the expression "world" was used in the New Testament to designate opposition to Christ. Cardinal Ruffini of Palermo suggested that the mystery of suffering was not given proper emphasis. Archbishop Sigaud of Diamantina (Brazil) expressed the fear that the *schema* opened a door to every conceivable false philosophy, culminating in Marxism. Archbishop Sigaud was the leading spirit of the best-organised conservative group in the Council. It called itself The International Group and claimed to reflect always the traditional teaching of the Church.

Interspersed among these criticisms were several expressions of appreciation and of hope that with some correcting, the *schema* would prove acceptable.

On Thursday September 23, the cardinal moderator put to the vote the question whether the assembly thought the general discussion had gone on long enough. Everybody rose to signify assent. A further question was then voted on: whether the Council should proceed to discuss the various parts of the *schema* in detail. The vote was favourable: 2 111 to 44.

The first speaker on the introduction was Cardinal Cardijn, founder of the Young Christian Workers. He treated the Council to one of his rousing rhetorical efforts. He could be as powerful in Latin as in English or French. He wanted specific treatment of three subjects: youth, workers and the Third World, that is, the poverty-stricken territories of Asia, Africa and South America. He spoke vigorously about the need for special treatment of youth, half the population of the world, so different from the youth of former times and so much in need of special consideration.

Among others who spoke on the introduction was Cardinal Frings of Cologne who wanted it revised entirely. He found its description of the world inadequate. It did not seem to refer to the modern world created by industry. He was also unhappy about a confusion between Christian growth and human progress. Others supported the criticism for different reasons.

The discussion of Part I of the *schema* began on Friday morning. This part is known in other languages as An Essay in Christian Anthropology. In English this sounds strange as the word "anthropology" has a limited scientific meaning. In other languages it embraces all knowledge that has the human being as its object. The first part of the *schema* endeavoured to evaluate the place of the human family in the universe and in the mystery of salvation.

Two prelates from the East, Cardinal Meouchi, Maronite Patriarch, and Archbishop Ziadé of Beirut (Lebanon) criticised this "anthropology" for its lack of reference to the resurrection of Christ. The resurrection has always been a cardinal point of Eastern theology, which sees in Christ's rising the restoration of all creation.

A point that attracted a great deal of attention was the paragraph on atheism. Cardinal Seper of Zagreb (Yugoslavia) said that many today were convinced that atheism was a condition for appreciating the world and promoting its progress. They wanted the Council to examine this attitude thoroughly. Archbishop Marty of Rheims spoke on similar lines.

Cardinal Maximos IV (yes Cardinal, despite former denunciations!) Melkite Patriarch of Antioch, also concentrated his attention on atheism and insisted that the Church needed less theorising on the subject and more practical action to show that Christians were concerned with the fate of the poor and the suffering. The unconcern of Christians was one of the main causes of the spread of atheism.

Cardinal König of Vienna analysed the causes of atheism, both intellectual and practical. Cardinal Florit of Florence followed in the same line emphasizing, as an Italian preoccupied with the whole situation, that atheism was an essential ingredient of Marxism. Many Italians endeavour to deny this.

Bishop Hnilica, a native of Czechoslovakia, spoke movingly of his experience of atheistic Marxism in a concentration camp. The Ukrainian Auxiliary of Toronto, Bishop Rusnack, described the destruction wrought by Marxism on the Ukrainian community of Czechoslovakia.

Archbishop Garrone of Toulouse (France) expressed disappointment that the *schema* had not given a better appreciation of creation. Creation was not merely something known to reason. It was an article of faith and the Christian concept of creation saw God's creative presence in all reality. Hence the believer had the highest and noblest appreciation of the universe.

Bishop Elchinger, Auxiliary of Strasbourg, felt that the *schema* was missing the mark because it was much too theoretical. The modern world did not want to be told what the Church could do for it. It would be convinced only by deeds. Archbishop Bengsch of Berlin reflected the dissatisfaction of the German hierarchy and proposed that the first part of the *schema* should be cut substantially. It should not aim at giving an exhaustive treatment of any one subject. This was beyond its scope.

One of the best speeches was made by the new Father General of the Jesuits, Father Arrupe. He spoke convincingly about the weakness of Catholic methods of communication. The Church had the truth but it could not get it across to the modern world, because the communication was clothed in abstract and incomprehensible terms. Father Arrupe called for a thorough investigation into the present situation of the world, an elaboration of a plan of action on a world scale and absolute obedience to the Pope in implementing it. There was a sharp reaction in press circles to Father Arrupe's mention of atheistic domination of the means of communication (press, radio, cinema and television) and his description of Catholic shortcomings in this regard.

The debate on Part II of the *schema* on The Church in the World of Today began on Tuesday September 27. On Wednesday morning, Bishop Hengsbach of Essen (Germany) was called upon to introduce the debate on Part II which consisted of five chapters dealing with the world's most urgent problems. Bishop Hengsbach outlined the difficulties: how much to say and how much to leave out in the treatment of a complicated problem which could have different dimensions in different parts of the world. He referred especially to the problem of reaching any sort of decision on nuclear war. Everybody deplored it but should it be totally outlawed, even in self-defence? After this introduction the Council began to examine Part II of the *schema*, chapter by chapter. The first chapter was on marriage – as thorny a question as nuclear war, if not more so.

Three great concerns became apparent in the debate:

1. The need for a powerful reaffirmation of the Church's teaching on marriage and related topics;

2. The need to foster fuller appreciation of the personal values in marriage with particular emphasis on conjugal love;

3. Where do we stand on birth control?

Cardinal Ruffini, as usual, set the ball rolling, this time with a powerful call for a return to the traditional view of marriage with its distinction between the primary purpose, procreation and the education of children, and its secondary purposes, mutual support and satisfaction of the sexual instinct. His Eminence was a good, clear and logical speaker but there was a hardness and inflexibility about his style that won few supporters. There were not many listening to him who would be satisfied with the old presentation of marriage that reduced it almost to a mathematical formula of purposes, rights and obligations.

A few other speakers supported him, more concerned about maintaining old positions than deepening the theological appreciation of marriage.

Cardinal Colombo of Milan shared his concern about emphasising the Church's traditional stand against birth control, but his approach was entirely different, sympathetic and humane. He praised the *schema* for its evaluation of the personal relationship of conjugal love.

Some fine speeches were made in favour of the second trend, the appreciation of conjugal love. The leader was Cardinal Léger of Montreal. He criticised the chapter of the *schema* as being a little illogical, extolling conjugal love but defining marriage merely as "an institution for the procreation and education of children". He advocated a definition describing marriage as a community of life and love which finds its fulfilment in the procreation and education of children. He was followed in this line by Bishop De Roo of Victoria (British Columbia, Canada) who spoke movingly of the part played by true conjugal love as an expression of the sacrament of matrimony, the development of the married couple and their Christian influence outside the home. Archbishop Urtasun of Avignon and Bishop Reuss, Auxiliary of Mainz, also supported this trend.

Cardinal Browne examined the concept of conjugal love with cold, philosophical accuracy. It didn't sound like the same thing at all.

Cardinal Suenens expressed the hope that the Council would call for expert scientific research on a massive scale to provide the Church with the data necessary for the guidance of the faithful. He also advocated an annual renewal of marriage vows as a liturgical feature of married life.

Cardinal Heenan and Cardinal Rossi of Sao Paolo (Brazil) raised the burning issue. Cardinal Heenan was the more explicit. He said that if nothing could be said about birth control it would be better not to publish anything about marriage, for to speak about marriage and not to mention the major problem of today would create a very curious impression, for instance, that the Church had no answer and was unable to maintain her previous stand against birth control.

That certainly was the question: how long could the Church wait for the papal decision that was to be based on the investigations of the special commission set up by Pope John XXIII?

Among other points referred to in the debate were the spread of abortion, the need for governments to do something about the increase of sexual immorality, the praiseworthiness of adopting poor, disabled and handicapped children, the effect of poverty and starvation on home and family life, and the need for a concerted world-wide effort to come to grips with this problem.

Cardinal Conway of Armagh (Ireland) and Bishop Taguchi of Osaka (Japan) wanted more precision in the statement about parents having the right to limit the number of their children.

Archbishop Djajasepoetra of Djakarta (Indonesia) complained that the treatment of marriage in the *schema* was typically Western. In the West love preceded marriage, but often in the East and in Africa marriage came first and love came trotting after.

Archbishop Zoghby, Melkite Vicar General for Egypt (who resigned when his superior, Patriarch Maximos IV, accepted the red hat, but retracted later) startled the assembly by advocating relaxation of the "no divorce" rule in the case of a deserted innocent party. He maintained that such people were not called by God to perpetual continence and it could not be imposed upon them. He cited the tradition of some oriental churches in favour of this. Cardinal Journet, a Swiss theologian, replied to him the next day, citing numerous gospel texts and pointing out that the leniency of the oriental churches had originated from the example of civil law.

The debate came to an end on Friday October 1. Just so as to leave no stone unturned, Bishop Hacault, Auxiliary of St Boniface (Canada) called for an appreciation of the positive values in polygamy.

At the end of the debate on marriage there were a few speakers, backed by 70 signatures, on topics that had appeared earlier. One of these was by Bishop Ddungu of Masaka (Uganda) asking for some stronger and clearer words against racial discrimination.

The Council then passed on to the discussion of culture, the second chapter of Part II of the *schema*. The discussion of this topic was no more inspiring than the previous year's. The subject was vast and amorphous and had no immediate crisis zones that stirred up passionate debate in the Church. This was probably because Catholicism had been so long out of touch with the marching wing of modern culture. Only 12 speeches were made on the subject. The word "culture" was taken in its broadest meaning, referring to whatever is involved in the work, philosophy, science and art of the human family.

The first speech and the best was made by Bishop Elchinger, Auxiliary of Strasbourg, who pointed out that the great concern of the Church with modern culture was the pastoral one: how to get in touch with it. The Church needed theologians with the ability, training and freedom of movement to enter into meaningful communication with the means at the source of modern cultural developments.

The French bishops were well to the fore in this debate. Archbishop Blanchet, Rector of the Catholic Institute of Paris, regretted the absence from the *schema* of a strong reference to the philosophy of science, something that would give a coherent view of scientific involvement and achievement.

Archbishop Veuillot, Coadjutor of Paris, reflected the disappointment of French Catholic scientists with the *schema* when he spoke of its lack of realism and urgency in regard to the place of science in modern culture and the anguish caused by the moral uncertainty about where science is taking the human race.

Bishop Lebrun of Autun (France) was a little more cheerful when he spoke appreciatively of the place of sport in modern culture and regretted that it had been overlooked in the text.

The newly-named and not yet consecrated Archbishop of Turin, Mgr. Pellegrino, showed the spirit that was coming into the Italian hierarchy when he spoke up strongly for freedom of research in the Church.

Bishop Spülbeck of Meissen (East Germany) welcomed the chapter on culture and its references to science but warned against over-optimism in the appreciation of the scientific mind. It was a mind governed by experiment and measure and had little inclination for faith or philosophy. Theologians could not communicate with the scientific mind unless they understood it thoroughly.

Another German, Bishop Frotz, Auxiliary of Cologne, returned to his feminine theme of the previous year when he spoke up for the rights of women. He wanted more implicit mention of the special and indispensable part played by women, married or single, lay or religious, in the development of culture.

There was an unexpected intrusion into the discussion of culture when Archbishop Zoghby, Melkite Vicar General for Egypt, got up to explain that when he had pleaded the case of the deserted innocent party in a marriage, he had not advocated divorce but some sort of dispensation similar to the Pauline and Petrine privileges. It sounded like a distinction without a difference but apparently he had been moved to this attempt at clarification by the wave of publicity that had followed his former speech and by the interpretations that had been put upon it.

The debate on culture came to an end on Monday morning, October 4, with the thoughts of all accompanying the Holy Father on his flight to New York.

The previous Friday the Secretary General had announced the probable ending of the general sessions in St Peter's by October 17. All debates would be over by then, but a great deal of work would remain to be done dealing with amendments to the *schemas* debated in the present period.

The Council completed the discussion of Part II of the *schema* on The Church in the World of Today on Friday October 8. During this fourth week of the period it dealt with the last three chapters of Part II: Socio-Economic Life, The Life of the Political Community, The Community of Nations and The Promotion of Peace.

The discussion on economic and political life was accompanied by the same sense of dissatisfaction as had characterized the debate on culture the week before. The Council was not at home in these fields. It was out of its depth in matters in which few of the assembly had any professional competence. It is one thing to enumerate the chief economic problems of our times. It is quite another to discuss them intelligently if you are not a sociologist or an economist. The *schema* described the problems fairly well: resources, capital, labour, economic co-operation, the poverty in so much of the world and the growing disparity between the rich and the poor nations. It also indicated what the Christian response should be. But the brief and condensed treatment left one with an impression of exceedingly simple solutions to excessively thorny problems.

Cardinal Siri of Genoa, who opened the debate, found the *schema* unbalanced. It proposed solutions to economic problems without taking the technical complications into account, for instance, the participation of workers in the ownership and control of industry. Cardinal Bueno y Monreal of Seville took an opposing view, that the *schema* had too much of the old Western individualistic spirit and did not sufficiently encourage the participation of the workers. Bishop Franic of Split, Yugoslavia, supported this view.

Two German bishops, Hengsbach of Essen and Höffner of Münster, found the *schema*'s economic considerations and proposals out-of-date and inadequate.

Two cardinals spoke strongly about the workers. Cardinal Wyszyinski of Warsaw said that they got fair treatment neither from the Marxist nor the capitalist system. A new social outlook was needed based on authentic Christian teaching. Cardinal Cardijn pleaded the cause of the workers with his usual vehemence and eloquence. He emphasised, as he had done before, the three themes dearest to his heart: the workers, youth and the underprivileged Third World of Asia, Africa and South America.

Bishop Himmer of Tournai (Belgium) and Bishop Larrain of Talca (Chile) spoke on economic progress, the former to warn of its dangers and to emphasise the efforts that are necessary for it to achieve its full human and Christian dimensions, the latter to advocate the right of all to share in economic progress and to point out the injustice and danger of excluding people. Bishop Larrain quoted the saying of Paul VI: "Development is the new name for peace".

Bishop Echeverria of Ambato (Ecuador) and Bishop Anoveros of Cadiz (Spain) laid stress on the growing social consciousness of modern times.

Archbishop Castellano of Siena (Italy) and Bishop Patteli of Tucuaremvo (Uruguay) deplored the scanty mention of agriculture in the *schema*.

Archbishop Garcia y Sierra of Burgos (Spain) thought the *schema* was taking the Church too far out of its own field and too deeply into economics, while Bishop de Vito of Lucknow (India) found its language too theological and not likely to mean much to those who were most concerned: the poverty-stricken and starving millions.

A theme that recurred on the lips of many speakers was the need for an organisation of some sort connected with the Holy See to promote social justice in word and deed. This idea was suggested by Cardinal de Arriba y Castro of Tarragona (Spain), Archbishop Angelo Fernandez, Coadjutor of Delhi, Bishop Mar Gregorios of Trivandrum (India), Bishop Sanstrom, Auxiliary of New York and Director of Catholic Relief Services, and Father Gerald Mahon, Superior General of the Mill Hill Congregation.

In the long run this may prove to be the most valuable outcome of the debate, backed as the proposal was by a deep realisation among the bishops of the extent of world poverty and malnutrition. As Father Mahon so vividly pointed out, during the 12 months between the two debates on *Schema XIII,* an estimated 35 000 000 died of starvation.

The debate on the political community went by almost unnoticed. It came at the end of Tuesday morning, October 5, as the assembly was preparing to receive the Holy Father on his return from New York and as representatives of the diplomatic corps and press were streaming into St Peter's. There were only four speakers.

Bishop Del Campo of Calahorra (Spain) said that relations between government and citizens were just as important as economic relations. Tax evasion needed particular attention. The Council must insist that tax laws are binding on conscience and that governments must take the steps necessary to re-establish confidence in the fiscal system and put an end to fraud and injustice.

Bishop Beitia of Santander (Spain) wanted more religion in political life, such as the official recognition by governments of Christ and his Church. The confusion of the functions of Church and state dies hard. One could have thought there had never been a discussion of religious liberty.

Archbishop Paraniak of Poznan (Poland) spoke of the problem of collaboration with an atheistic and totalitarian regime.

I praised the *schema* for reflecting the *aggiornamento* in advocating a Christ-like spirit in the Church's attitude to governments but pointed out that sometimes this Christ-like attitude involves standing firm on the Church's own freedom and the rights of people adversely affected by the action or the neglect of government.

After the dullness of the debates on culture, economics and politics, it was good to feel the Council coming to life again as it plunged into the question of peace and war. Here was an issue that was much more directly a Church issue: a problem that needed brave tackling.

The Joint Commission responsible for *Schema XIII* had given much study to the problem and had come up with quite a good chapter in the revised *schema*. Its approach was dynamic and constructive. Peace was a positive value to be worked for, to be earned. It demanded broad-mindedness and international co-operation in all fields, particularly the economic. Developing nations needed help and encouragement. The population explosion was to be faced and met with wholehearted economic expansion. War was the supreme horror. Total war, atomic, biological, chemical and conventional was grossly immoral. Nevertheless, force might have to be used against an aggressor. The balance of terror was a frightful and lamentable situation, and yet in some ways it kept the peace. The only hope was to persuade the nations to outlaw war and to set up a world authority to enforce the ban. In the meantime, however, nations might possess atomic arms to deter others. Minor wars were to be stamped out by removing the causes: injustice and discrimination. In regard to conscience, no-one should obey orders that conflicted with the divine law. However, in case of honest doubt, the presumption was in favour of authority. Provision must be made for conscientious objection.

The debate on all this opened late on Tuesday October 5, as the assembly waited for the Holy Father to arrive after his return from New York. Cardinal Alfrink spoke first, asking for a stronger text concerning the balance of terror, disarmament and conscientious objection. Cardinal McCann of Cape Town was next, supporting the idea of a central organisation for justice to help remove the causes of war.

On Wednesday and Thursday the debate continued and was prolonged into Friday by several speakers who claimed the right to intervene after the closure on the strength of 70 supporting signatures.

The French hierarchy gave the lead. Three cardinals, two archbishops and two bishops made a formidable array of speakers out of a total of 25. If oratory, indignation, passion and pleading could conjure war off the face of the earth, the seven French prelates would have done it. They brushed aside distinctions between just wars and unjust wars, little wars and big wars, combatants and innocents. They pleaded for stronger condemnations of war, for the outlawing of nuclear weapons, for the education of public opinion, for appeals to the conscience of statesmen, for the rights of conscientious objectors and the recognition of the power of non-violence.

The most powerful of their advocates was Bishop Boillon of Verdun, where 1 300 000 French and German soldiers died in the First World War. It was a magnificent display – yet not one could bring himself to say what the Christian pacifists wanted to hear: that one side should disarm even if the other did not and accept the consequences. And the calmer among the French prelates recognised explicitly the right of self-defence, even nuclear. It was necessary to remember the technicalities of language in this discussion of peace and war. It was confusing at times to hear speakers saying that there were no more just wars, yet by implication admitting the right of self-defence. What they meant was that no-one had the right to start a war in this day and age, for there was no proportion between the damage a war could do and the wrong that the would-be aggressor was trying to put right.

But the big question for the Christian conscience was precisely this question of self-defence. Does the Christian conscience in this nuclear age require unilateral disarmament? There were 20 women praying and fasting in Rome during the week of the debate. The object of their prayer and fasting was probably that the Council would say yes. One day, perhaps, the Church may say it, but not yet. In the meantime the Christian pacifists were keeping the bishops squirming – "men of little faith"!

The next most active group in the debate were the English. Abbot Butler led off criticising an ambiguous sentence about the right to possess nuclear arms solely to deter the enemy. He also discussed the question of conscience and called for a stronger statement on conscientious objection and the removal of the clause about presuming the authority right in doubtful cases involving military action. Archbishop Beck of Liverpool and two other English bishops supported him in this.

Archbishop Beck accepted the possession of nuclear weapons as a dangerous but necessary "occasion of sin", until a world authority was created that could stamp out war entirely.

Two Spanish bishops were less squeamish. They laid plenty of emphasis on the right of self-defence. One thought that conscientious objection should be a matter for the government to decide.

Bishop Carli of Segni (Italy), who defended every fossilised position with the skill of an expert swordsman, cut and thrust vigorously at the statement favouring conscientious objection.

The idea of a secretariat or central organization for social justice came up again in three speeches at least.

A minor engagement was fought over the population explosion. Bishop Simons, a Dutch missionary bishop from Indore (India), maintained that food production would never catch up with population, so there was only one thing for it: birth control by all available means. Bishop Gaviola of Cabanatuam (Philippines) hit back strongly the next day. Bishop Marling of Jefferson City (USA) also spoke on the need for more attention to the population problem. Archbishop Roep of Monaco repeated his plea of the previous year for a wide-open right to emigrate and so spread the population to where the food is.

One of the great speeches was that of Cardinal Ottaviani, who called for a complete condemnation of war and the use of every possible means to eliminate it. He spoke strongly about totalitarian governments, the fostering of civil war by communists, the need for sanctions against aggressors, and made a powerful plea for a world republic. Some of His Eminence's suggestions were a little unrealistic, but his sincerity was so obvious and his eloquence so warm that he got a good round of applause. It must have been a pleasant memory to balance so many memories of the battles he had fought and lost.

Another good speech was made by Bishop Philbin of Down and Connor (Ireland) who spoke on Friday October 8, in the name of 70 supporters, strongly criticising the whole *schema* for its intellectual approach to the world's problems and apparent neglect of the grace of Christ.

The debate on peace ended with the passionate oratory of the Bishop of Verdun.

The next topic for debate was The Missionary Activity of the Church. This *schema*, characterized as "dry bones" in the now historical speech of Bishop Lamont of Umtali (now Mutare), Zimbabwe, had been rejected by the Council in the third session. It had come back filled out with flesh and blood.

It consisted of five chapters. The first one dealt with the theology of mission and endeavoured to describe as accurately as possible what mission is. Much theological ink had flowed over this issue because, since it became fashionable to look aghast at the de-christianised condition of France and refer to it as a "mission country" there had been hot discussion as to whether de-christianisation was missionary work in the strict sense of the word. This is where the Anglophone mind gives up. What does it matter whether or not the situation is strictly missionary or not, the work of evangelisation has to be done both in old countries that are losing the faith and new ones that have never had it? But the Anglophone mind is not the human mind in its entirety and the Latin segment of humanity likes to get its ideas clear before it goes into action. Of course, it has to be constantly on the watch lest after an uproarious debate it forgets to go into action.

The *schema* took a broad view of the mission of the Church, tracing it back to the mission of the Son from the Father in the mystery of the Blessed Trinity and of the Holy Spirit from them both. It described the mission of the Church as the work by which the messianic people of God, obeying the command of Christ and moved by the love of the Spirit, bring salvation to people who do not yet believe in Christ. It also indicated that, in the strictest sense of the word, missionary activity aims at establishing the Church where it does not as yet exist.

The second chapter traced the stages of establishment from the first contacts (pre-evangelisation) through evangelisation proper to conversion, catechumenate and the formation and growth of Christian communities.

The third chapter dealt with the training of missionaries, the fourth with the co-ordination of mission work and the fifth with the co-operation of those engaged in the missionary apostolate: bishops, priests, religious, laity.

In the speeches that were made from Friday October 8 to Wednesday October 13 the points about which there seemed to be major concern were the urgent necessity of the missionary apostolate, the participation of the whole people of God, the place of ecumenism and the role of mission institutes: religious orders and congregations and the like.

The question of the urgent necessity of the missionary apostolate had arisen from the realization that the great majority of people are not Catholics and not even Christians. God must have some way of saving them. There must be much that is of the true God and of Christ the Redeemer in whatever religion or philosophy of life they adhere to. And if so, why worry to send missionaries to them? This would only complicate matters.

Cardinals Frings, König and Journet spoke about this and the absolute need for the Church as the means of salvation, though people could be saved by belonging to it only subconsciously, so to speak. Those who were saved without knowing the Church were really saved through the overflow of grace from it. But without the living, visible, conscious Church there would be no grace and consequently no overflow. So the stronger the Church the more abundant the overflow. Archbishop Cordeiro of Karachi (Pakistan) emphasised that the aim of the Church is to procure the glory of God in people and that the Church could not rest content as long as people did not explicitly adhere to Christ and consciously reflect the glory of God.

Several speakers, including Cardinal Alfrink of Utrecht (Holland) and Bishop Corboy of Monza (Zambia) emphasized that mission work is the function not merely of the hierarchy but of the whole people of God. Bishop McGrath of Santiago Veraguas (Panama) drew out the implications of this in regard to the laity.

Cardinal Frings spoke of the ecumenical dialogue which plays such an important part in missionary activity and so fully involves the laity. Cardinal König also referred to ecumenism while Father Degrijc, Superior General of the Missionaries Scheut, made it the theme of his whole speech.

The undercurrent of misunderstandings that sometimes occur between mission institutes and bishops came to the surface occasionally. Cardinal Zoungrana of Ouagadougou (Upper Volta, now Burkina Faso) devoted his speech to a passionate defence of mission institutes, but he was followed on the same day by the strange phenomenon of two African bishops of Rwanda and one from Burundi in quick succession expressing criticism of these institutes. Since there was only one mission institute in the area, the White Fathers (now Missionaries of Africa), it was evident that there was a little family and possibly tribal feuding in the background.

Latin America raised the question again of why many of their areas, though strictly missionary in character, were not treated like the areas under the Propagation of the Faith. The complaint has a long history behind it, a history of sensitivity characteristic of the countries of Spanish and Portuguese colonization about being termed mission countries.

Cardinal Suenens criticised the *schema* for not emphasising enough the practical apostolic training of missionaries. Bishop Koppmann of Windhoek (South West Africa, now Namibia) also referred to mission training and regretted the lack of reference to mission theology. He also sounded a note of caution concerning the dispositions of people to be evangelised. They have their good points and their proximities to Christianity, but there are many problems to overcome.

Archbishop Yu Pin of Nanking (then Rector of the Catholic University of Formosa, now Taiwan) also spoke of training and the need to help missionaries adapt to the culture of the country to which they went.

Father Arrupe, General of the Jesuits, criticised much mission propaganda as childish and sentimental. Mission work had frequently to be adapted to very advanced cultures as in Japan. The Church needed proper organs of information to make this known and create the proper image.

, Two speakers were most emphatic about the need for better organization: Father Queguiner, Superior General of the Foreign Missions of Paris, and Bishop De Reeper of Kisumu (Kenya). Bishop De Reeper said that when he returned to his territory, the question that would interest his priests most would not be whether the Council had succeeded in defining missionary activity, but rather in organising funds to promote it. His eloquent tirade indicated that he, like most missionary bishops, was pretty tired of the endless battle to find the money necessary to keep going and to expand.

The debate closed on Tuesday October 12. Bishop Lamont spoke in the name of 70 Council fathers to record his thanks that the "dry bones" had been given flesh and blood. That seemed to be the end of the discussion on missions.

But it wasn't. Ten more speakers rose on Wednesday, each in the name of 70 supporters, to repeat much of what had been said before and to ensure that the Council would be "kept in" on Saturday to finish the last debate, the one on The Ministry and Life of Priests. How popular these 10 speakers were can be left to the imagination.

A lay auditor from Togoland, Eusebe Adjakpley, Secretary for Africa of the International Federation of Catholic Youth, finally wound up the discussion on the missions. He cut a fine figure in his multicoloured West African toga, standing in the pulpit usually occupied by the Secretary General of the Council, and spoke an impeccable French.

The debate on The Ministry and Life of Priests which began on Thursday October 14, had already had its most dramatic moment a few days earlier. It was on Monday at the end of the day's sitting that the Secretary General read a letter from the Holy Father to Cardinal Tisserant, head of the Council of Presidents, recommending that the question of clerical celibacy not be discussed in the Council. The applause that greeted this letter indicated a genuine sense of relief on the part of a large number of Council fathers. A number of speeches had been prepared drawing attention to the problem being encountered in the modern world and the disturbing number of cases in which the law of celibacy seemed to be becoming a burden too heavy to be borne.

The Holy Father's letter created an angry sensation among the press people around the Council. They felt that it was a departure from freedom of speech and the public airing of information about delicate problems that should characterize the Church in modern times, and therefore a retrograde step.

The Holy Father signified his intention not only of upholding celibacy but of confirming it though he also asked for written submissions from any Council fathers who wanted to express an opinion on the matter.

The *schema* on The Ministry and Life of Priests treated in its first part of the nature of the priesthood, its identification with the priesthood of Christ and its relation to the episcopate. Priests formed with their bishop, who was their leader, one *presbyterium* for the joint exercise of the priesthood of Christ. In this *presbyterium* they were communicators of the Word, ministers of the Eucharist and leaders of the people of God.

Special passages were devoted to the relations between bishop and priest, among priests themselves, and with the laity.

The second part of the *schema* emphasised priestly sanctity, showing how it was related to priestly functions, and dealt with the evangelical councils and celibacy. The *schema* ended with a reference to remuneration and social insurance. Generally speaking, the *schema* was well received, many Council fathers commenting on the great improvement over the previous draft which had been rejected in the third period. But the debate had no real highlights and no significant controversies.

Some found that the theological description of the priesthood was still insufficient. Others that the need for priestly sanctity was not presented with sufficient logic and coherence.

The main issues that engaged the attention of speakers were:

1. The need for a theological evaluation of the priesthood that would be a real inspiration to priests under the present difficult conditions of life in the modern world;

2. The relations between bishop and priests. Some stressed the crisis of obedience and the need for a deep spirit of faith to render obedience possible. Others emphasised that the characteristics of priestly obedience must be initiative, responsibility and maturity.

Cardinal Meouchi criticised the *schema* for reflecting too occidental and legalistic a spirit. Cardinal Bea sympathized with this view and pointed out how the *schema* seemed to present celibacy as an essential adjunct of the priesthood, whereas this was not the case in the Eastern rites.

Cardinal Doi of Tokyo found the *schema* insufficiently mission-minded. Cardinal Léger found it too timid in associating priestly sanctity with apostolic work.

Cardinal Heenan spoke of the need for a close family spirit among priests and the danger of being a lone wolf. He felt that there was need for more fraternal connection among priests and that the schoolboy spirit of not reporting allowed unfortunate situations to drift into disaster. He also spoke of the necessity of strong priestly leadership for the lay apostolate and cited as an example the spirit of the Legion of Mary. His mention of Frank Duff, present as a lay auditor, brought a round of applause.

Bishop Leven, the Auxiliary of San Antonio, Texas, brought some life into a rather dull discussion on the final day with his passionate appeal on behalf of the forgotten men, the curates or assistant priests. He maintained that they had no rights under canon law except the right to ecclesiastical burial.

The final day was indeed something of an anticlimax. There had been so little expectation of a session that day that many had made other plans and at least 500 were missing from their places in St Peter's.

When the speech of an African bishop from Cameroon was brought unceremoniously to an end at about 12.15 on that day, October 16, by order of the Cardinal Moderator it could very well have been the last contribution to the debates of the Second Vatican Council but, as it was still possible for further speakers to stand up in the name of 70 supporters, when the Council reconvened on October 25, the last word may not yet have been said.

During the week under review voting was completed on three documents: Priestly Formation, Christian Education and Relations with Non-Christian Religions. Christian Education had had some heavy votes against it, but not enough to hold it up. Many Council fathers were dissatisfied with it either because it was too explicit about Catholic schools or not explicit enough. The document had suffered from a change in Council procedure which provided for a reduction in size of some *schemas* and curtailment of conciliar treatment. From being at one stage a full-blown *schema* on Catholic schools it had been reduced to a Declaration on Christian Education.

Non-Christian Religions also came in for some adverse voting mainly because of the Jewish question. Some votes were cast against it because it treated the Jews too well, others because the reference to the whole Jewish nation not being guilty of deicide had disappeared, though in fact a more satisfactory formula had been inserted.

So, on Saturday October 16 we broke up for a week, the next plenary session being due only on Monday October 25.

In the meantime, of course, many commissions would be busy with amendments to the *schemas* on Priestly Formation, Christian Education, Religious, Non-Christian Religions, Lay Apostolate, the Missions, The Life and Ministry of Priests. The Church in the Modern World with all its implications and complications would prove to be a nail-biting, midnight oil-burning experience for those involved in it.

By now the Council had reached the stage of operating in broken time. There would be three long recesses: October 17 to 24, October 30 to November 9, November 20 to 30 and even the plenary sessions held in St Peter's took little more than an hour-and-a-half. To fill in the intervals between votes the Secretary General indulged in an abundance of announcements couched in the most gracious and often humorous Latin. At school we had never dreamed that Latin could be humorous, but the surname of the Secretary General was not Felici for nothing. When even he ran out of ideas and Latin quips other means were used to maintain interest. On Friday October 29, the assembly was regaled by a German choir singing Russian hymns in the Palaeoslavic (ancient Slav) liturgical language. There were very few *non-placets*.

On Monday and Tuesday October 25 and 26, the time was occupied to some extent by 12 speakers, each of whom had managed to recruit 70 supporting signatures. They continued the debate on The Ministry and Life of Priests without adding anything particularly new to what had been said already. The last of the 12 to speak was Archbishop Pellegrino of Turin, newly enthroned. He spoke, as befits a man with an academic background, on study in the priestly life, both of profane and sacred subjects. His was the last such contribution to the Second Vatican Council.

As voting continued on several texts, ample use was made of the qualified vote in regard to religious freedom. The top 200 who had opposed religious freedom at every turn made their last great stand by this means. *Modi,* i.e. amendments, were mass-produced on every unwanted passage or phrase and made available to all who were willing to use them. Bishop van Velsen of Kroonstad (South Africa), who served on the Secretariat for Christian Unity, the body responsible for religious freedom, remarked that the Secretariat found it easier to calculate the amendments by weight than by number – 32 kilos.

However, not all the amendments were from the same camp. Quite a few came from progressives who were unhappy about a passage that had been inserted into the first section of the *schema.* This passage was a very strong statement of faith in the one true Church. Its purpose was to make quite clear that though Catholics believed in religious liberty they did not accept that one religion was as good as another. While this was true, it was a little disconcerting to have it flung in your face from the front page of an ecumenical document on freedom. As someone said, it was meant to buy the diehards. But they were not for sale. They were still wed to the proposition that because God had revealed, we were not free. They seemed unable to distinguish between the moral obligation to believe when you are convinced you ought to believe and the psychological fact that people cannot believe any other way but freely and therefore can never be constrained, especially by political pressure. No-one can shake off their past easily and one has to admit that 32 kilos of amendments were nothing in comparison with the weight of historical pressure bearing down on the last of the conservatives. Despite the bombardments of amendments, Religious Freedom received a two-thirds favourable vote on every section and was also set for final revision preparatory to ultimate adoption.

On Thursday October 28, the third public session of the Council was held for the promulgation of five completed conciliar texts: The Decree on the Pastoral Office of Bishops in the Church, the Decree on the Training of Priests, the Decree on the Up-to-date Renewal of Religious Life, the Declaration on the Relation of the Church to Non-Christian Religions and the Declaration on Christian Education.

The qualified vote was fairly extensively used in the case of the Mission *schema* and resulted in one chapter not meeting with approval. This chapter dealt with the Roman Congregation (i.e. department) in charge of missions, the Congregation of Propaganda Fide. Many Council fathers wanted bishops' conferences to have the right to elect their representatives on this Congregation. The support they rallied for their cause resulted in the chapter failing to secure the requisite two-thirds majority of *placets*. The *schema* on the Ministry and Life of Priests was also heavily loaded with amendments but not in sufficient numbers to hold up any of its chapters.

During the first half of November the topic of indulgences was brought up for discussion. It was not a topic on the Council agenda but it appears that the Holy Father had expressed the wish to get the opinion of bishops concerning the matter. However, on Saturday November 13, the process was discontinued. In announcing this the Secretary General added that one could not give unqualified assent to some of the statements that had been made in the reports about indulgences. With that stiff reprimand to eminent cardinals and the conferences they represented, the matter rested.

On the day before that, Friday November 12, another little episode indicated that the conservative-progressive tensions were still at work. The Secretary General announced that he had been asked if the lectures given at Domus Mariae were official or had been authorised by the Secretariat of the Council. His reply to both was a categorical negative. Domus Mariae is a hostel owned by Italian Catholic Action and housed many South American and Italian bishops during sessions. Everybody knew that the lectures were not official. Everybody knew that they were not authorised by the Secretariat of the Council, which goes for the myriad other lectures given in Rome on the periphery of the Council. Why the question and why the answer? Because, no doubt, on the list of lecturers figured the names of such as Edward Schillebeeckx and Hans Küng.

The Constitution on Divine Revelation and the Decree on the Apostolate of Lay People were promulgated on 18 November, and the Decree on Ecumenism and the Decree on the Catholic Eastern Churches on 21 November. The last four had to wait until the final working day of the Council, 7 December 1965.

Voting on The Church in the Modern World began on Monday November 15 and on Tuesday a record must have been established with 15 votes completed. The pace of voting increased as every effort was made to finish the work before the deadline of 7 December. The *schema* was taking conciliar shape but it was a pity that it had to be rushed so much at the end. It was noticeable that the work of sub-committees on various chapters had not been firmly pulled together by a co-ordinating hand. For instance, in response to criticism of the overoptimistic tone of the previous draft, some sub-commissions seemed to have introduced as much as they could about sin, suffering and anguish. The accumulation was a little depressing.

Depressing it may have been, but it was nothing in comparison with the fatigue that was building up among the members and consultants of the Commission on the Church in the Modern World. Midnight oil was being consumed by the tankful in order to get the text ready for promulgation on Tuesday 7 December, the last working day of the Council.

Rumours leaked out from the Joint Commission of contentious debates into the late hours; of amendments proposed by the Pope to the text on marriage which the Joint Commission felt it could not accept without invading the territory of the Pope's own commission on birth control; of efforts to strike a balance in the text on peace and war between condemnation of the horror of total war and recognition of the right of defence. However, the work was done for better or for worse and the amended *Schema XIII* appeared in the Council on Saturday 4 December and received final acceptance at the last general session on 6 December. But not without one last eruption, paradoxically concerning the chapter on peace, which read as follows:

> Every act of war directed to the indiscriminate destruction of whole cities or vast areas with their inhabitants is a crime against God and humanity, which merits firm and unequivocal condemnation. The hazards, peculiar to modern warfare consist in the fact that they expose those possessing recently-developed weapons to the risk of perpetrating crimes like these and, by an inexorable chain of events, of urging people to even worse acts of atrocity. To obviate the possibility of this happening at any time in the future, the bishops of the world gather together to implore everyone, especially government leaders and military advisers, to give unceasing consideration to their immense responsibilities before God and before the whole human race.

Archbishop Hannan of New Orleans, USA, feared that this could sound like a condemnation of his country for its possession of nuclear weapons. Cardinals Spellman of New York and Sheehan of Baltimore and seven other Council fathers, including myself, supported him in a paper he circulated. Archbishop Hannan and his supporters came under severe criticism for a day or two. It looked as if we were in favour of atomic warfare but what we were really trying to emphasise was the value of deterrence. In their turn, two prominent members of the Commission on *Schema XIII* circulated a letter in which they made a number of points, including this one: "Nowhere in numbers 80 and 81 (referring to paragraphs of the *schema*) is the possession of nuclear arms condemned as immoral". But how could possession without the intention of using be a deterrent? Catholic theology has always considered an evil intention as culpable as the deed intended. Perhaps the nine of us were wrong to support Archbishop Hannan but we could not help being convinced that the United States, without a nuclear deterrent, would have given Khrushchev an extremely powerful position in world politics.

In due course the nuclear storm subsided and we attended a very beautiful ecumenical service in St Paul's Basilica on the Saturday evening of 4 December. The Pope presided. Council fathers and observers from other churches participated. There were scriptural readings, prayers and hymns in Latin, French, English and Greek. Catholics and representatives of other churches took their turns or joined their voices as the occasion demanded. Pope Paul spoke briefly but deeply and movingly. There was brotherhood. There was community. There was a catch in many voices. What a long, long way we had come since 25 January 1959 when, in the precincts of this same basilica Pope John XXIII, not quite three months after his election to the papacy, had told a group of cardinals of his intention to call a council. According to an entry in his diary those cardinals had accepted the announcement with something like silent and respectful attention.

Chapter Six

The Commission on Seminaries, Academic Studies and Catholic Schools

This commission, like all the others, had come into existence during week one of the first period of the Council in October 1962. My election to serve on this commission was announced on 22 October 1962. This account of the commission's work provides a case study of one commission's method of operation.

For its agenda it had inherited from the Central Preparatory Commission two *schemas* relating to priestly formation: one on the fostering of ecclesiastical vocations and the other on the formation of candidates to the priesthood. The latter consisted of six chapters:

1. Preface and the General Organisation of Seminaries
2. Spiritual Formation
3. Discipline
4. Programme of Studies
5. Pastoral Formation
6. Post-Seminary Formation.

These chapters contained some excellent material but it was obvious that the Commission had not gone very deeply into the aim of priestly formation before drawing up the various chapters. This had resulted in the strange phenomenon of Chapter 4 on the Programme of Studies being submitted to the Central Preparatory Commission along with the *schema* on vocations four months before the other five chapters of the *schema* on formation. Since Chapter 1 on The General Organisation of Seminaries contained the description of the aim of seminary formation, it appears that this had not greatly influenced the chapter on studies.

The *schema* reflected the departmental thinking of the past. There were some good cross-references linking one aspect of formation with others; for instance, the importance of theology and liturgy for the spiritual life and the insistence on parallel development of pastoral and intellectual formation. But the general impression was of linking separate elements from without and not showing their internal unity.

There were four distinct parts of the training of seminarians: the spiritual, the disciplinary, the intellectual and the pastoral. Disciplinary training was carefully distinguished from spiritual, though described in language that tended to emphasise their identity. The treatment of disciplinary formation began in typical scholastic style: description, definition, errors... The errors were given prominence.

In regard to the curriculum of studies there was the traditional watertight division between the two years of philosophy and the four years of theology, and the separate consideration of theology and scripture. One good point, however, was that the *schema* accorded a measure of liberty to local hierarchies in shaping the curriculum. The treatment of pastoral formation was good, but suffered from the two sharp distinctions from other aspects of formation. It was obvious that there was no general strategic objective, no clearly-defined overall aim. The lack of unity was emphasised by a wordy and repetitive style that produced few highlights. The *schema* mentioned two reasons for allowing seminarians to interrupt their studies: first, to dedicate themselves more intensely to spiritual formation and secondly to exercise the diaconate before priestly orders. The *schema* also recommended, albeit with much hesitation and many safeguards, the initiation of seminarians into the pastoral life through practical experience of apostolic work. The old conviction still shone through that the best way to train a person for a complex job was to keep that person away from it for as long as possible.

A progressive step in the *schema* was the insistence on the proper training of seminary staff.

The Second Draft: 1962

The two *schemas* emerged from the Central Preparatory Commission as one, the *schema* on vocations now constituting the first chapter on the formation of candidates for the priesthood. It was published in 1963 after the first session of the Council in the fourth volume of the *Schemata Constitutionum et Decretorum*. It totalled about 9 000 words. The Preparatory Commission responsible for it had also prepared three other *schemas:* one on Catholic schools, one on academic studies and a third on the reverence due to the Magisterium of the Church in the teaching of sacred subjects. In due course the first two were blended into the Declaration on Christian Education and the third fell away entirely.

The Third Draft: March 1963

At the end of the first session of the Council Pope John announced new regulations for the revision of Council *schemas* and appointed a Co-ordinating Commission to see to their implementation.

On December 18, 1962 the Co-ordinating Commission addressed a questionnaire to the Council Commission on Seminaries, Academic Studies and Catholic Education regarding the matters that should be dealt with in the revised *schemas*. On January 30, 1963 this questionnaire was followed up by brief instructions on what the *schema* should contain. In the light of these the Commission went to work.

Its first work meeting was held on February 21, 1963. Owing to the short notice given only 14 out of 25 members were able to attend. The Commission divided into three sub-commissions: one on priestly formation, one on schools and academic studies and the third on the preparation of material for canon law. The work had to be finished in about 10 days so that the documents could be presented to the Co-ordinating Commission on March 10. This was obviously rushing things a bit. Perhaps the rush was due to Pope John's desire to have all the Council documents in shape before his death which he knew could not be far off. Or perhaps it was due to the difficulty Roman circles experienced in understanding the work involved in preparing a Council document.

Some members of the Commission on Seminaries and Schools had responded to the invitation to submit ideas by outlining or drafting new *schemas,* but the one accepted as the basis for discussion was the abridgment of the original *schema* carried out by the consultor, Father P. Dezza SJ. He had reduced the *schema* to about one-third of its length. Father Dezza was a master of concision. His skill in this regard left its mark on the *schema.* It is among the most muscular and sinewy of Council documents. But this style has the drawback, if such it is, of leaving the casual reader with the impression of a rather cold and dry document, lacking inspiration. It is only when one begins to study it closely that one realises the explosive possibilities of seemingly innocent phrases.

Father Dezza's abridgment had not redeemed the *schema* from its original sin of departmentalism. This point was placed squarely in the centre of debate at the Commission meeting and vigorously hammered out. As a result the pastoral aim of priestly formation was clearly formulated. This formulation was not easily achieved. I found myself almost alone in a whole day's argument about the necessity of formulating clearly the aim of priestly formation. In this I was a faithful disciple of St Thomas Aquinas on the paramount importance of what he termed the *causa finalis,* the "final cause", the aim. As a result the pastoral aim of priestly formation was clearly formulated in the section of the revised *schema* entitled The Aim of Formation and the Organisation of Seminaries. The pastoral aim was to train candidates for the threefold function of the priesthood now explicitly formulated: the ministry of the word, the ministry of worship, and the priestly service of the community.

The clear formulation of aim is a big step towards the realisation of structure in matters both theoretical and practical. In the light of a clearly-formulated aim everything else acquires shape and proportion. So it was with the *schema* on priestly formation. After the formulation of the goal, the relationship between parts of the *schema* began to emerge and the internal structure of each part began to take shape.

The division of the *schema* into chapters gave way in the abridgment to a division into sections. At the end of the Commission meeting the *schema* consisted of a preface and five sections:

1. Ecclesiastical Vocations

2. The Aim of Formation and the Organisation of Seminaries

3. Spiritual Formation

4. Studies

5. Post-Seminary Formation.

The document was far from perfect but good progress had been made. The treatment of spiritual formation showed more clearly its internal relationship with the intellectual and pastoral formation. The correlation of philosophy and theology had been more strongly emphasised. The need had also been recognised to initiate students from the beginning of the course into a vision of the priesthood, strongly scriptural in character, that would enable them to absorb and integrate all aspects of their training. The description of theological formation had become more dynamic, with insistence on the central position of scripture, the importance of the historical development of doctrine, and the necessity of making theology relevant to spiritual growth and human experience.

Practical pastoral formation had been included in the section on studies.

There had been some controversy about the position of the section on spiritual formation. This had always been given first place among the aspects of formation in order to emphasise its primacy. It was now questioned whether this was correct, and I was the main questioner. The importance of spiritual formation was not doubted, but the point was made that spiritual formation must be adapted to vocation, and should therefore be treated logically after intellectual and pastoral formation, which set the pattern for the life of a priest and seminarian. This one I lost, and spiritual formation continued to take first place geographically.

I am sorry that at the time I did not have available a beautiful passage from the writings of St Francis de Sales, which can now be found in the breviary for the memorial of this saint on 24 January:

> At the Creation God commanded the plants to bear fruit, each according to its kind, and likewise commands Christians, the living branches of the vine, to bear fruit by practising devotion according to their state in life. The practice of devotion must differ for the gentleman and the artisan, the servant and the prince; for widow, young girl or wife. Further, it must be adapted to their particular strength, circumstances and duties. Is the ordinary life of a Carthusian

suited to a bishop? Should those who are married practise the poverty of a Capuchin? If workers spent as much time in the church as religious, if religious were exposed to the same pastoral cause as a bishop, such devotion would be ridiculous and cause intolerable disorder.

Quite clearly, according to St Francis de Sales, consideration of spiritual life, of devotion, should come *after* consideration of one's calling in life.

Another lost battle was fought over the treatment of seminary discipline. This theme led quite a nomadic existence until it finally settled down in its true home, the section on spiritual formation. It had begun there in the early days of the Preparatory Commission but, in the *schema* presented to the Council (the first draft), it had emerged with a chapter to itself. Its house had been destroyed in the abridgment and it had been given lodging in the section on the general organisation of the seminary. Here it remained for the time being, despite a determined effort to move it back to its original home with spiritual formation. It retained, with some slight softening, a note of lamentation over the rebellious spirit of the times.

The new draft was accepted by the Co-ordinating Commission, approved by Pope John a month before his death, for discussion in the Council, and distributed with other *schemas* to the Council fathers.

The Fourth Draft: November 1963

The *schema* on Priestly Formation did not come in for much criticism at this stage, due mainly to the preoccupation of the bishops with the far more contentious issue of revelation and the Church. Seminaries would have to wait their turn. Nevertheless a significant number of comments was sent in by individual bishops and by some national and regional conferences.

Here is the place to pay tribute to the Secretary of the Commission, Father Augustin Mayer OSB, Rector of St Anselm's College, Rome, whom I have already mentioned in Chapter Four. He proved himself a most efficient and indefatigable worker in sending out texts for comment, co-ordinating the replies, cross-checking with other commissions and ensuring that everything was ready for meetings. The written comments he was continually eliciting from bishops all over the world meant that a consensus had substantially been reached before the debate in the *aula*. His easy command of Latin and of four modern languages made him a brilliant interpreter. When situations became tense he was the personification of the *Pax Benedictina*.

During the second session of the Council, the Commission considered comments that had been submitted, not without some misgiving, as the revised *schema* had been approved for debate and there did not seem to be much point in discussing alterations before the debate took place. However, different parts of the *schema* were allotted to three sections of the Sub-Commission while sections of the Sub-Commission on Catholic Schools and Academic Studies worked on various aspects of their topic. Amendments were formulated in the hope that permission would be given to incorporate them in a new text before the debate in the *aula*.

The changes reflected style and emphasis rather than the substance of the *schema*. With regard to seminaries, a more detailed and systematic treatment was given to practical pastoral formation, but this theme was again divorced from the section on studies.

The Fifth Draft: Schema *of Propositions: March 1964*

The permission to publish the revised text came towards the end of the session when, on November 29, 1963 new instructions were issued by the Co-ordinating Commission concerning all *schemas* that had not yet been discussed up to that date. New texts were to be ready by March 1964, and amendments to the previous texts were to be published side-by-side with the original. A report on the work of the Commission was to be provided, and amendments that had not been accepted were to be dealt with in an appendix.

Before these instructions could be acted upon there were further developments. Urgent meetings of the Co-ordinating Commission held after Christmas resulted in what appeared to be a panic decision. Either the officials controlling the Council had become afraid that if its work went on at the pace of the first and second periods it would never end, or the Holy Father himself wished to see work concluded with a third session in 1964. An instruction of January 23, 1964 laid down that outstanding *schemas* were to be drastically pruned and, incredible as it may sound, some were not even to be debated – just voted on. The *schema* on Priestly Formation was one of these. It had to be reduced to a series of votable propositions by the end of March 1964. So back the Commission members went to Rome to participate in a second great surgical operation from 3 - 9 March.

Two drafts of propositions had been compiled, from which the Commission had to choose one as the basis for further discussion. It chose Draft A which was an 850-word summary in 20 propositions of the 1963 *schema* as amended during the second session.

The Commission set about its work without much enthusiasm. The skeleton before it looked most uninviting. However, interest revived as the work progressed and at the end the 20 propositions had been reduced to 19 and the 850 words had been expanded to about 1 000.

There were three positive achievements on the credit side to balance the heavy loss through editing.

First, the passage granting to local hierarchies ample liberty of adaptation was promoted to the beginning of the *schema*. It became Proposition 1 and governed now not merely the programme of studies but the entire system of priestly formation.

The second achievement was the significant improvement in the treatment of spiritual formation. Previously this section had displayed little by way of theological order and emphasis. The defect was now remedied. The section acquired depth and luminosity from the new structural arrangement. The following themes were brought into orderly and progressive relationship: identification and communion with Christ the Priest; the Word of God in the liturgy as a source of spirituality; the theological virtue; priestly spirituality in its ecclesial dimensions of union with the bishop in the service of God's people; evangelical simplicity; the role of discipline in the seminary, its human requirements and its contribution to maturity and responsibility; the importance of the social virtues.

The third achievement has just been referred to: the integration of the treatment of seminary discipline into the section on spiritual formation. In the reduction of the text the pessimistic references to the spirit of insubordination were eliminated.

Despite these achievements, the document did not look too convincing. It was far too lean. To make up for this it was decided to request that the former text should be printed along with it. This would serve a double purpose: provide the Council fathers with a fuller understanding of the propositions, and possibly inspire a general demand for the re-inclusion of much of the discarded material.

The *schema* of propositions duly appeared with a lengthy appendix containing the former text and a full report on the history of the *schema*.

The Sixth Draft: October 1964

When the Council reassembled for the third period in September 1964 there was confident expectation that the authorities would relent and permit a debate on the reduced *schemas*. This hope was fulfilled when, on September 25, it was announced that there would be a short discussion on each of these *schemas* followed by voting with the right to amend. Thus only one stage of the procedure was to be omitted. An immediate jump was to be made from the stage of debate to the voting and amending stage. This was not entirely satisfactory as the two stages in the polishing of other *schemas* had proved invaluable in giving them genuine conciliar shape and balance. However, it was better than nothing.

The reaction of the Council fathers to the meagre propositions had been just what the Commission had hoped for. In written comments submitted before the third session many expressed their desire to see the flesh put back on the bones. Duly authorised, the Commission set about this task and worked briskly to have a new text, the sixth in the history of the *schema*, ready for the debate in the *aula*.

In size this draft was a compromise between the propositions and the previous text, leaning towards the latter. It was 2 000 words in length. It introduced one important new idea: that of dividing the student body of large seminaries into smaller groups to provide better for personal formation while retaining unity of direction and scientific training.

The debate on the *schema* took place from November 12 to November 17 with interruptions on Thursday 13 and Sunday 16. The *schema* was accorded a remarkably benevolent welcome despite the murderous mood the fathers were in after that treatment of the mission *schema* and the one on religious life. Father Augustin Mayer, like a good chief-of-staff, had made careful preparations for the debate. Commission members had been selected and primed, ready for the fray. But there was no fray.

Apart from one outright condemnation by a Polish bishop the debate, after the presentation of the text by Bishop Carraro of Verona (Italy), resolved itself into a chorus of praise with an occasional suggestion as to how the text could be improved. From the moment a warm burst of illegal applause greeted the intervention of the first representative of the Commission to speak after the presentation, Archbishop (later Cardinal) Colombo of Milan, the *schema* never looked back. Archbishop Garrone of Toulouse (France), in the name of 70 fathers, had special praise for the *schema*'s achievement in aptly and concisely applying the teaching on the Constitution on the Church to its subject matter. "A pity", he added, "this had not been done in other *schemas*". Archbishop Garrone later, as Pro-Prefect of the Sacred Congregation of Seminaries and Universities, had the job of promoting the implementation of the decree.

Cardinal Döpfner made an important contribution to the debate in regard to training for celibacy. Cardinal Léger raised the great bone of contention: the mention of St Thomas Aquinas as the authoritative Doctor of the Church. "Woe to the Church of one doctor", he warned. The battle over St Thomas was not unexpected. It had already been fought to an uneasy truce in the Commission. Letters had been circulated urging the unique position of St Thomas. In the course of the debate and after it masses of *modi* (amendments) were handed in suggesting how the great doctor's position could be defined. It would have taken the wisdom of Solomon to reconcile them.

The vote of acceptance of the *schema* resulted in the record score of 2 076 to 41.

The Final Text: 1965

The Commission met in Rome from April 26 to May 4, 1965 to apply the finishing touches to its work in the light of the proposed amendments. The battle over St Thomas flared up again and the decree ultimately compromised by being rather vague about a "philosophical patrimony perennially valid" and being more specific about the guidance of St Thomas in systematic theology. Explicit mention of the necessity of major seminaries was added to the *schema*. The treatment of formation for celibacy was given its eschatological dimension, and something more was said about the role of philosophy, the method of teaching it and its relationship to theology.

The final voting on the *schema* took place during the fourth session of the Council from 11 to 13 October. This revealed some minor misgivings among Council fathers about the treatment of minor seminaries, the general organisation of major seminaries and the teaching of philosophy. But they were not serious enough to hold up the decree. It was promulgated on 28 October 1965.

Chapter Seven

The Last Two Days:
7 and 8 December, 1965

Tuesday 7 December, saw the Council fathers assembled for the last time in St Peter's. It was the tenth and last public session. There were many "lasts": last votes, last announcements, last promulgations. The boredom, frustration and occasional outbursts of that last month were forgotten in the realisation that an experience given to few, to very few, in the long history of the Church, and of the world, was coming to an end. There is something a little sad about many endings. There is a deep pathos in a great ending.

Vatican II ended with the promulgation of Religious Freedom, the Missionary Activity of the Church, The Ministry and Life of Priests, and The Church in the Modern World.

The Council concluded with the ending of something else that had lasted 911 years: the mutual excommunication in Constantinople of the Patriarch of Constantinople and other Eastern ecclesiastics by Roman legates and of the Roman legates and the Holy See they represented, by the Patriarch of Constantinople and his Synod. So had begun the tragic schism between the Catholic and Orthodox Churches.

If ever there was a moment when St Peter's was well nigh bursting with emotion that was it. Many saw only through their tears the grandeur of the scene as Cardinal Bea standing on the right of the Holy Father read the message of reconciliation. On the Pope's left was the strikingly handsome figure of the Delegate of Athenagoras, Patriarch of Constantinople, Metropolitan Meliton of Heliopolis. And when His Holiness held out the document to the Metropolitan and took him in his arms many, and that included me, could not bear to look.

On 8 December, the Feast of the Immaculate Conception, the last farewells were said in St Peter's Square when a great phalanx of the people of God assembled with their chief pastor and their bishops and clergy for a Mass that reflected in its sense of community and intensity of participation the incredible liturgical progress of four short years. One realised then, however, that no matter how much the vernacular may mean to us, we must never entirely lose the Latin, never lose the ability to assemble a quarter of a million people and send the sonorous Gregorian phrases in wave after wave to the very gates of heaven. Perhaps when we have learnt to love the singing of God's praises in our own tongue we should find the occasional use of Latin and Gregorian a delightful and inspiring change. Perhaps ...

There were seven messages to the world: to people in government, to intellectuals, artists, women (obviously not exclusive categories), the poor and suffering, the workers and young people.

When Cardinal Liénart, reading the message to people in government, cried out that all the Church demanded of them was liberty, many a tough old hand of the French Revolution must have turned in his grave and wondered what side he had been on at the time.

When Jacques Maritain, looking immensely old and frail, went up to receive a copy of the message to intellectuals, the whole Church of God, represented by that conciliar assembly, paid tribute to one who had done so much to make a new Catholic understanding of human freedom possible.

The Second Vatican Council ended with the final invocations of the blessing by the Holy Father and his ringing valediction: "Go in peace". The response was the heartiest and most enthusiastic *"Deo gratias"* that most had ever heard.

Then the bishops walked along Bernini's colonnade and made off in their buses for the last time in a volume of vocal farewells and a forest of waving hands.

They had begun their journey back to their dioceses where they must endeavour to lead the great effort of bringing the Council decrees to life in the communities which they served.

The first step had been taken in the realisation of Pope John's dream. The Church, through her thinkers and pastors, had taken a long searching look at herself and seen what parts of her very being must be explored more deeply and lived more fully and what, on the other hand, she had gathered around herself on the pilgrimage of great historical epochs and could now happily discard.

She had seen herself as the People of God, the Body of Christ, the Temple of the Holy Spirit, the Universal Sacrament of Salvation with the varied and multiple functions of her members. She had seen how the glory of the word had come to her and the pattern of her worship and the meaning of her mission. She had seen with new pride what her laity is and what it must do in the world. She had seen how all people in some way are hers and must be loved accordingly so that in freedom they may seek and find her. She had seen how her religious must be renewed and how her priestly candidates must be trained for the great pastoral tasks of the future.

She had seen too, but more darkly, more confusedly, what the world means to her, the unfolding of God's designs, in the fulfilment of the Kingdom.

All this she had seen through the eyes of her pastors and searchers. Now she must see it through the eyes of all her priests and people, see it through their eyes and live it in their minds and hearts and hands. That was the great task awaiting us.

Endnotes

1.   Archbishop Hurley told the editor this was Archbishop Marcel Lefebvre.

2.   After all, Christ sent me not to baptise, but to preach the gospel; and not by means of wisdom of language, wise words which would make the cross of Christ pointless. The message of the cross is folly for those who are on the way to ruin, but for those of us who are on the road to salvation it is the power of God. As scripture says: *I am going to destroy the wisdom of the wise and bring to nothing the understanding of any who understand. Where are the philosophers? Where are the experts?* And where are the debaters of this age? Do you not see how God has shown up human wisdom as folly? Since in the wisdom of God the world was unable to recognise God through wisdom, it was God's own pleasure to save believers through the folly of the gospel. While the Jews demand miracles and the Greeks look for wisdom, we are preaching a crucified Christ: to the Jews an obstacle they cannot get over, to the gentiles foolishness, but to those who have

been called, whether they are Jews or Greeks, a Christ who is both the power of God and the wisdom of God. God's folly is wiser than human wisdom, and God's weakness is stronger than human strength. Consider, brothers and sisters, how you were called; not many of you are wise by human standards, not many influential, not many from noble families. No, God chose those who by human standards are weak to shame the strong, those who by human standards are common and contemptible – indeed those who count for nothing – to reduce to nothing all those that do count for something, so that no human being might feel boastful before God. It is by him that you exist in Christ Jesus, who for us was made wisdom from God, and saving justice and holiness and redemption. As scripture says: *If any want to boast, let them boast of the Lord.*

3. An extract from this speech can be found on pg. 162.

4. The word Tridentine refers to the period since the Council of Trent which met on and off between 1545 and 1563 and set up the Catholic defences against Protestantism.

5. See p 164 for an extract from this speech.

6. Friday 4 October. I have since realised that Cardinal Ruffini spoke after Cardinal Spellman of New York who referred in his intervention to the diaconate.

7. Saturday 11 October.

8. I wrote of myself in the third person because I hadn't disclosed that I was the Council correspondent for *The Southern Cross.*

Denis Hurley's Addresses in the Council

These excerpts from addresses given by Archbishop Hurley during the sessions of the Second Vatican Council give an impression of his contributions to the Council and highlight the breadth of his interests and concerns. Though the speeches were delivered over 40 years ago, they remain remarkably relevant.

On the Pastoral Objective of the Council

(*Acta Synodalia,* vol. I, Period I, Pars III, Congregatio Generalis XII, 19 November 1962, pp. 198-200)

I regard the present debate to be of the utmost value, because it concerns an absolutely fundamental issue, the purpose of the entire Council. On this purpose all are agreed, thanks be to God. We all say that the purpose of the Council is pastoral and this is what we all understand from the splendid words of the happily reigning Supreme Pontiff. There is no disagreement about this point. But – and it is a very big "but" – there is extreme disagreement about the interpretation of the word "pastoral".

Some declare that the Council can act pastorally simply by defining the truth, by safely storing the seed of the Gospel in the granary of dogmatic definitions. Others deny that defining truths suffices to attain the Council's pastoral objective, and they want the Council to speak in such a way that its very way of speaking will make it clear that truth is not merely to be safeguarded, but to be proclaimed; that the seed of the Gospel is not to be stored up in the granary of dogmatic definitions but to be scattered and sown throughout the world.

This then is the difference between the two sides: whether it is possible for the Council to be pastoral simply through definitions that safeguard truth; or whether its pastoral character requires such a way of expression that whoever hears or reads its declarations will experience the power and sweetness of the truth.

If there is anyone who denies that it is possible for the Council to speak in such a way, then I suggest that the very beautiful schema prepared by the Secretariat for Christian Unity and entitled *De Verbo Dei* be printed and distributed to the conciliar fathers. That schema, as we have heard from a number of fathers, breathes the sweet beauty of Sacred Scripture, and there is nothing that touches the hearts of believers and nonbelievers alike more than the fragrance of the scriptures....

The division about what belongs to the pastoral nature of the Council far exceeds the limits of the present debate. But I am absolutely sure that this division will enter into nearly all future debates. By the kindness of the Supreme Pontiff I was a member of the Central Preparatory Commission and, as I remember it, the most frequent intervention on the various *schemata* – particularly those regarding faith and morals – pointed to their insufficiently pastoral character. Yet after so many such interventions I was amazed to discover that the *schemata* had been amended only slightly, and very slightly indeed, in a pastoral direction. After the debate of these last several days I now know the reason, namely, that those assigned the task of amending the *schemata* did not understand the word "pastoral" in the same sense as those who made interventions.

We are therefore at a crisis point in the Council and as far as I can see we will experience this same division in the debate on 90% of the *schemata*. What is to be done? I see now that when in the central commission we complained about the non-pastoral character of the *schemata*, we were voices crying in the wilderness. But there was no one there to hear our cry, no one who could and should have been concerned with this defect in the preparatory work. There was no central direction. There was no person or commission to give a clear interpretation of the pastoral objective of the Council, to direct and coordinate the labours of the individual commissions toward its declared purpose, to establish limits to the topics that would be presented to the Council. Therein lies the basic defect of the preparatory work; therein, so to speak, lies the original sin of this Council.

Esteemed fathers, we cannot spend ten or 20 years debating *schemata* of a 1000 pages and on every page face the same division about the meaning of the word "pastoral".

I do not question the usefulness of the debates of these past weeks, since they have brought to light the disagreement over the interpretation of the purpose of the Council. But now that this point has been made, we cannot argue endlessly about every individual manifestation of this disagreement. The issue must be resolved either by a general debate and vote in the Council *aula* or by the work of a special commission to be established by the Supreme Pontiff to deal with the issue between the first and second session of the Council. And if such a commission is established, it should receive a broad mandate to attend to the reviewing and shortening of *schemata* and to the improving of the order of their debate.

Only in this or a similar way can the Council be redeemed from the original sin of the preparatory work and reach a successful outcome.

* * * *

(*Acta Synodalia,* vol. I, Period I, Pars IV, Congregation Generalis XXXIII, 3 December 1962, pp. 197-199)

It is not pleasant to play the role of devil's advocate time and again in the conciliar debates, but in this stage of, so to speak, the Council's purgative way, there seems to be no escaping the task.

For the most part I am not greatly pleased with the schema *De Ecclesia* because of a defect running throughout almost all the preparatory work for the Council: a lack of unity and coordination. A number of fathers have complained about the inclusion in this schema of chapters on bishops, on the states of perfection, on the laity and on ecumenism. I cannot understand how the work in preparation for a Council on unity could have been itself so lacking in unity.

For the solution of this problem it seems that there is nothing left but to propose again that between the first and second session the entire preparatory work be redone under the direction of a central and – excuse the word – centralising commission, having the task of expressing clearly, in accord with the mind of the Supreme Pontiff, the purpose of the Council and of ensuring that the means necessary for achieving that purpose are applied, as His Eminence, Cardinal Léger (Cardinal Paul Léger, Archbishop of Montreal) has already said this morning.

As to the purpose of the Council, there is practically no need for defining truths, since they are not in any danger that would call for conciliar consideration. Indeed I would venture to say that it is neither appropriate nor desirable to constrict certain teachings within the theological formularies of the past, since we are in the midst of a very fruitful stage of theological ferment arising from many causes, particularly from the renewed study of Sacred Scripture, of the documents of the fathers and Church history, and from a growing concern for the needs of our contemporaries.

That concern is a pastoral concern, which must be the supreme concern of this Council, convened not to define truths but to renew the pastoral activity of the Church. And with the help of God that activity will have as one of its foremost results an increased ecumenical effectiveness.

The nature and properties of "ecumenicity" have been clearly presented to us (especially by His Eminence Cardinal Bea and His Excellency Bishop de Smedt); other fathers have spoken about the pastoral aspect. Permit me also to say a few things about the pastoral issue, in order that this effort, however small, may serve to make the idea clearer and sharper.

It belongs to the pastoral office to propose the truth to people in such a way that they are able to embrace it and so to live by it. The first requirement for this is a suitable way of presenting doctrine that consists not simply in adapting words and language, but in a manner of speaking that is not academic or rhetorical but plain and ordinary, yet precise; that is not juridical or desiccated, but is imbued with a kind of unction and love for God and neighbour.

In addition to this mode of expression, a further requisite is that doctrine be developed and explained so that of itself and as doctrine it has the power to give an answer to the questions with which people truly grapple about their final end, about God and his Christ. The truth should not, of course, be changed nor diminished, but must be examined with deeper insight, brought back again to its source, developed more profoundly and extensively, and renewed in such a way as to be not only doctrine true in itself but doctrine *for the people* to whom we are sent. It must become teaching that has the effective and actual power to answer the just demands and questions of people. Our speech must not just say *something*, even something true, but must seek to say something to the people of these times. Let us remember the scholastic adage: "Whatever is received is received according to the mode of the recipient". And let us therefore speak in the Council in such a way as to give a new impulse to the preaching of the Gospel in today's world. Paul the Apostle dared to preach the Gospel to the Greeks in the language of the Greeks. The mediaeval doctors dared to express Christian truth in scholastic concepts and vocabulary. It therefore is the Church's tradition to accommodate its preaching to the needs of the people and of the times.

The Council of Trent called for, so to speak, a new type of bishop, and in St. Charles Borromeo found the perfect model: a type of bishop who was no longer the feudal lord of the Middle Ages, no longer the humanist of the Renaissance, but a bishop who is a pastor in the face of the needs of post-Tridentine society. We have been sent to a very different kind of world. It is not like the post-Tridentine world, which at least in intention and in principle was favourable to religion; our world has little or no regard for religion, yet it struggles intensely with the problems of human existence on this earth and of the development of the world. Since we are the appointed pastors of this world and its people, we must search for some apt and, if need be, new way of speaking to them, or rather we must be present to them in the name of Christ and for the sake of Christ. Does not this new world need some new type of evangelical pastor, a pastor not less doctrinal than a Tridentine pastor, but one who is not content to present people with "doctrine *in se*", who is concerned with presenting doctrine of a kind or formulated in such a way that it responds to their questions? Was that not the meaning of the address of the Supreme Pontiff delivered in the Council *aula* on 11 October? May God grant that from the Second Vatican Council a new generation of pastors may emerge, worthy to be compared to the great generation of Tridentine pastors, but who are pastors fully attuned to the world of this age and to its people!

On the Constitution on the Liturgy

(*Acta Synodalia*, Vol. I, Period I, Pars I, Congregatio Generalis IV, 22 October 1962, pp. 327-328)

Since all that I wished to say has already been well said by others (although perhaps not by His Excellency [Archbishop Vagnozzi] the last speaker), moved by the charism of brevity, I yield my right to speak. (The following remarks were submitted in written form).

It is undoubtedly a favourable sign that the schema proposed for the first debate is the schema on the liturgy. It is a most beautiful *schema*, filled, to use its own words, with a "warm and living love for scripture" (SC art.24). We must fervently hope that the other *schemata* will be enlivened by the same love. We should thank the preparatory commission from the bottom of our hearts for a *schema* so well composed.

What pleases me most is the *schema's* lucid exposition of the true and genuine nature of the liturgy and its importance in the life of the Church. As the text makes so clear, the primary and supreme purpose of the Church is to give glory to God. The Church by its entire nature strives for the salvation of souls, or to put it in terms better suited to our times, for the salvation of the people of God. But the salvation of the people of God is the glory of God, according to the words of Psalm 105 (106): "Save us, O Lord our God, and gather us from among the nations, that we may give thanks to your holy name and glory in your praise" (verse 47).

The more therefore that anything in the Church glorifies God, the more directly does it contribute to the purpose of the Church. But the supreme means, although as the *schema* notes not the only means, of giving glory to God is the liturgy, and the primary manifestation of the Church is the full and active participation of the entire holy people of God in liturgical celebrations.

A further point relative to the liturgy deserving of the fullest consideration is that the Church cannot give glory to God without thereby receiving immediately and abundantly from the divine generosity the most precious gifts – the gifts of divine life, of faith, hope, love, and apostolic zeal. The liturgical movement must always have a two-fold direction: the movement of the people's worship, prompted by the Holy Spirit, toward God the Father through Christ the Head; and the movement from God the Father towards his people through Christ the Head in the Holy Spirit. These gifts build up the body of Christ, the people of God and the Christian community.

The *schema* explains this idea very well by citing words from the Acts of the Apostles: "And they devoted themselves to the apostles' teaching, and fellowship, to the breaking of the bread and to the prayers.... praising God and having favour with all the people" (Acts 2:42, 47). These words point out very well the three elements that make up the principal outward expressions of the Church's life and apostolic activity, namely, teaching, liturgy, and "favour with all the people", or the witness of a Christian life. By its nature the life of the Church is apostolic and missionary in character, and to form an apostolic spirit those three elements are necessary – teaching, liturgy and the witness of Christian life.

If we wish to renew the apostolic spirit in the Church (and this, I think, is an aim of this ecumenical Council), it will be necessary to reform the liturgical life, not apart from catechetical and moral renewal, but in close conjunction with them. And this reform can come about, it seems to me, only if the exposition in this *schema* of the importance of the liturgy is enthusiastically embraced and if the *schema's* intent concerning the participation of the faithful and the adaptation, structure, and language of the liturgy is faithfully pursued.

On the Declaration on Religious Freedom

(*Acta Synodalia*, vol. III, Period III, Pars II, Congregatio Generalis LXXXVIII, 22 September 1964, pp. 515-518; excerpt)

[...] There is one aspect of the question which I wish to consider, namely, the classical argument for the union of the Catholic Church with the State. It is necessary to deal with this argument, since to many of us it may seem to vindicate the so-called ideal condition, one, that is, which the Church of its nature desires to attain which it can with regard to its relations with civil society and its directive organism, called "the State". If the classical argument retains its force, our declaration cannot be said to be complete and accurate and must be emended at least in regard to the following proposition: "the civil powers possess no direct capacity and competence to determine or regulate the citizens' relations with their Creator and Saviour".

The classical argument in its simpler and principal form runs as follows: Since each person is a social being by nature, each is obliged to worship God not only as an individual but also in a social manner. In order that this social obligation may be fulfilled, civil society as such is bound to acknowledge and worship God, and indeed in the manner in which God himself has indicated, namely, through the Catholic Church. Civil society is therefore bound to show special respect toward the Catholic Church and to provide it with assistance.

We all accept the principle, namely: Since each person is a social being by nature, each is obliged to worship God not only as an individual but also in a social manner. But the fallacy in the argument seems to consist in this, that from that accepted principle it makes a jump to the conclusion that therefore civil society must ensure the fulfilment of this obligation. I call this a fallacy because if God has established a special society in which people may fulfil their social obligation to worship, by that very fact civil society is exempt from such a duty. For it is a basic principle of Catholic sociology that civil society should do for its members only those things which they cannot either do for themselves or through some other society, for example, the family.

But in fact God has established a special society in which people can fulfil their obligation of social worship, namely, the Church. Under the New Testament, therefore, no obligation or competence is left to civil society in this regard. Therefore the following proposition of our *schema* is entirely acceptable: "The civil powers possess no direct capacity and competence to determine or regulate the citizens' relations with their Creator and Saviour."

We must further consider that if, in virtue of the argument for union of Church and State, we hold that civil society of its nature has an obligation regarding divine worship, we implicitly assert the direct power of the Church over civil society. For the direct power of the Church extends to every area where the obligation regarding divine worship exists. And it should be noted that this is not a question of the power of the Church over civil society by reason of subject matter, that is, in regard to temporalities; to admit that civil society as such has an obligation in any way to have concern for social worship is to imply the power of the Church over civil society by reason of the very constitution of civil society.

Such a direct power of the Church over civil society must not be admitted. Therefore in our times and in keeping with today's understanding of these ideas the teaching on union between Church and State must be abandoned. There need be no fear that this would lead to harm for the Church; rather it should be expected to work for its advantage. Without that union the Church strives much more to exercise its influence on all members of society and does not place its hope and trust in help expected from the State.

Finally, a further argument against religious freedom that is drawn from people's inadequacy regarding religious truth, seems to me to be quite weak. We must recognise that people, both as individuals and as part of society, progress in the natural order from ignorance to the possession of truth, only slowly and through difficult paths, fraught with snares and pitfalls. This progress necessarily implies the danger of erring. And history in fact teaches us that people have never attained any important truth without first experiencing error. Those therefore who want human rights to depend on the possession of the truth implicitly deny to people the right of thinking, inquiring, discussing and writing.

The conclusion is that freedom and rights belong to people not because they have already attained the truth, but in order that they might reach it. And if this conclusion applies to the natural order, it applies *a fortiori* to the supernatural order, for in elevating humankind God has not lessened human freedom but sanctified it.

On the Church in the Modern World

(*Acta Synodalia*, vol. III, Period III, Pars V, Congregatio Generalis CVII, 22 October 1964, pp. 341-343; excerpt)

Although there are some good points in this *schema*, it seems to have a basic defect, which, as many have remarked, consists in the *schema's* having been composed before its purpose was clearly settled. On the contrary, the destination of a journey should be known before the journey begins.

His Excellency, the relator, has described the *schema's* purpose in paragraph 12 of his report: "The issue is to promote more and more a dialogue with all people, so that they may be heard concerning their ideas, conditions, and problems, and so that they in turn may know the mind of the Church regarding the more important conditions, trends, and problems of our times."

If this purpose had been settled before the *schema* was composed and if it had been kept firmly in mind, we would not now be deploring its many defects. Among these I note the following.

1. In chapter 1 paragraph 5 (of the report on the *schema*) it is stated that the *schema* must explain "the importance of earthly things for the total human vocation." But it seems to me that "to explain" exceeds the scope of the *schema* since the *schema* takes as its objective to promote dialogue, not to give a full explanation of the truth. To promote dialogue is not to look for explanations from oneself alone but from all the parties to the dialogue, *as was well pointed out yesterday by His Excellency Archbishop Wojtyla, Archbishop of Cracow* (emphasis in original). And in fact there is no explanation in the *schema*, and it would be amazing if there were one, since theology itself has not yet arrived at a true explanation of the issue in question. This chapter of the *schema* seems not even to suspect the things that are being discussed in recent times about the value of the natural order and its relationship to the supernatural end of humankind....

Having said these things, I gladly declare that I accept the purpose of the *schema* as stated by His Excellency the relator in his report: "The issue is to promote more and more a dialogue with all people...."

But with regard to the method of achieving this purpose, I humbly suggest that it should not be in the manner of a simple exposition of truth but in the manner of an exhortation to all orders and members of the Church: to ourselves the bishops and other fathers of the Council, to priests and all religious, to laypersons in a special way – to parents, owners, workers, scientists, scholars – to all, so that we may show ourselves, according to our individual order, office and capacity, to be concerned about the problems of the world and about the need for working and cooperating with others to find solutions. Such an exhortation, elaborated with pertinent arguments, could serve as the *prooemium* of the *schema*.

After the *prooemium* there should be a discussion on the more important problems of the times, including suitable considerations and suggestions that may lead to finding a way of solution.

The first and greatest problem is clearly the theological problem of the true value of the natural order and its relationship to the supernatural end of humankind. Mention should be made of the ideas that have lately begun to be circulated and which have their origin principally in the splendid vision, religious and scientific, evolutionary and eschatological, of that illustrious son of the Church, Pierre Teilhard de Chardin.

The issue is the idea of the presence of God in the world, a presence that is always creative, and of which St Thomas has written so beautifully. This is an idea also based on St Paul's doctrine of cosmic Christology, on which Cardinal Meyer has spoken so well, an idea that sees an intimate connection between the presence of God in the world and, since the incarnation, the presence of Christ through his death and glorification. But there is a great problem that remains to be clarified, namely, whether the creative activity of the word, with which people cooperate in fulfilling their own work in the world, is now the creative action of the word incarnate and how this creative activity is related to the work of salvation. This, if I am not mistaken, is the greatest theological problem of this century.

There should also be a discussion of the particular problems that the *schema* already treats, but care must be taken to ensure that this treatment does not take on the appearance of being a simplistic and merely theoretical solution of problems that are extremely difficult and complex. As has already been said, the objective of the *schema* is not to present definitive solutions, but rather to urge the members of the Church of whatever order and condition to find solutions to the problems and to work with other people to apply these solutions. [...]

* * * *

(*Acta Synodalia*, vol. IV, Period IV, Pars III, Congregatio Generalis CXLII, 5 October 1965, pp. 395-397; excerpt from speech on Ch. IV of the *Schema* of the Pastoral Constitution on the Church in the Modern World, delivered in the name of 70 bishops)

[…] The paragraph on relations between the Church and the political society is well marked by the spirit of *aggiornamento*. Nor does it limit itself to juridical issues between the two so-called perfect societies. Our hope is that the term "perfect society" may disappear from our theological language, for it causes confusion in determining the relations between the Church and the political society. For the Church is called a society only in an analogical sense and its true nature is hidden in the mystery of God. It is also impossible to divide human activity sharply into the spiritual and the temporal, for all human acts in the temporal order belong also to the spiritual order because of their moral orientation.

For this reason there is need to qualify an expression used in paragraph 89, namely: "The Church, not wanting in any way by reason of its task and its competence to be confused with civil society…." It is true that the Church does not wish to be confused with civil society. But it does wish to have an influence on civil society, because it seeks to consecrate all human activity, forming Christian consciences in such a way that people as citizens and as leaders of the earthly city can imprint a Christian direction on social and political life.

For this reason I propose that the words in question be emended more or less as follows: "Because the Church is at once a sign and a witness of human transcendence, it does not wish to involve itself in any way in matters pertaining to the political society, except to form the consciences of people toward the right and faithful fulfilment of their civil responsibilities."

The new spirit is also evident in the statement of paragraph 89: "But (the Church) does not place its hope in privileges offered by civil authority. Indeed the Church will gladly renounce the exercise of certain legitimately acquired rights, when it is clear that such exercise would cast doubt upon the sincerity of its witness or that new conditions of life demand a different arrangement."

This is well put. We must acknowledge that in spite of the efforts of the authorities and members of the Church to avoid conflict with the civil powers, such conflicts will arise. They will arise because the true freedom of the Church is denied or because the Church is forced to defend human rights to life, peace, a just distribution of wealth, or a true social, cultural, and political freedom.

In the past we have perhaps insisted too much on the rights of the Church and the antiphon "The Church claims the right" was too frequently repeated in theology and by the magisterium. Please God in the future we will be concerned with at least as much zeal for human rights. And this, I hope, will be the result of the *schema* The Church in the Modern World. In defending the freedom of the Church regarding human rights we will hardly be able to avoid conflict with civil authority. The difficulty will be to conduct ourselves in such conflicts as witnesses to the love of Christ.

Therefore I ask that to the text be added, for example, at the end of the chapter, words along the lines of the following: "The Church cannot agree in essentials to the denial of this freedom (that is, freedom to proclaim the faith). Nor as mother and teacher of all can the Church tolerate injustices committed or permitted by the public authority against the people of any race or religion, and particularly injustices against the poor. The Church must raise its voice against such abuses of power, and it will at times come into conflict with the civil powers, but without ever ceasing to bear witness to Christ's love."

On the Dogmatic Constitution on the Church: Bishops in the Church

(*Acta Synodalia*, vol. II, Period II, Pars II, Congregatio Generalis XLIV, 9 October 1963, pp. 364-366; excerpt)

Permit me to say a few things about this Chapter II, by touching on two themes: first on the ministries of bishop; second, on the role of priests.

[...] We may immediately notice a great disproportion in paragraph 19, which treats of the (bishop's) office of teaching and contains no less than 50 lines. At first glance this does not seem great, if we fail to notice that 41 of these lines are on infallibility, which leaves only nine lines on the general office of preaching the word, the greatest ministry of the Church, given the time and labour expended on it. Not that the importance of things is to be measured merely by prolixity of words – but the great verbal disproportion here may lead to a like disproportion of ideas.

This consideration aside, the contents of the paragraphs cited are rightly and well put, if we consider only principles. For by the very nature of episcopal ministry it belongs to the bishop to teach, to sanctify, and to rule. But if we look at practice, at the reality itself, what do we see? The ministry of teaching and sanctifying in their daily actuality and in nearly all its aspects is fulfilled not by the bishop but by priests.

To 99 out of a 100 of his flock the bishop appears as an unfamiliar and remote figure, a complete unknown at the personal and human level. It is up to him to establish general directives, to arrange and organise diocesan business, to coordinate the various projects and undertakings. But he most often has no direct hierarchic influence upon his flock; this is left to the priests, through whom the bishop does almost everything else in the diocese. They are the bishop's hands and feet, his eyes and ears and voice. Just as no one can act except through bodily organs, so too all the things that the bishop wishes to accomplish, all that he may hope to be done, depend completely on his priests to be put into effect. We all know that in the reading of pastoral letters whether the bishop's words sound like the trumpet of the archangel or like a list from the telephone directory depends completely on the priests.

From this it is clear that the bishop exercises the offices of teaching, sanctifying, and ruling above all by leading his priests. Since in today's circumstances it is all but impossible for the bishop to draw near to his people directly, his greatest concern must be to provide his priests with pastoral leadership. Thus he can accomplish through them what he cannot do of himself. I think that this must be said explicitly in the *schema*; indeed a special paragraph should be drawn up on the bishop's pastoral leadership, namely, on how he should direct, organise, inspire, encourage, and assist his priests. But if it should be said that since this matter belongs to the practical order, it does not fit in with the character of a dogmatic constitution, I would answer by saying that even a dogmatic constitution must pay attention to *facts*. And the chief fact about the ministry of the bishop (particularly his office of teaching and sanctifying) is that in these times this ministry is being carried out by his priests, and therefore it is incumbent upon the bishop to provide the best leadership and support possible.

I confess that in all these things I speak as one less wise (2 Corinthians 11:23), since I am aware that I am incapable of showing in what this role of leadership consists. Still, I am sure that this is a most serious issue that should be dealt with in the *schema*. If in the last decades there seems to have been a slow response to the appeals of the Supreme Pontiffs concerning the social apostolate, missions, the apostolate of the laity, catechetical and liturgical renewal, the explanation, in my opinion, lies above all in the fact that we bishops have been unequal to the fulfilment of our leadership role. We have lacked the ability to present the papal encyclicals to our priests as living teachings so that they could then communicate them as living teachings to the people of God. Sad to say, the impulse towards Catholic renewal has not originated with us, but with special groups of priests and laity.

I am therefore completely convinced of this: when the *schema* treats of the episcopal office it must clearly state the principle that the fulfilment of this office consists above all in providing strong and gentle pastoral leadership to his priests, who, with the cooperation of religious and laity, must carry out the work that we ourselves cannot do.

From this serious consideration what naturally follows as a conclusion is the great importance of the order of the presbyterate for the carrying out of hierarchic ministries.... In order therefore that the priesthood may be dealt with as it deserves, I propose that Chapter II be divided into three articles, so that it treats clearly and distinctly each level of the hierarchy – episcopacy, priesthood, and diaconate.

* * * *

(*Acta Synodalia*, vol. II, Period II, Pars V, Remarks submitted in writing on the Dogmatic Constitution on the Church: the Conferences of Bishops; pp. 320-321)

During this debate I have now heard many times the admonition that the decisions of conferences of bishops do not possess juridic force. With great admiration I have listened to expositions on how great conferences have functioned successfully now for many years without their decisions having any juridic power. As a member of a hierarchy that has experienced the great generosity of the conference of bishops of Germany let me publicly in this Council *aula* offer my deepest thanks both to the entire conference and in particular to its beloved president Cardinal Joseph Frings.

In our conference of South Africa we have always successfully used the same principle (denying juridic force), as experience attests. In this matter we are indebted to His Excellency Martino Lucas, who when he was the Apostolic Delegate laid the main foundations of our conference; it is therefore pleasant to recall that we have learned the practice of collegiality first from the representative of Peter.

So much for the past, and I gladly grant that juridic power was not very necessary to the conferences of the past. What of the future? If matters are placed in the hand of the conferences to be decided juridically – liturgical matters, for example – they are undoubtedly decided by the conferences juridically. We cannot avoid the issue. This is the price of the "decentralisation" that we all desire. If we wish to exclude all juridical power from the conferences of bishops, we reject "decentralisation" and acknowledge ourselves to be incapable of assuming collegial responsibility. It would be a shame to admit such a thing in today's world, which more and more tends toward unity and in which we see nations prepared to lay aside their particular rights in order to foster and promote international collaboration.

Furthermore, if the conference of bishops lacks all juridical power, for individual cases special delegation from the Holy See will be required, and from this in the course of time the result may be that quinquennial faculties are granted not simply to the individual bishops but also to the conferences of bishops.

Esteemed fathers, we are no longer deliberating in secret. Each and every item that we hear in the *aula* is shouted from the housetops; and in my opinion this is a good thing. Let us therefore ask ourselves: how do our words sound in the ears of the wide world? Do they sound like the words of people wanting only their own way, who on the one hand claim for themselves the right to share in ruling the universal Church, but on the other hand in the running of their own dioceses do not wish to impose any limitation or form of limitation on themselves, nor to resign because of advanced age, nor to accept the decisions of brothers in the episcopate?

It has been said that the faithful are disturbed by the constraint of monarchical episcopal power. My own experience at least contradicts this. But when laws and their application differ from one diocese to another, then the faithful cry out in complaint: "Is it ever going to be possible for you bishops to agree with one another?"

Shaping English Liturgy: Studies in Honour of Archbishop Denis Hurley. Edited by Peter C. Finn and James M. Schellman, (Washington DC: The Pastoral Press, 1990).

Denis Hurley Interviewed about the Council

Interviewer: John R. Page

**1. What was your capacity at the Council? Were you also a
member of the Central Preparatory Commission?**

I attended the Second Vatican Council in my capacity as Archbishop of
Durban, South Africa. I was appointed a member of the Central Preparatory
Commission and attended all its meetings except the third in January 1962.
At the first session of the Council I was elected a member of the commission
on seminaries, universities and Catholic schools. (The word "schools"
was later changed to "education".)

2. How many sessions of the Council did you attend?

If by "sessions" is meant the four periods of the Council, I attended them
all. If the word refers to the general assemblies in St. Peter's, I also attended
all of these.

3. What was the most significant moment at the Council for you?

The most significant moment for me was when, in September, 1964, it
was announced that we had given a very impressive vote to chapters I, II
and III of the *schema* on the Church. Chapter I deals with the mystery of
the Church; chapter II with its membership, the people of God; and chapter
III with the hierarchy, and includes the very important section on episcopal
collegiality.

**4. Of all the documents of the Council, which one is most
significant for you and why?**

The four constitutions – on the Church (*Lumen Gentium*), the liturgy
(*Sacrosanctum Concilium*), revelation (*Dei Verbum*) and the Church in

the modern world (*Gaudium et Spes*) – vie with each other in significance, but in the end, the most significant is the Constitution on the Church, for a number of reasons.

First, in chapter V, *Lumen Gentium* sets out the great overriding purpose of the Church: the pursuit of holiness, a holiness that consists of the gift of divine life, the inestimable privilege of enjoying in our human life the presence of Christ and his Father and of the Holy Spirit, a presence inspiring the practice of and growth in love of God and love of creation, especially of its human dimension, the climax of known creation.

Secondly, in chapter VII, we read of the goal of humanity and of all creation in the glorious mystery of Christ in heaven.

Thirdly, in chapters II, III, IV and VI, we are given the varieties of membership of the Church and also its organisation, in regard to which the important issue of the collegiality of the bishops with and under the primacy of the pope is dealt with in chapter III. Finally, the role of the Blessed Virgin Mary as model of the Church is beautifully described in chapter VIII.

A slightly disappointing feature of all this is that holiness – the great purpose of the church – and love, its most important manifestation, are not given all the emphasis they deserve. Without entering into the detail on the Constitution on the Church in the Modern World, love should shine out as the greatest potential the Church has when influencing the world, promoting peace and dealing with poverty.

5. What's the most important teaching that came out of the Council?

The most important teaching to emerge from the Council is what has been said in the answer to the preceding question, and the involvement of the Church in the world as explained in *Gaudium et Spes*.

6. Whom do you feel was the most significant figure at the Council?

In my opinion Cardinal Leo Joseph Suenens (1904-1996), Archbishop of Mechelen and Brussels, was the most significant figure in the Council. I say this for three reasons: first, because of the part he played in giving shape and balance to the agenda of the Council; secondly, because of his membership in a number of controlling organs of the Council; and thirdly, because of his magnificent contribution to discussions held in general assemblies of the Council. (Contributions to discussions came to be known as "interventions", a word adopted from languages of Latin origin.)

Prior to the Council, Leo Suenens had served as auxiliary bishop of Mechelen and Brussels; on December 15, 1961, he was named archbishop of that diocese and shortly afterward was appointed a member of the Central Preparatory Commission. I met him for the first time when he attended the fourth meeting of the commission held in February, 1962. He made no great contribution to that, being content to observe and reflect. It did not take him long to realise what several of us in the commission were concerned about: lack of clear purpose and a disorderly agenda. He came back to the next meeting a cardinal, having been created such on March 19, 1962.

He came back with a very clear plan for the agenda of the Council. It consisted of two parts rejoicing in the Latin names of *Ecclesia ad intra* and *Ecclesia ad extra*. I was very impressed, and after the meeting lost no time in congratulating the cardinal on what he had placed before us. It was a remedy for my anxieties and an answer to my prayers!

The Council was launched on October 11, 1962. During its first period which concluded on December 7 that year, it dealt with three major topics: liturgy, revelation and the Church, along with two topics of less importance. The *schema* on the liturgy had been well prepared and was accepted as a Council document, subject to revision. But the *schemas* on revelation and the Church proved unacceptable, and total revision was called for.

Before this first period of the Council came to an end, the Holy Father accepted what had been asked for in the Central Preparatory Commission and set up a coordinating commission of seven cardinals, one of whom was Cardinal Suenens. On December 4, His Eminence addressed the assembly and put forward his *Ecclesia ad intra, Ecclesia ad extra*, which was greeted with loud and prolonged applause.

"Moderators" were also appointed; basically their role was to preside over general assemblies but, as the Council progressed, they seemed to pick up other responsibilities. Again, Cardinal Suenens was one of the moderators. So the leadership to guide the Council through the rest of its history was in place, and Cardinal Suenens occupied a key place in it.

Within the coordinating commission, items on the agenda of the Council were assigned to various members for care and attention. Cardinal Suenens was allocated two major ones: an *ad intra* item, The Church, and an *ad extra* item that ended up as The Church in the Modern World (*Gaudium et Spes*). He was obviously carrying a very heavy load.

This did not prevent him from taking a prominent part in the discussion of various *schemas*. He had the advantage of a splendid backup of academic persons: theologians and other experts based at the University of Louvain. Among them, the most important was Monsignor Gerard Philips (1899-1972), who also became the principal writer of *Lumen Gentium*, the Constitution on the Church.

A characteristic of the great debates in the Second Vatican Council was that the bishops of the western European bloc – France, Germany, Switzerland, Austria, Belgium and Holland – had the advantage of a magnificent pool of theologians, scripture scholars, historians, liturgical experts and prominent promoters of lay apostolate, social concern and catechetics. It was this combination that brought the theological and other revivals forcefully into the consciousness of the Council and neutralised and almost extinguished the traditional grip of the Roman Curia on the Catholic outlook. The struggle between these two tendencies was the drama of the Central Preparatory Commission and the first period of the Council. Clearly, Cardinal Suenens was a prominent, if not the most prominent, leader of the western European bloc. He was well served by his own particular Belgian brigade based in Louvain.

Along with all this, he was amply endowed with the gift of enthusiasm. This had become evident in his promotion of the lay apostolic movement known as the Legion of Mary. In the Council he strove to have the significance of the term Catholic Action broadened to include movements like the Legion. His enthusiasm for the Council was unbounded, and in the last period of his life, so was his enthusiasm for the charismatic movement.

Cardinal Suenens, during the treatment of the *schema* on the Church, introduced the topics of the permanent diaconate and the recognition of a variety of charisms, that is, special aptitudes and activities originating from the Holy Spirit and of great importance to the laity as well as clergy and religious. In the discussion on holiness, he pointed out how unbalanced was the list of canonisations, with 85% pertaining to members of religious institutes and 90% to three European countries.

On October 23, 1964, Bishop Emilio Guano (1900-1970) of Leghorn in Italy – rapporteur of the joint commission (doctrine and lay apostolate) responsible for the *schema* that became the Pastoral Constitution on the Church in the Modern World – announced that the question of artificial birth control would be removed from the competence of the Council since there already existed a special commission to deal with it.

Despite that, on October 29, Cardinal Suenens went ahead with his intention of speaking to the issue. He said it would be highly necessary that a commission of the Council work with the commission already established by the pope for the consideration of this question. (He was referring to the Commission on Population, Family and Birth set up by Pope John XXIII.) He said that the issue of birth control should be considered from two points of view: firstly, in regard to Church doctrine, that while the Gospel is unchangeable, doctrines relating to it will always be open to examination. It was possible, the cardinal thought, that in regard to marriage, too much emphasis had been laid on the Scriptural injunctions "increase and multiply", but not enough on "they will be two in one flesh". The commission should investigate whether we had not urged the duty of procreation to the detriment of conjugal communion and put this in some jeopardy.

The commission, the cardinal said, should also face up to the population explosion, evident in many parts of the world; we should examine this problem in order to assist the Church, "the light of the nations", to make known its mind. The commission should also give attention to what was emerging from scientific research which was continually unveiling new dimensions of our humanity.

"I adjure you, brothers," exclaimed the cardinal, "let us avoid another trial of Galileo. One is enough for the Church."

After a few more considerations, including the assurance that the final decision rested with the Holy Father, Cardinal Suenens moved into his peroration: "Venerable brothers, we have no right to be silent. Let us not fear studies about this issue. At stake is the salvation of souls and of our families, even of the world. Let us remember the word of the Lord: 'Truth' – both natural and supernatural – total and living truth – 'will make you free'. I have spoken. Thank you." It must be remembered that the Latin word *dixi*, meaning "I have spoken" was the usual way of terminating an intervention.

One can imagine what a meal the world (media) made of this speech. The news of it rumbled and roared around the globe to the extent that His Eminence found himself constrained to refer to it at the end of his contribution to the debate on missions on November 7. He maintained that he had been misrepresented. He had not said that the teaching on birth control should be changed; he had merely called for a thorough examination of the issue in the light of doctrine and science and had clearly indicated that the final decision rested with the Holy Father.

Pope Paul VI could not have been too pleased with this contribution of Cardinal Suenens to the debate on the family. Possibly it inaugurated the cooling-off in relations between pope and cardinal. Whatever the truth of this the cardinal persevered in his vigorous participation in the Council and played a full part in the backroom struggle between the promoters of Church reform and the guardians of the establishment, the Roman Curia. Despite an unending series of setbacks, the Curia never gave up its resistance to change, relying on papal decisions to give it victory in a few skirmishes in the overall campaign.

Before the end of the Council, Cardinal Suenens had the enormous task of nursing what was first known as *Schema XVII* and later *Schema XIII* through a difficult first debate, through a midnight-oil-burning period of revising and correcting, to final acceptance and promulgation as the Constitution on the Church in the Modern World on December 7, 1965, the last working day of the Council.

Because all this left him with time to spare, he ran his own series of discussion groups on various Council topics.

7. What was the most significant statement from the Council and why?

I would consider that the most significant statement from the Council is the conclusion to section 17 of the Constitution on the Church (*Lumen Gentium*), which reads as follows:

> Thus the Church both prays and works so that the fullness of the whole world may move into the people of God, the body of the Lord and the temple of the Holy Spirit, and that in Christ, the head of all things, all honour and glory may be rendered to the Creator, the Father of the Universe.

Being an ardent disciple of Teilhard de Chardin, I consider this the most significant statement from the Council because it brings together the being of God, Father, Son and Holy Spirit, and the being of the universe created by the Father and destined in Christ, its head, to give the Father full honour and glory through the Church that is the people of God, body of the Lord and temple of the Holy Spirit.

8. What has happened that you never imagined would happen?

The outcome of the renewed vision on the relationship between the Church and the world resulted in a far-reaching unsettlement of priests and religious, the abandonment by many of their chosen state of life and a drastic drop in vocations to the priesthood and religious life.

9. What hasn't happened?

The collegiality of bishops. As things stand at present, it depends on the pope how collegiality is practised and developed. Pope Paul VI took a small step in the direction of collegiality when he established the Synod of Bishops; but this is not really a collegial institution because, as the *motu proprio* describes its identity and operation, only the pope is authorised:

* ❖ to convoke the synod whenever this would seem appropriate and to indicate the place where it will be held;
* ❖ to approve the election of members in keeping with the prescriptions of sections V and VIII;

❖ to decide the agenda at least six months before the synod is held;

❖ to decide the programme;

❖ to preside over the synod himself or through others.

The synod is a permanent body and all its meetings have conformed to these prescriptions.

It fell to me to represent the Southern African Catholic Bishops' Conference in some of the early synods. I deplored the absence of theologians. To a very large extent, theologians made the Second Vatican Council. (See Appendix on page 188.)

10. Is there any issue you regret that the Council did not address?

There are two issues that I regret the Council did not address: priestly celibacy and birth control in marriage.

11. What has been the most significant liturgical achievement and what do we yet need to do to implement full, conscious and active participation?

The most significant liturgical achievement has been a better understanding of the liturgy and much better participation. Even better and fuller participation will depend upon the training of seminarians and young priests in the line of sensitivity to all dimensions of the liturgy.

12. In your opinion, should there be a third Vatican Council, and what topic(s) would you bring to the table?

In my opinion there should not only be a third Vatican Council but an arrangement should be made for a council of the Church every 25 years, so that every generation could experience a council and benefit from its impact. However, for ecumenical councils to achieve the best results, I think we should remember the Council of Jerusalem and include others besides bishops as members: representatives of priests, deacons, men and women religious, and lay women and men. This might make it difficult for all bishops of the world to attend, but each episcopal conference could have representatives, as in the case of the present Synod of Bishops. Careful research will be necessary to work out how a huge and multilingual gathering of that nature should be organised. We have many examples to learn from in the great conferences that have been held in recent times on a great number of topics in various parts of the world.

This proposition concerning ongoing councils would be the main topic to be brought to the table of Vatican III.

13. *What Council teaching was the most difficult to implement in the local churches?*

I think the most difficult teaching of the Council to be implemented in the local churches is the teaching on war – first, because the teaching itself is not devoid of complexities, and secondly, because it is not easy to have the clearer parts accepted by those who feel urged to embark on war.

14. *Is there any special historical or cultural significance that Vatican II occurred in the 1960s? Could it have happened earlier, later in your opinion?*

If Vatican II had not occurred in the 1960s it might never have occurred up to the present time. Blessed John XXIII was unique in his conviction and courage about the necessity and value of the Council. The early 60s was a providential time, bringing together as it did the vision and courage of Pope John and the results achieved in an impressive array of revivals in the Church: scriptural, theological, apostolic (especially in the matter of the lay apostolate), liturgical and catechetical.

Reproduced with permission from: Prendergast, Michael R. and Ridge, M.D., *"Voices from the Council"*, (Portland, Oregon: Pastoral Press, 2004)

Appendix

Archbishop Hurley added the following Appendix to his answer to *Question 9* of his interview with John Page.

Question 9: Concerning the Collegiality of Bishops

It is worth considering the contrast between certain sections of the Constitution on the Sacred Liturgy of Vatican II, namely, section 22 (1), (2) and (3) and sections 37, 38, 39 and 40 of the same Constitution and passages from the Instruction on "The Authentic Liturgy" (*Liturgiam Authenticam*) of the Congregation for Divine Worship and the Discipline of the Sacraments of May 7, 2001.

1. The Constitution on the Sacred Liturgy (1963)

22. (1) Regulation of the sacred liturgy depends solely on the authority of the Church, that is on the apostolic see, and, in accordance with law, on the bishop.

   (2) In virtue of the power conferred on them by law, the regulation of the liturgy within certain defined limits belongs also to various kinds of groupings of bishops, legitimately established, with competence in given territories.

   (3) Therefore no other person whatsoever, not even a priest, may add, remove, or change anything in the liturgy on their own authority.

37. Even in the liturgy the Church does not wish to impose a rigid uniformity in matters which do not affect the faith or the well-being of the entire community. Rather does it cultivate and foster the qualities and talents of the various races and nations. Anything in people's way of life which is not indissolubly bound up with superstition and error the Church studies with sympathy, and, if possible, preserves intact. It sometimes even admits such things into the liturgy itself, provided they harmonise with its true and authentic spirit.

38. Provided that the substantial unity of the Roman rite is preserved, provision shall be made, when revising the liturgical books, for legitimate variations and adaptations to different groups, regions and peoples, especially in mission countries. This should be borne in mind when drawing up the rites and rubrics.

39. Within the limits set by the standard editions of the liturgical books it shall be for the competent territorial ecclesiastical authority mentioned in article 22:2 to specify adaptations, especially as regards the administration of the sacraments, sacramentals, processions, liturgical language, sacred music and the arts – in keeping, however with the fundamental norms laid down in this Constitution.

40. In some places and circumstances, however, an even more radical adaptation of the liturgy is needed, and this entails greater difficulties. For this reason:

    (1) The competent territorial ecclesiastical authority mentioned in article 22:2 must, in this matter, carefully and prudently consider which elements from the traditions and cultures of individual peoples might appropriately be admitted into divine worship. Adaptations, which are considered useful or necessary, should then be submitted to the Apostolic See, to be introduced with its consent.

    (2) To ensure that adaptations may be made with the requisite care, the Apostolic See will, if needs be, grant permission to this same territorial ecclesiastical authority to permit and to direct the necessary preliminary experiments over a determined period of time among certain groups suitable for the purpose.

    (3) Because liturgical laws usually involve special difficulties with respect to adaptation, especially on mission lands, people who are experts in the matters in question must be employed when they are being formulated.

2. *Instruction of the Congregation for Divine Worship and the Discipline of the Sacraments (2001)*

6. Ever since the promulgation of the Constitution on the Sacred Liturgy, the work of the translation of the liturgical texts into vernacular

languages, as promoted by the Apostolic See, has involved the publication of norms and the communication to the bishops of advice on the matter. Nevertheless, it has been noted that translations of liturgical texts in various localities stand in need of improvement through correction or through a new draft. The omissions or errors which affect certain existing vernacular translations – especially in the case of certain languages – have impeded the progress of the inculturation that actually should have taken place. Consequently, the Church has been prevented from laying the foundation for a fuller, healthier and more authentic renewal.

7. For these reasons it now seems necessary to set forth anew, and in light of the maturing of experience, the principles of translation to be followed in future translations – whether they be entirely new undertakings or emendations of texts already in use – and to specify more clearly certain norms that have already been published, taking into account a number of questions and circumstances that have arisen in our own day. In order to take full advantage of the experience gained since the Council it seems useful to express these norms from time to time in terms of tendencies that have been evident in past translations but which are to be avoided in future ones. In fact, it seems necessary to consider anew the true notion of liturgical translation in order that the translations of the sacred liturgy into the vernacular languages may stand secure as the authentic voice of the Church of God. This instruction therefore envisions and seeks to prepare for a new era of liturgical renewal which is consonant with the qualities and traditions of the particular churches, but which safeguards also the faith and unity of the whole Church of God.

16. As regards the decisions of the conferences of bishops for the introduction of a vernacular language into liturgical use, the following are to be observed (cf. No. 79):

   a) For the legitimate passage of decrees, a two-thirds vote by secret ballot is required on the part of those in the conference of bishops who have the right to cast a deliberative vote.

b) All of the acts to be examined by the Apostolic See, prepared in duplicate, signed by the president and secretary of the conference and duly affixed with its seal, are to be sent to the Congregation for Divine Worship and the Discipline of the Sacraments. In these acts are to be contained the following:

    i) The names of the bishops, or of those equivalent to them in law, who were present at the meeting.

    ii) A report of the proceedings, which should contain the outcome of the votes pertaining to the individual decrees, including the number of those in favour, the number opposed and the number abstaining.

    iii) A clear exposition of the individual parts of the liturgy into which the decision has been made to introduce the vernacular language.

c) In the *relatio* is to be included a clear explanation of the language involved as well as the reasons for which the proposal has been made to introduce it into liturgical use.

22. Adaptations of the texts according to Nos. 37-40 of the Constitution *Sacrosanctum Concilium* are to be considered on the basis of true cultural or pastoral necessity, and should not be proposed out of a mere desire for novelty or variety nor as a way of supplementing or changing the theological content of the *editiones typicae*; rather, they are to be governed by the norms and procedures contained in the abovementioned instruction *Varietates Legitimae*. Accordingly, translations into vernacular languages that are sent to the Congregation for Divine Worship and the Discipline of the Sacraments for the *recognitio* are to contain, in addition to the translation itself and any adaptations foreseen explicitly in the *editiones typicae*, only adaptations or modifications for which prior written consent has been obtained from the same dicastery.

23. In the translation of texts of ecclesiastical composition, while it is useful with the assistance of historical and other scientific tools to consult a source that may have been discovered for the same text, nevertheless it is always the text of the Latin *editio typica* itself that is to be translated.

30. In many languages there exist nouns and pronouns denoting both genders, masculine and feminine, together in a single term. The instance that such a usage should be changed is not necessarily to be regarded as the effect or the manifestation of an authentic development of the language as such. Even if it may be necessary by means of catechesis to ensure that such words continue to be understood in the "inclusive" sense just described, it may not be possible to employ different words in the translations themselves without detriment to the precise intended meaning of the text, the correlation of its various words or expressions, or its aesthetic qualities. When the original text, for example, employs a single term in expressing the interplay between the individual and the universality and unity of the human family or community (such as the Hebrew word *adam*, the Greek *anthropos* or the Latin *homo*), this property of the language of the original text should be maintained in the translation. Just as has occurred at other times in history, the Church herself must freely decide upon the system of language that will serve her doctrinal mission most effectively and should not be subject to externally imposed linguistic norms that are detrimental to that mission.

31. In particular: To be avoided is the systematic resort to imprudent solutions such as mechanical substitution of words, the transition from the singular to plural, the splitting of a unitary collective term into masculine and feminine parts, or the introduction of impersonal or abstract words, all of which may impede the communication of the true and integral sense of a word or an expression in the original text. Such measures introduce theological and anthropological problems into the translation. Some particular norms are the following:

   a) In referring to almighty God or the individual persons of the most Holy Trinity, the truth of tradition as well as the established gender usage of each respective language are to be maintained.

   b) Particular care is to be taken to ensure that the fixed expression *Son of Man* be rendered faithfully and exactly. The great Christological and typological significance of this expression requires that there should also be employed throughout the translation a rule of language that will ensure that the fixed expression remains comprehensible in the context of the whole translation.

c) The term *fathers*, found in many biblical passages and liturgical texts of ecclesiastical composition, is to be rendered by the corresponding masculine word into vernacular languages insofar as it may be seen to refer to the patriarchs or the kings of the chosen people in the Old Testament or to the fathers of the Church.

d) Insofar as possible in a given vernacular language, the use of the feminine pronoun rather than the neuter is to be maintained in referring to the Church.

e) Words which express consanguinity or other important types of relationship such as *brother, sister*, etc., which are clearly masculine or feminine by virtue of the context, are to be maintained as such in the translation.

f) The grammatical gender of angels, demons and pagan gods or goddesses, according to the original texts, is to be maintained in the vernacular language insofar as possible.

g) In all these matters it will be necessary to remain attentive to the principles set forth above in Nos. 27 and 29.

32. The translation should not restrict the full sense of the original text within the narrower limits. To be avoided on this account are expressions characteristic of commercial publicity, political or ideological programmes, passing fashions, and those which are subject to regional variations or ambiguities in meaning. Academic style manuals or similar works, since they sometimes give way to such tendencies, are not to be considered standards for liturgical translation. On the other hand, works that are commonly considered "classics" in a given vernacular language may prove useful in providing a suitable standard for its vocabulary and usage.

76. In implementing the decisions of the Second Vatican Council, it has become evident from the mature experience of the nearly four decades of the liturgical renewal that have elapsed since the council that the need for translation of liturgical texts – at least as regards the major languages – is experienced not only by the bishops in governing the

particular churches but also by the Apostolic See for the effective exercise of her universal solicitude for the Christian faithful in the city of Rome and throughout the world. Indeed, in the Diocese of Rome, especially in many of the churches and institutes of the city that depend in some way on the diocese or the organs of the Holy See as well as on the activity of the dicasteries of the Roman Curia and the pontifical representations, the major languages are widely and frequently employed even in liturgical celebrations. For this reason, it has been determined that in the future the Congregation for Divine Worship and the Discipline of the Sacraments will be involved more directly in the preparation of the translations into these major languages.

92. So that there might be unity in the liturgical books even as regards vernacular translations and so that the resources and the efforts of the Church might not be consumed needlessly, the Apostolic See has promoted, among other possible solutions, the establishment of "mixed" commissions, that is, those in whose work several conferences of bishops participate.

93. The Congregation for Divine Worship and the Discipline of the Sacraments erects such "mixed" commissions at the request of the conferences of bishops involved; afterwards the commission is governed by statutes approved by the Apostolic See. It is ordinarily to be hoped that each and every one of the conferences of bishops will have deliberated the matter of the abovementioned establishment of the commission as well as of the composition of its statutes before the petition is submitted to the Congregation for Divine Worship and the Discipline of the Sacraments. Even so, if it is judged opportune by that dicastery due to the great number of conferences or the protracted period of time required for a vote of particular pastoral necessity, it is not excluded that the statutes be prepared and approved by the same dicastery, after consultation, insofar as possible, with at least some of the bishops involved.

Reflections on
Vatican II

The Historical Significance of Denis Hurley's Contribution to the Second Vatican Council[1]

Philippe Denis OP

Denis Eugene Hurley started writing his memoirs on his retirement as archbishop of Durban, but because of his many commitments he did not complete the work before his death. The only section that was nearly ready for publication dealt with the Second Vatican Council. This says a great deal about his priorities. Many people remember Hurley as the man who defied the apartheid regime and promoted the cause of social justice in the Catholic Church of Southern Africa. Interestingly, it was not this aspect of his life that he first finalised for publication. "We did too little too late" was his usual answer when a visitor asked him to speak about his memories of apartheid. He much preferred to talk about Vatican II, an event which had left a deep mark on him. He was immensely proud of having participated in the Council and was eager to share his experience with as many people as possible. He started, while still in Rome, by chronicling the conciliar proceedings for the South African Catholic newspaper *The Southern Cross*. Back in South Africa, he gave countless talks on the Council, one of the last at St Joseph's Theological Institute, Cedara, on the occasion of the encyclical *Pacem in Terris'* 40th anniversary, six months before he died.

The Second Vatican Council had a profound influence on the Catholic Church in Africa. It opened the way to indigenisation and inculturation and assisted the new generation of bishops in dealing with the problems of the post-independence era. Vatican II greatly contributed to the transition from a missionary Church to a local Church. Most observers agree, however, that the African bishops failed significantly to influence the work of the Council itself. The African representation – 260 bishops of a total 2 358 at the first session in 1962 – had relatively little weight in the final outcome of the Council. The themes discussed were perceived as "too European" not only by the 61 African-born bishops, present at the opening of the Council, but also by the missionary bishops. The importance of the Second Vatican Council for the African continent lies in the way it was received.[2] Yet not all the African bishops were ill-at-ease with the procedures of the Council and its day-to-day working. A minority succeeded in having their voices heard, and they actively participated in the conciliar event. One of these bishops was Hurley. His declarations, especially during the first session, evoked considerable attention. If his participation in the Central Preparatory Commission of the Council went relatively unnoticed, his role in the Commission for Priestly Formation and Catholic Education can rightly be described as crucial. From the start, he belonged to the group of progressive bishops. The Suenens, Liénarts and Frings saw him as one of theirs.

Archbishop Hurley's biography still needs to be compiled. So far, little has been written on his participation in the Council.[3] This is not because of a lack of sources.[4] They are plentiful. My only purpose, in this essay, is to give a brief outline of the subject. It is hoped that another student of history will deal more appropriately with it in future.

Archbishop Hurley's papers are kept in good order in the Archdiocesan Archives in Durban.[5] They extensively document his participation in the Council. His correspondence with Eric Boulle, his vicar general, and Geoff de Gersigny, his bursar, in particular, is of great value. The archbishop's papers also contain the drafts of his interventions *in aula* and numerous other significant documents. Also of interest, as mentioned above, is his chronicle of the Council, published weekly in *The Southern Cross* during the second, third and fourth sessions.[6] Written with frankness and humour, these articles provide first-hand information on the progress of the discussions, the mechanisms of the assembly, the theological issues at stake and the personalities of the principal actors. Archbishop Hurley's own speeches and written statements are now to be found in the *Acta Synodalia Sacrosancti Concilii Oecumenici Vaticani II,* the official Roman publication.[7] One can also make use of the accounts he gave of the event, after the closure of the Council. These relate mainly to the work of the Commission for Priestly Formation and Catholic Education.[8] Lastly, I should mention the oral sources. For the purpose of this paper, Archbishop Hurley graciously agreed to be interviewed by one of my then students, Fr Alan Henriques,[9] and by myself on several occasions.[10] I also interviewed Bishop Gerard van Velsen[11] as well as Fr Dominic Scholten,[12] who was the secretary of the Southern African Catholic Bishops' Conference.[13]

The Preparation of the Council

On 25 January 1959, four months after his election, Pope John XXIII announced an ecumenical council. In June, Archbishop Hurley, like all the Catholic bishops and major superiors in the world, received a letter from the Cardinal Secretary of State calling for suggestions for the Council.[14]

By that time, Hurley was already a prominent figure in his Church. Born in 1915 in Cape Town to a family of Irish immigrants, he had joined the Oblates of Mary Immaculate soon after matriculation. His ordination took place in Rome in 1939, when he was about to complete his studies in theology. His ecclesiastical career progressed very rapidly. His first appointment was as curate of Emmanuel Cathedral, Durban. In December 1943, he became the superior of a new Oblate house of studies in Prestbury, Pietermaritzburg. His interest in theological education dates from that time. Three years later, he was appointed vicar apostolic of Natal and consecrated bishop. At the age of 31, he was the youngest bishop in the world. When the hierarchy was established in Southern Africa in 1951, the Natal vicariate became the Archdiocese of Durban and he became its first archbishop. He was one of only five South African-born bishops at the time. In 1952, he became the president of the Southern African Catholic Bishops' Conference. He was still holding this post when the announcement of the Council was made.

At first, Archbishop Hurley did not know how to respond to the call for suggestions for the Council:

> I looked at [the letter] and I wondered why the Church needed a Council. There seemed to be no crisis. Many bishops, I think, felt the same, especially in English-speaking parts of the world where the Church seemed to be in good shape, with churches well-attended, schools flourishing and vocations multiplying.[15]

Only eight bishops from South Africa, Swaziland and Basutoland responded to Cardinal Tardini's request. Like many other bishops, Hurley did not see the Council as a priority. At the time, his main concern was the preparation of the plenary session of the bishops' conference due to be held in January 1960.[16] "Having missed the deadline", he wrote, "I came to the conclusion that I should resign myself to making no positive contribution to the agenda of the council".[17]

However, on 21 March 1960, the secretary of the Antepreparatory Commission of the Council sent a reminder and this time he responded:

> I rolled up my sleeves, pulled out my Latin dictionary and grammar and sent off my conclusions in what I hoped was comprehensible Latin. Little did I suspect that every document pertaining to the Council would be published in the record, the *Acta*. The halting Latin of my humble suggestions lies enshrined in one of the mighty tomes of those *Acta*.[18]

Hurley's suggestions – or *vota* as they are usually called – were actually among the most elaborate of those coming from Southern African bishops. The majority of the 25 Southern African *vota* dealt with rather minor problems of ecclesiastical discipline and liturgy. The same trend was observed in other parts of Africa.[19] Owen McCann, on the other hand, insisted on the need to redefine Catholic doctrine, in response to communism, positivism, materialism and all the errors of the time. Interestingly, one of these errors, according to the archbishop of Cape Town, was "racialism". He urged the Council to invite all nations, classes and individuals to work for peace.[20] Bishop Gerard van Velsen's *vota* also expressed new concerns. He pleaded – already! – for a relaxation of the celibacy rule for African clergy and recommended that the Church's laws give precedence to charity over discipline in order to promote unity with the "dissident brethren".[21]

Hurley's *vota* consisted of two parts. In the first he outlined what he thought the *Tractatus dogmaticus* should contain. Quite remarkably, most of the issues he listed in this section of his *vota* were later to be discussed at the Council, namely, the Church as Body of Christ, the collegial government of the Church, the priests as co-helpers of the bishops, the role of laity in subordination to the hierarchy, the relationship between

Church and state and the imperatives of Christian freedom. Under the heading *Tractatus practicus,* he made several recommendations concerning the relationship between the local Churches and the Holy See, the periodicity of episcopal conferences, the liturgy of the Church, Catholic Action, the catechesis of adults and children and the training of priests. What was to become one of his main contributions to the Commission for Priestly Formation and Catholic Education two years later found its first expression here:

> The training of candidates to the priesthood in seminaries should take more into account the pastoral necessities. The current curriculum appears too theoretical. It does not provide a real understanding of Christ's Mystery (of the whole Christ, Head and Body) and a full grasp of the liturgical and apostolic work of the Church. Not enough importance is given to the art of announcing the mystery in words as well as in writing. It would be better to give a first overview of Christ's Mystery to the seminarians, to the best of their abilities, before they begin the course of philosophy. At the same time they should be taught how to speak and write properly. In this way, the priestly apostolate will be seen from the start as a practical service of the Divine Master. If the seminarians always keep this vision and this objective in sight, they will benefit more from the study of philosophy, theology and other ecclesiastical sciences.[22]

The Archbishop of Durban did not mention apartheid in his submission although he had often criticised it publicly. He does not explain this significant omission in his memoir on the Council. Was it, as Étienne Fouilloux suggests[23], because he did not think that apartheid was a question for the Council to take up?

Not long after he had sent his *vota* to the Antepreparatory Commission of the Council, Hurley was nominated to the Central Preparatory Commission of the Council, the commission established to co-ordinate the work of the various preparatory commissions.[24] He received the news, he wrote in his memoir on the Council, "to my utter surprise and delight".[25] By his own admission,[26] the appointment was probably attributable to the fact that the Holy See had an out-of-date report on the Southern African Catholic Bishops' Conference, which named him as the president, a position from which he had stepped down in February 1960. The new president was Archbishop McCann. Two other African bishops were appointed to the Central Preparatory Commission: Bernard Yago, the Archbishop of Abidjan, and Jerome Ratokomalala, the Archbishop of Antananarivo.

The task of the Central Preparatory Commission was to review and co-ordinate the position papers – or *schemata* – submitted by the other commissions. Ten in number, these commissions were charged with specific areas of doctrinal, pastoral and canonical concerns. They were all headed by curial officials. Also active in the preparation of the Council was the Secretariat for Christian Unity, an entirely new institution in which Gerard van Velsen, the Bishop of Kroonstad, participated. Born in Holland, this Dominican bishop had gained some experience in ecumenical affairs through his involvement in the Afrikaans apostolate in South Africa.[27]

The Central Preparatory Commission was dominated by conservative curial cardinals. Hurley soon realised that not much could be expected of a commission thus constituted:

> It did not take long to notice that the members of the Central Preparatory Commission were divided into conservatives and progressives and the curial representatives, mainly cardinals serving in Rome, were preponderantly conservative. The procedure gave the curial representatives an enormous advantage. After we had gone home after each session, a team of them sifted through our votes and amendments to formulate the final text for the Council. The playing field was anything but level.[28]

Hurley expected a lot more from the Council. His assessment of the then situation of the Catholic Church found expression in the January 1962 issue of the Irish theological magazine *The Furrow*. Atheistic communism and secularism, he explained, posed a fundamental challenge to Christianity. The Church had already started responding to this new situation. A "radical renewal" was underway with a return to the scriptural sources in doctrine, a renewal in liturgy and catechesis and the flowering of the lay apostolate. More, however, was necessary. The Church as a whole, and especially its priests, were in need of reform:

> These developments are bound to result in a transformation in the ordinary life and activity of the Church. This must inevitably entail a transformation in pastoral methods. Unless the change of methods is

dramatically pursued a first-class crisis will result, for there is no better way of promoting a crisis than by allowing a situation to drift into change without adjusting the approach of those most directly involved in the situation.[29]

The Central Preparatory Commission was miles away from sharing these perspectives. As time went on, Hurley became "more and more despondent" about the kinds of documents that would constitute the agenda of the Council. But he was not prepared to give up. He established contacts with members of the Commission who shared his frustration. Most of them were bishops from countries north of the Alps; hence the name *transalpini*.[30]

At the November 1961 meeting of the Commission, Hurley supported König, Döpfner, Bea and Alfrink in their criticisms of the document *De fontibus revelationis* prepared by the Curia.[31] The agenda of the meeting, he wrote in his memoir on the Council, caused some misgivings:

> We did not seem to be dealing with the main issues which should be engaging our attention in so important a matter as a general council. [...] I was very critical of the formula for a new profession of faith. I thought it was far too defensive and negative, too concerned with the errors of the time. I suggested that it was inviting us to believe *against* rather than *in*. I found it sadly lacking in the growing understanding of Jesus and gift of the Holy Spirit. I also found it too triumphalistic in its appreciation of how the Church appears in the eyes of people.[32]

On 18 April 1962, Hurley sent Cardinal Suenens a memorandum containing his suggestions for a revision of the work of the Central Preparatory Commission. In his opinion, the Council's opening should be postponed until the preparatory texts could be carefully revised. On 4 May, he discussed the matter with Cardinal Frings, and gave a copy of his memorandum to Cardinal König.[33] "They all agreed", he later commented, "but saw no way of remedying the situation".[34]

The Commission completed its work in July 1962. A series of seven preparatory documents, duly approved by the pope, was sent to the bishops for comment in early August. For many of them, it was too late. Hurley, like all missionary bishops, was already on his way to the Council. He found the *schemata* only on his arrival in Rome.[35]

The Opening of the Council

Archbishop Hurley arrived in Rome on Tuesday 9 October 1962, two days before the opening of the Council, after an extended trip through Katanga and Congo. He soon renewed the contacts established earlier with the *transalpini* bishops. He also met the French theologian Yves-Marie Congar with whom he had exchanged letters during the previous year. [36]

The seven preparatory documents had now been read by all the bishops. Products of the neo-scholastic theology taught in the Roman schools, they caused disappointment and distress among those who expected the Council to bring about a renewal of the Church. Only the document dealing with the liturgy seemed responsive to the current needs.

A group of progressive bishops and theologians, however, was preparing a counter-offensive. A reply to the preparatory documents, hastily written by the Dominican Edward Schillebeeckx and duplicated in Latin and in English, was communicated to all the conciliar fathers already assembled in Rome before the opening of the Council. The distribution continued afterwards. During the first days of the Council, 300 copies of this document were handed over to Bishop Jean-Baptiste Zoa and Bishop Joseph Blomjous, the respective secretaries of the French-speaking and English-speaking sections of the recently-founded General Secretariat of the Episcopal Conferences of Africa and Madagascar. [37]

In September and early October, a *Projet de déclaration initiale,* written by Marie-Dominique Chenu with the assistance of Congar, had circulated among progressive bishops. This document, substantially rewritten, was to become the *Message to the World,* adopted by the conciliar assembly at its third congregation on Saturday 20 October 1962. Thirteen bishops received the initial document. Archbishop Hurley was one of them. Except for Cardinal Léger, the archbishop of Montreal, he was the only bishop on the list drawn up by the two Dominicans, who was not from Europe. [38]

The Council opened on Thursday 11 October. On Saturday 13 October the bishops met again for the election of the commissions. Sixteen members had to be elected for each of the 10 commissions. The Curia expected its candidates to be voted in without difficulty. But an alternative list, prepared by the Belgian bishops in association with the other European episcopates, was also circulating, more or less secretly, during the days before the vote. This list included Hurley's name as member of the Commission for Seminaries, Studies and Catholic Education.[39]

At the beginning of the session, Archbishop Felici, the Secretary of the Council, told the bishops to record the names of their candidates in booklets provided for that purpose. "There was", related Hurley, "an agonising silence of about two minutes while those of us who knew what was brewing thought we had been sold out. But in due course the voice of Cardinal Liénart came over the public address system, protesting that we had not had enough time to know who to vote for. Cardinal Frings supported him and the Council of Presidents upheld the objection. So the meeting was adjourned."

During the following two days, intense lobbying took place. The progressive bishops tried to canvass support from all the world's episcopates. The final outcome of the vote, however, was uncertain. The conservative bishops, led by the curial cardinals, also tried to mobilise support. In his correspondence, Hurley shows himself to have been an acute observer of the Council's political dynamics. He shared his analysis with his Durban correspondents on 16 October, the day of Cardinal Liénart's historic intervention:

> The best organisation was put together by the Central Europeans – France, Germany, Austria, Holland and Belgium. In due course, they were joined by Switzerland, Scandinavia, Poland, Yugoslavia and other Iron Curtain countries. The Latin Americans were also well organised. They have about 600 votes. The United States had its own tight organisation (with about 240 votes) but did not seem to be doing much horse-trading with the others. The English, Irish, Australians and New Zealanders published their own list of candidates. Africa was quietly into the field with continent-wide consultations controlling about 300 votes and Asia was split between India and Ceylon on one side and the Far East on the other.
>
> As there was not enough time to achieve complete international organisation, it is hard to see how the voting will turn out. Central Europe is giving the most vigorous leadership with Cardinals Frings, Liénart, Suenens, Alfrink and König at the centre of things; but Central Europe does not control a great number of votes. However, its influence is extended through German, French, Dutch, Belgian,

Austrian and Swiss missionaries. Most of Africa will, I think (or hope), fall in behind it.

If South America is conservative and unites with Italy and the United States, we are sunk. Those three regions could control at least half the votes. But there is no sign of such a tragedy yet. Italy may wake up to the pleasant surprise that the rest of the world has not such a *timor reverentialis* of the Curia – and after that, anything could happen. With Curial officials and missionaries, Italy has nearly 500 votes.[40]

The rest is history. Two days later, a clear majority opting for change emerged. The minority did not disarm, however, and, until the end of the Council, compromises had to be negotiated. Archbishop Hurley was elected as a member of the Commission for Seminaries, Studies and Catholic Education with 930 votes. He was the member of the commission with the tenth-highest number of votes, out of 16. The first to be elected, Patrick O'Boyle, Archbishop of Washington, received 2 059 votes. The commission included nine additional members, nominated by the pope. On 28 November 1963, another four members were elected by the assembly. Three more were nominated by the pope in 1964 and 1965.

Hurley was the only member of the Southern African Bishops' Conference to be elected to a conciliar commission during the first period of the Council. Six other African bishops, Jean-Baptiste Zoa (Yaoundé, Cameroon), Laurent Rugambwa (Bukoba, Tanzania), Andre Perraudin (Kabgayi, Rwanda), Joseph Blomjous (Mwanza, Tanzania), Joseph Malula (Kinshasa, Congo-Kinshasa) and Jean Van Cauwelaert (Inongo, Congo-Kinshasa), were elected with him. A further six African bishops were nominated by Pope John XXIII, namely, Jerome Rakotomalala (Antananarivo, Madagascar), Stephanos I. Sidarouss (Alexandria, Egypt), Araste Mariam Yemmeru (Addis Ababa, Ethiopia), Bernard Mels (Luluabourg, Congo-Kinshasa), Bernard Yago (Abidjan, Ivory Coast) and Victor Sartre (Beroe, Madagascar).[41] Bishop van Velsen (Kroonstad), a member of the Secretariat for Christian Unity since 1960, retained his post at the opening of the Council, like all the other members of the Secretariat. In November 1963, Archbishop Owen McCann (Cape Town) was elected to the Commission for Bishops. Finally, in January 1964,

Pope Paul VI nominated Emmanuel 'Mabathoana (Leribe, Basutoland) to the Commission for Missions.

Interventions in aula *and Written Submissions*

Apart from being an active member of the Commission for Seminaries, Studies and Catholic Education, Archbishop Hurley drew attention by the number of speeches he delivered during the plenary sessions. During the four conciliar periods, he spoke 10 times and submitted four written interventions. Only one African bishop, the Tanzanian Cardinal Laurent Rugambwa, spoke more frequently, with 15 oral interventions. Two bishops, Sebastiao Soares de Resende (Beira, Mozambique) and Elie Zoghby (Nubia, Egypt), delivered the same number of speeches as Hurley.[42]

Hurley was, by far, the most "visible" South African bishop during the Council. Archbishop McCann, who was the president of the Southern African Bishops' Conference at the time, delivered four speeches, one on behalf of the Conference and three in his own name. He submitted five written interventions on behalf of the Conference and four in his own name. Bishop van Velsen (Kroonstad) delivered one speech and submitted one written intervention. Archbishop Garner (Pretoria) and Bishop Green (Port Elizabeth) each delivered one speech. Archbishop Whelan (Bloemfontein) did not address the Council but submitted one written intervention.

Period	Congr.*	Date	Mode	Bishop	Conciliar Document
I	3	20.10.62	Oral	Hurley	*Message to the World*
I	4	22.10.62	Oral/Wri.	Hurley	*The Sacred Liturgy*
I	22	18.11.62	Oral	Hurley	*The Sources of Revelation*
I	-	-	Written	McCann	*The Sources of Revelation*
I	-	-	Written	McCann	*Means of Social Communication*
I	32	3.12.62	Oral	Hurley	*The Church*
I	-	-	Written	van Velsen	*The Church*
I	-	-	Written	McCann	*The Church*
I	-	-	Written	SACBC	*The Church*
II	40	3.10.63	Oral	van Velsen	*The Church*
II	44	9.10.63	Oral	Hurley	*The Church*
II	-	-	Written	McCann	*The Church*
II	52	21.10.63	Oral	Hurley	*The Church*
II	-	-	Written	Whelan	*The Church*
II	62	7.11.63	Oral	McCann	*The Church*
II	-	-	Written	Hurley	*The Church*
II	-	-	Written	SACBC	*The Church*
II	67	14.11.63	Oral	Garner	*The Pastoral Office of Bishops*
II	79	2.12.63	Oral	Green	*Ecumenism*
III	88	25.9.64	Oral	Hurley	*Religious Liberty*
III	-	-	Written	SACBC	*The Pastoral Office of Bishops*
III	-	-	Written	SACBC	*The Divine Revelation*
III	97	8.10.64	Oral	McCann	*The Church*
III	98	19.10.64	Oral	Hurley	*The Apostolate of Lay People*
III	107	22.10.64	Oral	Hurley	*The Church in the Modern World*
III	-	-	Written	SACBC	*The Training of Priests*
III	123	16.11.64	Oral	Hurley	*The Ministry and Life of Priests*
IV	131	20.9.65	Oral	McCann	*Religious Liberty*
IV	-	-	Written	Hurley	*Religious Liberty*
IV	-	-	Written	Hurley	*The Church in the Modern World*
IV	142	5.10.65	Oral	Hurley	*The Church in the Modern World*
IV	-	-	Oral	McCann	*The Church in the Modern World*

* Congr. = Congregation, i.e. occasion on which the Council assembled in plenary.

Hurley's first four interventions in *aula* were his most "political". They were meant to give support to the pastoral approach followed by the emerging majority. During the debate preceding the adoption of the *Message to the World*, on Saturday 20 October 1962, he recommended that the reference to the papal primacy be dropped, in order to take into account the sensitivities of the non-believers and of the "separated brethren".[43]

The discussion of the preparatory document on the liturgy started two days later. Deeply frustrated by the method of debate, which consisted in what seemed to be an endless series of monologues, Hurley thought it futile to deliver the address he had prepared and handed in the text. His main point was that liturgical reform should not be separated from catechetical and moral renewal. It was extremely important to develop lay participation and to adapt the structure and language of the liturgy.[44]

The debate on the sources of revelation is usually regarded as a turning-point in the first period of the Council. Hurley took an active part in it. After a week of speeches, from 14 to 21 November 1962, the document drafted by the Theological Commission was finally rejected. This was a momentous decision for the future of the Council. Hurley, whom Giuseppe Ruggieri described as "one of the most clear-sighted as to the real heart of the debate,"[45] threw all his weight into the discussion. Everybody agreed that the Council should be pastoral, he explained. But there was no agreement on the meaning of the word "pastoral". To be pastoral, was it enough to give a firm definition of the doctrine? Or was it necessary, also, to preach the Gospel to the world? It was because of this disagreement that 90% of the preparatory documents caused divisiveness among the conciliar fathers. The work of the Central Preparatory Commission, he concluded, was essentially flawed:

> What should we do? In the Central Commission, when we complained that the *schemata* were insufficiently pastoral, we were voices shouting in the wilderness. There was no body to listen to our clamour and to remedy the shortcomings of the preparatory work. There was no central direction. There was no body, nor any commission, to explain the pastoral purpose of the Council, to direct and co-ordinate the work of the various commissions according to the statutes and to decide which documents were to be presented to

the Council. This was the fundamental defect of the preparatory work.
It was, I would like to say, the original sin of this Council.[46]

In early December, Hurley added his voice to the criticisms directed
against the preparatory document on the Church by the majority of the
bishops. The text, according to him, needed a thorough revision. The
pastoral concern was to be "the supreme preoccupation of the Council".
The Council, he further said, "was not called to define old truths, but to
renew the pastoral action of the Church, which, with God's help, will
have an intensification of ecumenical activity as one of its most important
results".[47] But the battle was already won. The opposition to the document
was so widespread that a vote of the sort that had taken place on the
sources of revelation was considered superfluous. On 6 December 1962,
it was announced that Pope John XXIII had appointed a Co-ordinating
Commission to review all the prepared texts to decide which of them to
retain and to see how to bring these into conformity with the pastoral
orientation the Pope wished the Council to reflect.[48]

The public speeches and written submissions Hurley made during the
last three periods of the Council were not as momentous as those of the
first period. Many of them dealt with technical issues, which cannot be
reviewed here in detail. It should suffice to mention his interventions on
the relationship between Church and state, an important subject for a bishop
living in a Protestant country dominated by apartheid.

During the debate on religious freedom, Hurley emerged as a strong
proponent of the Church's independence from politics. He intervened on
this subject on two occasions. He first expressed his views on 25 September
1963, when the document prepared by the Secretariat for Christian Unity
was discussed for the first time *in aula*. In the modern world, he argued,
the Church no longer had any power over the state. And it was better so.
There was no need for the Church to be united to the state. For practical
purposes, like the negotiation of subsidies for Catholic schools, it was
enough to sign agreements with the state.[49]

The discussion of the revised document on religious freedom was only
held at the beginning of the fourth session and, because the issue was
extremely contentious, it continued until the very end of the Council. Hurley
made a written submission during the first part of the discussion, in

September 1965. He was in agreement with the general purpose of the document – the recognition that religious freedom was a Christian value – but had difficulty with its argument. In his view, the *schema* relied too exclusively on philosophical reasoning. Truth, according to this argument, had to be sought in human fashion, that is, by human inquiry. Therefore, one should not be coerced into religion against one's conscience. But, the Archbishop of Durban argued, the social dimension of religion also had to be taken into account. The role of political authority in matters pertaining to the truth had changed dramatically in recent times. It was this evolution that, according to Hurley, the document needed to highlight. Christian revelation, he went on, "taught the distinction of the spiritual order from the temporal". The history of the Church gave abundant evidence of this doctrine. The state has "no competence" in religious matters. It was true that, from the time of Constantine to the 20th century, the Church accepted that temporal society was obliged to recognise, uphold and promote the spiritual. But, in recent years, this proposition had been re-examined. "Now we are almost unanimous in rejecting state competence in religious matters and its obligation to the true Church".[50]

There is little doubt that, when writing this text, Hurley had in mind the problem of apartheid in South Africa. It was during the previous year, on 16 January 1964, that he delivered his famous Alfred and Winifred Hoernlé memorial lecture on "Apartheid: A Crisis of the Christian Conscience".[51] In this lecture, he demolished one by one the arguments in favour of apartheid. He thus appeared, to the dismay of his fellow Archbishop W. P. Whelan, as a resolute critic of the South African government. During the Council, the issue of apartheid was often discussed in private conversations.[52] Hurley even held a press conference on race relations in South Africa, on 15 November 1964.[53] But the subject was never debated *in aula,* either by the Archbishop of Durban, or by any of his fellow bishops.

Before concluding this review of Hurley's public interventions, let us say something about his eulogy – on 22 October 1964, during the discussion of the document on the Church in the Modem World – in honour of the French palaeontologist and theologian Pierre Teilhard de Chardin. In the times preceding the Council, one should remember, the Jesuit was the conservatives' *bête noire.* On 30 June 1962 the Holy Office had published a *monitum* about the theological and philosophical ambiguities and errors in Teilhard's work.[54] This did not detract from Hurley's eagerness to read the palaeontologist's writings, even before they were published as books. He had first heard of Teilhard as a student in Rome in the '30s, and he tried to contact him during his visit to South Africa in 1951, but his efforts had failed.[55] In his memoir on Vatican II Hurley explained the reasons for this lifelong fascination for the French Jesuit:

> It was not precisely the palaeontology of Teilhard that meant so much to me though I was deeply impressed by it. What contributed to my personal growth was Teilhard's vision of the cosmic Christ. Teilhard had had the good fortune to become acquainted with the early development of the revival of the Body of Christ theology promoted by the Jesuits in France in the early years of the 20th century. That vision of Christ, coupled with Teilhard's scientific picture, blossomed out into the magnificent totality of the cosmic Christ – the risen Jesus present not only in his Church but present too, as the Word of God in the physical universe in all its measurable dimensions.[56]

In his speech to the Council, Hurley commended Teilhard for having luminously described the relationship between the natural and supernatural orders. From his "splendid vision", which was "simultaneously religious and scientific, as well as evolutionary and eschatological", he argued, the Council had everything to gain.[57] This speech, Hurley commented later, in *The Southern Cross,* was responsible for "a minor controversy within the major debate". The following day, Benedictus Reetz, the Abbot of Beuron, expressed the view that Teilhard had not seen enough evil in the world and tended to reflect Origen's erroneous opinion that there was no eternal punishment. Later on, however, Bishop Spülbeck of Meissen, East Germany, came to the defence of Teilhard, pointing to the influence he exerted in scientific circles. The Marxists feared him because his work was based on science. "So", concluded Hurley, "it ended two-to-one in favour of Teilhard".[58]

Hopes and Frustrations

During the last three periods of the Council, the Archbishop of Durban achieved the *tour de force* of sending an article every week – anonymously – to *The Southern Cross*. As far as we know, he was the only bishop at the Council who played the role of a journalist.[59] This gave him the opportunity of sharing with the South African public his hopes for and questions about the Council.

This chronicle was, firstly, a pedagogical exercise. Week after week, he explained in simple terms the significance of often-complicated and tedious theological discussions. The former lecturer was at work, as this example will indicate:

> The Second Vatican Council finds the Church in the throes of a transition from a theology of concept to a theology of image. The concept was fine for defensive purposes but is not so good for progressive pastoral strategy. In swinging to the image, the Church finds itself in a "back-to-the-Bible" campaign. The Bible is God's poetry, God's word in glowing images. So, the argument in St Peter's from Tuesday to Friday on the first chapter of the schema on the Church, "The Mystery of the Church", revolved around the best expressions and images with which to present the hidden reality of the Church to the world of the 20th century.[60]

Hurley's chronicle of the Council is a magnificent piece of literature. Forty years after the event, it still reads like a novel. The most difficult subjects were treated with humour, and yet the seriousness of the issues at stake was never lost:

> Opposition to the permanent diaconate hinged mainly on the question of celibacy. Some hair-raising pictures were painted of the conjugal misery to which married deacons could be reduced – unfaithful and garrulous wives, delinquent sons and fashion-conscious beauty-queen daughters. Married deacons were also seen as the thin end of the wedge that would one day wreck the celibacy of the Western clergy in general.[61]

Particularly interesting were his descriptions of national characters. This was, for instance, how he described the intervention of an Italian bishop during the debate on collegiality:

The speaker was the young, newly-consecrated (five days previously) Auxiliary of Bologna, Bishop Bettazzi. He charged into the fray spraying a torrent of eloquent Latin and gesticulating magnificently. In 15 hectic minutes that galvanised a weary end-of-the-week assembly he marshalled an imposing array of theological witnesses to prove that the Italian tradition was as surely behind collegiality as any other.[62]

At the end of the debate on collegiality, when the *aggiornamento* theologians were publicly expressing their satisfaction, the Archbishop of Durban had this to say:

To the Anglo-Saxon mind this theological enthusiasm is a little incomprehensible. The pragmatic Anglo-Saxon is inclined to say that if worldwide episcopal collaboration is a good thing, why not get on with it without agonising over the academic theological implications? But the Anglo-Saxon mind is not the Latin mind nor the Transalpine. The Transalpines and the Latins must have theological and philosophical reasons for doing things. The Anglo-Saxons prefer to do them first and find reasons afterwards.[63]

Like all the other bishops, Hurley had moments of doubt, particularly at the end of the third period, when the minority persuaded the pope to add a conservative postscript to the document on collegiality. At times, he complained that the Council was dragging on, as if it were going to last for ever. At such moments, he felt rather despondent, as he told one of his South African correspondents:

The Council is becoming very boring. It takes oceans of words to cover a subject. It took us five weeks to get through the *schema De Ecclesia* and now we are launched into the debate on the administrative aspect of the episcopal office and further oceans of words are going to flow concerning relations between the Curia and the bishops and the powers of bishops conferences and so on. There is not even the excitement we had last year of throwing out *schema* after *schema* from the middle of November. We realise now that every time we throw out a *schema*, we add another year to the life of the Council. In this mood, we would be prepared to accept any old rag as a basis of discussion. No matter how good or how bad the *schema* is, the discussion lasts just as long.[64]

Such times of discouragement were, however, short-lived. Until the end of the Council, Hurley remained an active participant. Part of his time was devoted to the work of the Commission for Seminaries, Studies and Catholic Education, a subject to which we shall soon return. On 16 June 1965, he became a member of the Council for the Implementation of the Constitution on the Sacred Liturgy.[65] He also got involved in the reform of the liturgy in English. It was on his initiative that the International Commission on English in the Liturgy was established in October 1963.[66] As a member of the Episcopal Committee he took an active part in the work of the Commission, during and after the Council. There was a good spirit of co-operation, he wrote to Boulle and de Gersigny in November 1965, despite the "Homeric" battles with Professor H.P.R. Finberg, an English liturgist, over the use of "thou" and "you" in the liturgy.[67]

The Archbishop of Durban's final intervention, during the last week of the Council, concerned the issue of public defence. The document on the Church in the Modern World included a paragraph condemning nuclear war in no uncertain terms. But it also stated that governments could not be denied the right of lawful self-defence. In Hurley's view, this was an illogical position. "The out-and-out option", he wrote to his Durban correspondents a few weeks before the vote, "is that the bomb is so bad that the Council should come out in favour of unilateral disarmament – we disarm, the Russians and Chinese don't. [...] Some Americans are already upset because there is no commendation in the text of those who are defending what is left of the world's freedom at great sacrifice".[68] Hurley himself agreed with the American position. He did not express his views *in aula* but submitted a written intervention in which he suggested that the entire second part of the document on the Church in the Modern World, which included the controversial paragraphs on nuclear war, be suppressed and replaced with a statement of principle on the problems facing society in the modern world, at the end of the first part. The Council had not been able to look at those issues in detail, he argued. To say nothing was better than to make unprofessional assertions on difficult social and political matters.[69]

On 2 December 1965, Archbishop Philip Hannan of New Orleans, a former chaplain to paratroopers, circulated a petition recommending the rejection of the paragraphs concerning the use of nuclear weapons, on the grounds that "the possession of nuclear weapons has preserved freedom for a very large portion in the world". Hurley added his signature to those of nine other bishops, mostly from Northern and Central America.[70] The petition, however, failed to achieve its objectives. The document on the Church in the Modern World was voted unaltered, with a strong condemnation of the nuclear bomb only tempered by the recognition that the disarmament should be bilateral.[71] Thirty years later, Hurley still defends the position he took during the Council, but he puts it in a wider perspective:

> I felt that we had arrived at a huge contradiction between the right of self-defence and the possession of nuclear weapons. The contradiction, I fear, remains unsolved until we arrive at universal nuclear disarmament. Possibly in my supporting Archbishop Hannan the logic of my scholastic training was exerting too great an influence on me.[72]

The Conciliar Document on Priestly Formation

The Archbishop of Durban was voted onto the Commission for Priestly Formation and Catholic Education at the second congregation of the Council, on 16 October 1962. The theologians who had campaigned for his election knew him, among other reasons, from the article he had published in *The Furrow* on the pastoral training of seminarians. This article had been translated into several languages.[73]

But, as mentioned earlier, Hurley had already expressed his views on priestly formation in his submission to the Antepreparatory Commission of the Council of April 1960. He had also pleaded for a revision of the programme of priestly formation at the International Study Week on Missionary Catechetics held in Eichstatt, Germany in July 1960.[74] Johannes Hofinger, the organiser of this conference, had come to South Africa in 1959 to give a series of lectures on the catechetical renewal. Hurley's invitation to the International Study Week was a consequence of that visit.[75] In many respects, the opinions expressed in the paper delivered in Eichstatt anticipated those defended two years later in *The Furrow*.

Lastly, the Archbishop of Durban had tried to disseminate his ideas concerning seminary training at the Central Preparatory Commission. In June 1962, in particular, he had submitted to the Commission a detailed critique of the document drafted by the Preparatory Commission for Studies and Seminaries.[76] He returned to the subject in his memoir on the Council, explaining why he had disagreed with the document prepared by Curia officials for the February meeting of the Commission:

> In dealing with the paper on seminaries I was very critical of what had been placed before us, contending that while philosophy and theology were very important, the most important consideration should be the pastoral training of seminarians, providing them with the ability to speak and communicate well, to relate to people, to perform liturgy well and to exercise the kind of leadership that would be required from them as priests.[77]

His interest in theological education reached back to the days of his own training in Rome. It was on this rather unlikely ground, he explained to the journalist Desmond Fisher, that the seeds of the liberal ideas that were to make him, a quarter-of-a-century later, one of the leading figures of the *aggiornamento* were sown.[78] Soon after his ordination, he got involved in seminary training, as the rector of the newly-founded Scholasticate of the Oblates of Mary Immaculate in Pietermaritzburg. Once a bishop, he became the first President of the Board of Seminaries of the Southern African Catholic Bishops' Conference. He was serving in that capacity when the South African bishops assumed the responsibility for St Peter's Seminary, Pevensey, a seminary for black candidates for the priesthood, from the missionary congregation of Mariannhill.

In his article in *The Furrow*, Hurley insisted that priests should be, above all, "competent communicators of the faith". The chief object of the seminaries was not to promote academic knowledge but to impart "communicable knowledge". The current system, with a three-year course of scholastic philosophy followed by four years of theology, was unable, according to the Archbishop of Durban, to achieve this objective:

> At the end of this course of study the average seminarian has a fairly good text-book knowledge of the faith in terms of magisterial decrees and scholastic definitions. The big question is: has he a communicable

knowledge? Is he filled with fire and enthusiasm for the Word and
has he acquired the ability to propound it in an attractive and
compelling style to all manner of audiences? Ask the parishioners in
the pews. Ask the teachers in the schools.[79]

To improve the quality of priestly training, Hurley proposed a radical
restructuring of the seminary programme. In the first place, he suggested
the institution of an introductory year, during which the young seminarian
would receive "a thorough initiation into the Mystery of Christ". Secondly,
and this was the most revolutionary aspect of his proposal, he recommended
that the courses of philosophy and theology be integrated into one "sacred
science". This, he argued, was the approach of Thomas Aquinas. "One of
the great drawbacks of Catholic thought in modern times has been the too-
great insistence on the distinction between faith and philosophy, to the
detriment of both".[80] The whole seminary course, philosophy included,
had to be built up in such a way that it was "related to life".[81] In this way,
the principal objective of seminary studies, that is, the training of pastoral
priests, would be met.

The views expressed in this article exerted a fair amount of influence
on the Commission for Seminaries, Studies and Catholic Education. Hurley
failed, however, to convince the members of the commission to take into
consideration the entirety of his proposal, particularly the idea of integrating
philosophy and theology into one central course, with a heavy pastoral
component.

The commission had its first plenary session at the very end of the first
conciliar period, on 3 December 1963.[82] Its president, Cardinal Giuseppe
Pizzardo, played only a nominal role. Its most influential member was
Archbishop Dino Staffa, a curial official. Augustin Mayer, a German
Benedictine living in Rome, fluent in many languages and with great
organisational skills, served as secretary. Of all the *periti,* Paolo Dezza,
an Italian Jesuit, was the most active. German Mártil, the Rector of the
Spanish College of Rome, who later wrote a book on the work of the
commission, was another.[83] By-and-large, the conservative element
dominated, as Hurley told Cardinal Suenens shortly after the second
meeting of the commission:

> Unfortunately, it appears to have been a policy to appoint only "safe" men, men who can be relied upon to promote conventional curial and juridical views. They are nearly all Romans of Italian or Spanish origin, rectors or professors in Roman seminaries or employed in the Sacred Congregation of Studies. The Romans also include one Irishman (rector of the Irish College) and a German Salesian canonist. The only outsiders are three Americans who exert little influence and a French Dominican, Father Camelot, who does not say much. Father Dezza SJ is the best of the *periti,* but it would take some time to get him to shake off the Roman mentality completely. Father Mayer is also good.[84]

The first work session of the commission took place from 21 February to 2 March 1963. Owing to the short notice given, only 14 of 25 members were able to attend. The commission was divided into three sub-commissions: one on priestly formation, one on schools and academic studies, and the third on the preparation of material for canon law. Hurley was on the first sub-commission, with an Italian bishop as chair. The procedure was first to work in sub-commissions and then to report back to the entire commission.

The commission used as its starting point a document compiled by Paolo Dezza which combined the two *schemata* drafted by the Preparatory Commission for Seminaries and Schools during the preparatory phase of the Council, one on vocations and the other on the formation of candidates for the priesthood. As one could have expected, Hurley found this document quite unsatisfactory. In January 1963, he therefore submitted to the commission an alternative document entitled *De sacrorum alumnis formandis,* preceded by a critique of the document compiled by the Preparatory Commission for Seminaries and Schools.[85] His submission reproduced the views he had expressed in *The Furrow* article. The commission also followed a series of guidelines prepared by the Central Co-ordinating Commission in December 1962.

Given the composition of the commission, Hurley's suggestions were too radical to gain full approval. Only some aspects of his proposals were considered. On 28 February, Hurley wrote of his disenchantment to Eric Boulle and Geoff de Gersigny:

> You can imagine what little sympathy my draft *schemata* found here. Some made charitable comments on the interesting features they noticed, but by and large I think they were considered slightly crackpot.

He then proceeded to the analysis of what he thought had been his mistake:

> The fundamental tactical error on my part was to depart so radically from the previous order and arrangement. It meant that to understand what I was getting at, the traditionalists had to leave their customary categories and lines of thought. This, of course, was impossible.

He nevertheless managed "by hard arguing" to get a few amendments accepted, but, as he explained to his Durban correspondents, these remained "amendments to old views". His only hope was that the work of the commission would be rejected by the conciliar assembly:

> Perhaps that is all we can hope for the time being – until the Transalpini turn their guns on our work in the plenary sessions. How short-sighted, all the same, or just plain mean of those responsible to load the dice so overwhelmingly in favour of one view, when they must know by now they cannot hope to get away with it in the Council.[86]

The document that emerged from the meeting, a 12-page long *schema* divided into 27 articles, was little more than an abridgment of the original *schema*. Paolo Dezza, a "master of concision", was its author.[87] It was immediately submitted to the Co-ordinating Commission. This rush, according to Hurley, was due to Pope John XXIII's desire to have all the conciliar documents in shape before his death, which he knew could not be far off.[88]

Seeing that he could not make any further progress, Hurley decided to go directly to the Central Co-ordinating Commission. He wrote down his comments on the *schema* prepared by the Commission for Seminaries, Studies and Catholic Education and, on 18 March 1963, he sent them, with an accompanying letter, to Cardinal Suenens, one of the members of the Co-ordinating Commission.

In the letter, he recommended that "five or six new *periti*" be added to the commission so as to give "the right orientation and spirit" to its work. The *schema* on priestly formation could be amended, he further said, provided that "one good man with the ability to grasp theory and practice in a unified vision" helped Dezza and himself to put the finishing touches to the document. The *schema* on schools and universities, on the other hand, required "a total overhaul". Hurley suggested a few names as possible *periti*. First on his list was the American Jesuit John Courtney Murray.[89]

Hurley, in his comments, spelt out his objections to the *schema* on priestly formation. He commended the efforts made to indicate "both in general and in particular" that the whole orientation of priestly formation should be pastoral. But he had reservations about the paragraph on minor seminaries, which he thought was out of place. According to him, all references to minor seminaries were to be grouped under a special heading at the end of the document. His most important comment concerned the place reserved for spiritual formation in the *schema*. In his view, spiritual and pastoral formation were intimately related. Their separation, like the separation of practical pastoral formation from theology, was a manifestation of a "departmental" mentality which was prejudicial to the quality of priestly formation:

> The tendency to treat spiritual formation before doctrinal and pastoral formation betrays, I think, the old "departmental" mentality, according to which there is a real dichotomy between a priest's spiritual life and his apostolic life. It is not my intention to argue that doctrinal and pastoral training are more important than spiritual formation, but to maintain that doctrinal and pastoral training is *logically prior* to spiritual formation and that this logical priority should require the order of treatment.[90]

Hurley's letter to Suenens was communicated to the Secretary of the Council, Pericle Felici, who sent it, with other reactions, to the Commission for Seminaries, Studies and Catholic Education. It had no immediate effect. The composition of the commission remained substantially the same, and the *schema* on priestly formation was accepted, in principle, by the Co-ordinating Commission. It was then approved by Pope John XXIII for discussion in general congregation and distributed, with other *schemata*, to the Council fathers. The *schema* on schools, on the other hand, was sent back for revision to the *periti* residing in Rome, with the request to make it sound "more pastoral". "I doubt very much", commented Hurley, "whether they will be able to do this".[91]

Hurley's main achievement, if one looks at what the commission did during the intersession, was to bring to the fore the pastoral dimension of seminary training. The idea of an introductory year focussing on the mystery of Christ at the beginning of seminary training is also his.[92] But his suggestion that the spiritual and the pastoral training be considered together, instead of treating the spiritual formation as a separate topic and dealing with it at the beginning of the document, did not gain any support from the other bishops. He lost that battle, as he admitted in a recent interview:

> After a long discussion in which I was almost alone fighting for a definition of the object of priestly formation, they finally agreed to define the purpose of training for the priesthood. I think that helped a lot, because it brought out the pastoral dimension quite strongly. The only time I lost an argument was over spiritual training. To know what spiritual training the students should get, we need to see to what pastoral training and to what theology this spiritual training is related. It needs to be related to the whole process. But they did not agree with me on that. The spiritual training had to be the first. I had to go along with them. I could not win the argument.[93]

The commission met again during the second session of the Council to consider the various comments that the secretary had collected in the meantime. Some changes were made to the *schema* on priestly formation but they concerned the style and emphasis of the document rather than its content.[94]

During the second session, the commission received the injunction to reduce the draft to a series of votable propositions. The Co-ordinating Commission was so anxious to accelerate the conciliar process that it even considered submitting the document to the vote without discussion. But this plan was not entirely practical. When the Council reassembled for the third session in September 1964, the commission was asked to give more flesh to the document and it was subjected to a discussion in aula.[95]

Fearing a difficult debate, the Secretary of the Commission, Augustin Mayer, picked speakers from the commission to respond to the anticipated criticisms of the document. Hurley was one of them. He intervened at the end of the debate, on 16 November 1964, and insisted on what he thought was the key aspect of the document, that is, the "harmonious integration" of the pastoral, intellectual and spiritual aspects of priestly training, The purpose of seminary formation, he added, was to train "pastoral priests". Repeating an argument already used in *The Furrow*, he noted that Thomas Aquinas himself wanted to integrate, in a single approach, theology and philosophy.[96]

Unlike other texts presented during the same session, the *schema* on priestly formation was well received by the conciliar fathers.[97] The only bone of contention was the mention of Thomas Aquinas as an authoritative doctor of the Church, but a compromise solution was eventually found. On the whole, the document reflected the mood of the Council. This was due, in no small measure, to Hurley's influence on the commission. An observer noted at the time that "the author of the document [...] had somehow managed to escape from the predominantly conservative influence of the curial Congregation for Seminaries and Universities and to keep that influence at arm's length".[98] This anonymous homage primarily concerned Mayer and Dezza, the two main authors of the document, but it also referred to the Archbishop of Durban.[99] The most-praised paragraph was the first, which handed the responsibility of the seminary programmes to the episcopal conferences. This considerably reduced the power of the Congregation for Seminaries and Universities, of which, interestingly, Staffa was the secretary at the time of the Council.[100] Hurley, whose opposition to excessive ecclesiastical centralisation was well known, certainly contributed to the insertion of this paragraph at the beginning of the document.[101]

Archbishop Hurley and Vatican II

Hurley's contribution to the anti-apartheid movement in South Africa has been widely recognised, not only among the members of his Church but also in the ecumenical movement, nationally and internationally. But he fought many other battles. The Second Vatican Council is one of them. He was involved in its preparation and attended all four sessions, from 1962 to 1965.

Few people realise how important Hurley's contribution to this major historical event has been. There was no guarantee that the ecumenical Council called by Pope John XXIII in 1959 would produce any result at all: the Central Preparatory Commission, almost entirely dominated by Curial officials, was determined to maintain the *status quo* at any cost. It was because of the determination of a small group of progressive bishops, helped by theologians like Chenu, Congar, Küng, Rahner, Häring and Schillebeeckx, that the *aggiornamento* wanted by the Pope eventually took place. Hurley was one of these bishops. In September 1962, a month before the opening of the Council, he was on a list of 16 bishops identified by Congar and Chenu as key allies in the fight for a truly ecumenical event. From the start, he had a clear view of what the Council was meant to achieve, as shown by the *vota* he submitted to the Antepreparatory Commission in April 1960, his contribution to the International Study Week on Missionary Catechetics in July 1960 and his article on priestly ministry in the January 1962 issue of *The Furrow*.

Of all the South African bishops, he was by far the most active, as the number of oral interventions and written submissions shows. The speeches he delivered during the first period of the Council were particularly critical. He took an active part in the fight for the rejection of the documents prepared by the Central Preparatory Commission and the setting of a new agenda for the Council. Among the interventions he made during the last three periods, one can single out those in favour of the Church's independence from the state and his apologia for Teilhard de Chardin. Hurley's primary concern was to encourage and nurture the Church's pastoral commitment. Trained as a scholastic theologian, he was deeply conscious of the limitations that this traditional way of thinking imposed on the Church's ability to confront the challenges of modern society. He became one of the key members of the Commission for Seminaries, Studies and Catholic Education. Despite the fairly conservative composition of this commission, he succeeded in giving the document on seminary training a distinctly pastoral note. During all the meetings of the commission and again in plenary session, he pleaded for a "harmonious integration" of the pastoral, intellectual and spiritual aspects of priestly training. In theological education, the cardinal sin was "departmentalism". He was adamant that the philosophy and theology courses had to be integrated if the seminaries were to produce "pastoral priests".

Archbishop Hurley became an enthusiastic populariser of the Second Vatican Council. The conciliar event profoundly influenced him. It is worth noting that one of his strongest public denunciations of apartheid took place in 1964, between the second and the third periods of the Council. There is little likelihood that his subsequent involvement in the anti-apartheid movement would have been the same if he had not taken part in the Council.

The Archbishop of Durban was a son of the Council. But he was also one of its fathers – if one may be forgiven for using this politically incorrect term. It is hoped that this essay, incomplete as it is, will contribute to highlighting this essential aspect of his life.

Endnotes

1.   Revised and updated version of a paper read at the conference on the history of Vatican II organised by the Instituto per le Scienze Religiose in Bologna, Italy, in December 1996 and published three years later in M.T. Fattori and A. Melloni (eds), *Experience, Organisations and Bodies at Vatican II* (Leuven: Bibliotheek van de Faculteit Godgeleerdheid, 1999), p. 233-60. For a South African reprint see Philippe Denis, ed. *Facing the Crisis, Selected Texts of Archbishop Denis E. Hurley,* (Pietermaritzburg: Cluster Publications, 1997) p. 228-55.

2.   On the African participation in the Second Vatican Council, see Marie-Dominique Chenu, "L'Afrique au Concile", *Parole et mission,* 20 (January 1963), pp. 11-18, reprinted in his *L'Évangile dans le temps* (Paris, Cerf, 1964), pp. 647-53; Georges Conus, "L'Église d'Afrique au Concile Vatican II", *Neue Zeitschrift für Missionswissenschaft,* vol 30 (1974), pp. 241-55 and vol 31 (1975), pp. 1-18, 124-42; Claude Prudhomme, "Les évêques d'Afrique noire anciennement française et le Concile", in Étienne Fouilloux, ed., *Vatican II commence... Approches Francophones* (Leuven: Bibliotheek van de Faculteit der Godgeleerdheid, 1993), pp. 163-88; Claude Soetens, "L'apport du Congo-Leopoldville (ZaVre), du Rwanda et du Burundi au Concile Vatican II", *ibid.*, pp. 189- 208; J. P. Messina, "L'église d'Afrique

au concile Vatican II: origines de l'assemblée du synode des évèques pour l'Afrique", *Mélanges de Science Religieuse*, 3 (1994), pp. 279-95; Matthijs Lamberigts, "Der Beitrag Afrikas während der Konzilsdebatteüber die Liturgie", in Wolfgang Weiss, ed., *Zeugnis und Dialog. Die Katholische Kirche in der neuzeitlichen Welt und das II. Vatikanische Konzil. Klaus Wittstadt zum 60. Geburtstag* (Würzburg: Echter, 1996), pp. 186-207. The reception issue is discussed by Adrian Hastings, "The Council came to Africa", in Alberic Stacpoole, ed., *Vatican II by those who were there* (London: Geoffrey Chapman, 1966), pp. 315-23. See also Adrian Hastings, "The Post-Conciliar Church in Eastern Africa", in *African Catholicism. Essays in Discovery* (London: SCM and Philadelphia: Trinity Press International, 1989), pp. 122-37; Evangelista Vilanova, "The intersession (1963-1964)", in Alberigo, ed., *History of Vatican II*, vol. 3, pp. 481-84.

3.   On Hurley's participation in the Council, see Desmond Fisher, *Archbishop Denis Hurley* (Notre Dame, Indiana: University of Notre Dame Press, 1965), pp. 31-47. For a shorter version of this study, see *Men who make the Council: Portraits of Vatican II Leaders* (University of Notre Dame, Indiana, 1965). Re-edition in *Guardian of the Light. Tributes to Archbishop Denis Hurley OMI on the Golden Jubilee of his Priestly Ordination, 1939-1989* (Durban: Archdiocese of Durban, 1989), pp. 15-23.

4.   On the problem of sources for the history of Vatican II in Africa, see François de Medeiros, "Les archives africaines", in Jan Grootaers and Claude Soetens, *Sources locales de Vatican II. Symposium Leuven – Louvain-la-Neuve 23-25-X-1989* (Leuven: Bibliotheek van de Faculteit der Godgeleerdheid, 1990), pp. 95-97.

5.   These archives are kept in 24 boxes distributed as follows: Central Preparatory Commission (four boxes); 1st session (three boxes); 2nd Session (three boxes); 3rd Session (two boxes); 4th Session (two boxes); Commissio de Seminariis et de Educatione Catholica (four boxes); other commissions (six boxes).

6.   See Alan Henriques, "Vatican II in *The Southern Cross*" *Bulletin for Contextual Theology in Southern Africa & Africa* 4/1 (1997), pp. 31- 39. Hurley also expressed his views in an interview conducted at the end of the first period of the Council. See D. E. Hurley, "Freeing the Word of God", in V. A. Yzermans, *A New Pentecost. Vatican Council II: Session I* (Westminster, Maryland, 1963), pp. 276-83.

7.   Rome: Typis Polyglottis Vaticanis, five vol.

8.   Rome: Typis Polyglottis Vaticanis, five vol.

9.   Interview conducted in Durban on 21 February 1995.

10. Interviews conducted in Durban, April-October 1996.

11.   Interview conducted in Zwolle, Netherlands, on 23 January 1991.

12.   Interview conducted in Cape Town on 30 April 1992.

13.   Interview conducted in Cape Town on 30 April 1992.

14.   Cardinal Domenico Tardini, Secretary of State, to Archbishop Hurley, Rome, 18 June 1959. Durban Archdiocesan Archives.

15.   Hurley, Denis, "The Second Vatican Council" p.24.

16.   Hurley, "The Second Vatican Council" p. 24.

17.   Hurley, "The Second Vatican Council" p. 24.

18.   Hurley, "The Second Vatican Council" p. 24.

19.   For instance in Congo. See Soetens, "L'apport du Congo", p. 193.

20.   Acta et Documenta Concilio Oecumenico Vaticano II Apparanda. Series 1: Antepraeparatoria. Volume 2: Consilia et Vota episcoporum ac praelatorum. Part 5: Africa (Rome: Typis Polyglottis Vaticanis, 1960), p. 537. Vota dated 22 August 1960.

21.   *Ibid.*, pp. 543-44. *Vota* dated 6 October 1959.

22.   *Ibid.*, pp. 537-39. *Vota* dated 15 April 1960.

23.   Fouilloux, "The antepreparatory phase", p. 129.

24.   Archbishop Pericle Felici to Archbishop Hurley, Rome, 5 July 1960, Durban.

25.   Hurley, Denis, "Memories of Vatican II", in *Vatican II: Keeping the Dream Alive*, p. 9.

26.   Hurley, Denis, "The Second Vatican Council" p.24.

27.   Bishop Gerard van Velsen, interview conducted in Zwolle on 23 January 1991. Van Velsen (1910-1996), a Dutch Dominican who arrived in South Africa in 1937 and was consecrated bishop in 1950, was one of the six resident bishops invited to be members of the Secretariat for Christian Unity. See R. Burigana, M. Paiano, G. Turbanti and M. Velati, "La messa a punto dei testi. Le commissioni dell a fase preparatoria del Vatican II", in Fouilloux, ed., *Vatican II commence...*, p. 30; Philippe Denis, *The Dominicans in Southern Africa. A Social History (1577-1990)*, Leiden, Brill, 1998, pp. 184-86. Bishop van Velsen's life story, including his impressions of the Council, was recorded in 1988 by the Dutch journalist Cees Veltman *(HN Magazine. Hervormd Nederland Oecumenisch Opinieweekblad,* vol. 44, nr 6, 13 February 1988, pp. 6-9). His papers, kept in the Dominican Library in Pietermaritzburg, mostly contain official documents, which are easy to find elsewhere.

28.   Hurley, "The Second Vatican Council" p. 24.

29.   Hurley, "Pastoral emphasis in seminary studies", *The Furrow,* vol. 13, January 1962, p. 16; reprinted in Philippe Denis, ed., *Facing the Crisis,* pp. 12-24.

30.   According to Joseph Komonchak, the members of the Central Preparatory Commission who were critical of the prepared texts were the following: Alfrink (Utrecht), Döpfner (Munich), Frings (Cologne), Hurley (Durban), König (Vienna), Léger (Montreal), Liénart (Lille), Maximos IV (Patriarch of the Melchites), Montini (Milan) and Suenens (Brussels). See Komonchak, "The struggle for the Council during the preparation of Vatican II (1960-1962)", in Alberigo, ed., *History of Vatican II*, p. 304.

31.   Komonchak, "The struggle", p. 306.

32.   Hurley, Denis "Memories of Vatican II, p.12.

33.   For an account of this episode based on material provided by Archbishop Hurley, see Komonchak, "The struggle", pp. 340-42. See also G. Routhier, "Les réactions du Cardinal Léger à la preparation de Vatican II", *Revue d'histoire de l'Église de France*, vol. 80 (1994), p. 281. A copy of the memorandum submitted to the *transalpini* is kept in the Durban Archdiocesan Archives.

34.   Hurley, "The Second Vatican Council", p. 24.

35.   See Jan A. Brouwers, "Vatican II: derniers préparatifs et première session. Activités conciliaires en coulisses", in Fouilloux, ed., *Vatican II commence...,* p. 353. Only seven documents out of the approximately 70 that had been drafted by the Central Preparatory Commission were sent out.

36.   Hurley, Denis "Memories of Vatican II", p.18.

37.   Jan A. Brouwers, "Vatican II: derniers...", p. 364, The General Secretariat of the Episcopal Conferences of Africa and Madagascar was established on 17 October 1962. The group of African bishops, the first to be constituted at the Council, was important "because of the number of bishops involved and because of their repeatedly unanimous votes at the Council, which gave interventions in the name of the group an enormous influence" (Hilary Raguer, "An initial profile of the assembly", in Alberigo, ed., *History of Vatican II,* p. 189).

38.   André Duval, "Le message au monde", in Fouilloux, ed "*Vatican II commence*", p. 111; Klaus Wittstadt, "On the eve of the Second Vatican Council (July I - October 10, 1962)", in Alberigo, ed., *History of Vatican II*, vol. 1, p. 425. There is no trace, in Congar's papers, of Hurley's response. See Andrea Riccardi, "The tumultuous opening days of the Council", in G. Alberigo, ed., *ibid*, vol. 2, p. 52.

39. Archbishop Hurley to Eric Boulle and Geoff de Gersigny, Rome, 16 October 1962. Durban Archdiocesan Archives.

40. *Ibid.* The Durban Archdiocesan Archives contain a three-page typewritten document entitled "Impressions of the Council", dated 27 October 1962 and addressed to Douglas Woodruff, the editor of *The Tablet,* in which Hurley shared a similar, but more detailed, analysis of the forces at play.

41. See Conus, "L'Église d'Afrique", vol. 31, p. 3-5.

42. See Conus, "L'Église d' Afrique", p. 7.

43. *Acta Synodalia Sacrosancti Concilii Oecumenici Vaticani II,* vol. 1/1 (Rome: Typis Polyglottis Vaticanis, 1970), p. 238.

44. *Acta Synodalia,* vol. 1/1, p. 327-28. On this intervention, see Lamberigts, "Der Beitrag", p. 192 and "The liturgy debate", in Alberigo, ed., *History of Vatican II,* vol. 2, p. 112.

45. Giuseppe Ruggieri, "The first doctrinal clash", in Alberigo, ed., *History of Vatican II,* vol. 2, p. 266. In his essay on "La discussione sullo *schema constitutionis dogmaticae de fontibus revelationibus* durante la I sessione del Concilio Vaticano II" (Fouilloux, ed., *Vatican II commence...,* p. 316) Ruggieri highlights the "great lucidity" of Hurley's intervention.

46. *Acta Synodalia,* vol. 1/3, p. 199. See Ruggieri, "The first doctrinal clash", p. 250.

47. *Acta Synodalia,* vol. 1/4, p. 198. See Giuseppe Ruggieri, "Beyond an ecclesiology of polemics. The debate on the Church", in Alberigo, ed., *History of Vatican II,* vol. 2, p. 343.

48. See Joseph A. Komonchak, "The initial debate about the Church", in Fouilloux, ed., *Vatican II commence...,* p. 344.

49. *Acta Synodalia,* vol. 3/2, p. 515-18.

50. *Ibid.,* vol. 4/2, p.188-89.

51. Denis E. Hurley, *Apartheid: A Crisis of the Christian Conscience* (South African Institute of Race Relations, 1964); reprinted in Philippe Denis, ed., *Facing the Crisis,* pp. 58-76. This lecture was also published in *The Southern Cross* (22 January – 19 February 1964). Hurley's first major public pronouncements against apartheid date from 1957. It was at his instigation that, in the same year, the Southern African Bishops' Conference declared apartheid "intrinsically evil".

52. Cardinal McCann, interview conducted in Cape Town, 30 April 1992.

53. G. Vallquist, *Das Zweite Vatikanische Konzil* (Nuremberg, 1966), p. 204.

54. Komonchak, "The struggle", p. 243.

55. Hurley, Denis, "Memories of Vatican II", p.2. On Teilhard's visit to South Africa, see also Denis, *The Dominican Friars*, p. 137.

56. Hurley, Denis "Memories of Vatican II", p. 4.

57. *Acta Synodalia,* vol. 3/5, p. 342. See Norman Tanner, "The Church in the world *(Ecclesia ad extra)*", in Alberigo, ed., *History of Vatican II*, vol. 4, p. 285.

58. *The Southern Cross,* 4 November 1964. On this debate, see Antoine Wenger, *Chronique de la Troisième Session* (Paris: Centurion, 1965), p. 410; Xavier Rynne, *The Third Session. The Debates and Decrees of Vatican Council II, September 14 to November 21*, 1964 (London: Faber and Faber, 1965), pp. 125-26. Hurley quoted Teilhard de Chardin's *Le Milieu Divin* in the above-mentioned Alfred and Winifred Hoernlé memorial lecture on apartheid.

59. On the journalists at the Council, see Jan Grootaers, "L'information religieuse au début du Concile", in Étienne Fouilloux, *Vatican II commence... Approches francophones* (Leuven: Bibliotheek van de Faculteit der Godgeleerdheid, 1993), pp. 211-34; Alberto Melloni, "The beginning of the second period. The great debate on the Church", in Alberigo, ed., *History of Vatican II*, vol. 3, pp. 31-32.

60. *The Southern Cross,* 16 October 1963, quoted in Melloni, "The beginning", p. 48.

61. *Ibid.,* 30 October 1963.

62. *Ibid.,* 23 October 1963.

63. *Ibid.,* 13 November 1963.

64. Hurley to R.J. Coates, Rome, 6 November 1963. Durban Archdiocesan Archives.

65. See Finn and Schellmann, *Shaping English Liturgy,* p. 9. When the Council ceased to function in 1969, Hurley was appointed to the newly-established Congregation for Divine Worship. He remained a member of that Congregation until 1974.

66. Frederick R. McManus, "ICEL: the First Years", in Finn and Schellmann, *Shaping English Liturgy,* pp. 436-38. Hurley was elected Chairman of ICEL's Episcopal Board in August 1975. In subsequent years, he was re-elected several times to that office by the bishops of the board.

67. Hurley to Boulle and de Gersigny, 15 November 1965. Durban Archdiocesan Archives.

68. Hurley to Boulle and de Gersigny, 23 September 1965.

69   Durban Archdiocesan Archives. *Acta Synodalia,* vol. 4/3, p. 205-206.

70.   A copy of the petition, dated 2 December 1965, is kept in the Durban Archdiocesan Archives. On this episode, see *The Southern Cross,* 2 December 1965; Xavier Rynne, *The Fourth Session. The Debates and Decrees of Vatican Council II, September 14 to December 8, 1965* (London: Faber and Faber, 1966), pp. 225-30; Antoine Wenger, *Chronique de la Quatrième Session* (Paris: Centurion, 1966), p. 277.

71.   *The Church in the Modern World,* 79-82.

72.   Hurley, letter to the author, Durban, 31 October 1996.

73.   Hurley, Denis, "The Second Vatican Council", p. 25.

74.   Hurley, "The Bishop's Role in the Catechetical Renewal", in Johannes Hofinger, ed., *Teaching All Nations. A Symposium on Modern Catechetics* (Freiburg: Herder and London: Burns and Oates, 1961), pp. 341-56. This volume was originally published in German. It was also translated into French. The second part of Hurley's contribution (pp. 351-56) deals with seminary studies.

75.   Fisher, *Archbishop Denis Eugene Hurley,* p. 19.

76.   "Observationes super schemate De Sacrorum Alumnis Formandis", 11 June 1962. Durban Archdiocesan Archives.

77.   Hurley, Memories of Vatican II, p.14.

78.   Fisher, *Archbishop Denis Eugene Hurley,* p. 16.

79.   Hurley, "Pastoral Emphasis in Seminary Training", p. 18.

80.   *Ibid.,* p. 23.

81.   *Ibid.,* p. 27.

82.   On the work of the commission, see German Mártil, *Los Seminarios en el Concilio Vatican II. Historia y comentario* (Salamanca: Ediciones Sigueme, 1966); Denis E. Hurley and Joseph Cunnane, *Vatican II on priests and seminaries* (Dublin and Chicago: Scepter Books, 1967); A. Mayer and G. Baldanza, "Genesi storica del decreto "Optatam Totius", in A. Favale, ed., *Il decreta sulla formazione sacerdotale* (Torino, 1967), pp. 15-48; Jean Frisque,"Le décret *Optatam Totius. Introduction historique*", in J. Frisque and Y. Congar, eds, *Les prétres. Décrets "Presbyterium Ordinis" et "Optatam Totius". Textes latins et traductions françaises* (Paris: Cerf, 1968), pp. 187-89; Alois Greiler, *Das Konzil und die Seminare: die Ausbildung der Priester in der Dynamik des Zweiten Vatikanums* (Leuven and Paris, Peeters), 2003. For a short account of the conciliar debate on priestly formation, see Tanner, "The Church in the World", in Alberigo, ed., *History of Vatican II,* vol. 4, pp. 356-64.

83. Mártil, *Los Seminarios* . Mártil refers rather sympathetically to Hurley. See for example p. 51: "La idea sobre la que Mons. Hurley machacó insistentemente, de diversos modos, con una cierta noble rudeza, fue ésta: la formación sacerdotal no tiene más que un fin, el de preparar sacerdotes pastores."

84. Hurley to Suenens, [Rome], 18 March 1963. Durban Archdiocesan Archives.

85. Mártil, *Los Seminarios,* p. 50.

86. Hurley to Boulle and de Gersigny, Rome, 28 February 1963. Durban, Archdiocesan Archives.

87. Hurley and Cunnane, *Vatican II on priests and seminaries,* p. 174.

88. *Ibid.,* p. 173.

89. Hurley to Suenens, [Rome], 18 March 1963. Durban Archdiocesan Archives.

90. "Comments on the schema *De sacrorum alumnis formandis"*, [mid-March 1963]. Durban Archdiocesan Archives. A similar observation is made in Hurley and Cunnane, *Vatican II on priests and seminaries*, p. 174: "Father Dezza's abridgment had not redeemed the *schema* from its original sin of departmentalism".

91. Hurley to Whelan, [Durban], 4 April 1963. Durban Archdiocesan Archives.

92. See Karl Rahner, *Zum Reform des Theologiestudiums* (Freiburg: Herder, 1969), p. 55.

93. Hurley, interview conducted by Alan Henriques, Durban, 21 February 1995.

94. Hurley and Cunnane, *Vatican II on priests and seminaries,* p. 177.

95. *Ibid.,* p. 177-79.

96. *Acta Synodalia,* vol. 3/8, pp. 21-23. See Tanner, "The Church in the world", p. 363. On Thomism at the Council, see Joseph Komonchak, "Thomism and the Second Vatican Council", in A.J. Cernera, ed., *Continuity and Plurality in Catholic Theology: Essays in Honor of Gerald A. McCool, S.J.* (Fairfield, Conn., 1998), pp. 53-73.

97. The final vote of the decree on the training of priests (*Optatam Totius*) took place a year later, on 13 October 1965. It was promulgated on 28 October 1965.

98. Xavier Rynne, *The Third Session*, p.216. The real name of Rynne was Francis Xavier Murphy, a Redemptorist who published a chronicle of the Council in the *New Yorker.* See Jan Grootaers, "L'information religieuse au début du concile", p. 220.

99. On the authorship of the draft see M. von Galli and B. Moosbrugger, *Das Konzil. Kirche im Wandel* (Olten, 1965), p. 53.

100. *Ibid.*, p. 217.

101. This is suggested in Hurley and Cunnane, *Vatican II on priests and seminaries,* p. 177.

Denis Hurley and the Seminaries' Commission

Alois Greiler SM interviewed by Paddy Kearney

What was the main issue that the Seminaries' Commission wrestled with, and what was its main achievement?

The commission was generally seen as a minor one – the better periti and the attention of bishops and media focussed on the "major themes": church, religious freedom, ecumenism etc.

The seminaries' commission had to deal with two topics related to the universal church: priestly formation and catholic schools. The first it dealt with in the decree *Optatam Totius* which covered vocations, minor seminaries, major seminaries, the study of philosophy and theology, pastoral experience, the transition from major seminary to priestly life and ministry. The second, Catholic schools, it dealt with in the decree *Gravissimum Educationis* devoted to schools, universities, and philosophy and theology in a university context.

A major problem for this commisson was that the time for defining universal norms to apply to the whole church was over. So they had to struggle with balancing general principles and freedom for local churches. Some very conservative drafts and proposals were presented to the commission, and it had members and periti who pushed in that direction. Gradually however the commission as a whole opted for a more open approach – due to the secretary, Father (now Cardinal) Augustin Mayer OSB, Archbishop Hurley and others.

The "pastoral" decree on seminaries had to wait for basic decisions to come out of the lengthy discussions about church, bishops and priests that were taking place in other commissions. On the basis of these principles the seminaries' commission could then develop pastoral applications.

As indicated, the seminaries' commission succeeded in producing two decrees. The decree on priestly formation, in which Archbishop Hurley was deeply involved, received a lot of praise. It strongly supported decentralising formation according to the needs of local churches, but always linked to the universal church. It had a positive approach to many elements such as celibacy and other vocations, rather than an ascetic and negative view.

After a hundred years of neo-thomism dominating the study of philosophy and theology in the Catholic Church, this decree introduced a strong emphasis on the bible as the "soul of theology", using this phrase even before *Dei Verbum*, the constitution on the bible, did so. It also emphasised salvation history (a concept from the protestant theologian, Oscar Cullmann); as well as openness to ecumenism and interreligious dialogue, history and theological developments. The decree insisted on formation of the formators as a priority, and on accompanying young priests as they moved from seminary to parish. All this was new and important for the history of theology and for seminary training. Local churches had to reformulate their guidelines for priestly training according to *Optatam Totius*.

What was the significance of Archbishop Hurley's contribution to the Commission?

Hurley spoke from experience and need, from his perspective as a diocesan leader. In the commission he met others, both members and periti, who worked in the curia and had a more theoretical and principled approach, and some, who didn't make much contribution at all. Hurley was one of the most active participants. He had to overcome initial difficulties and get used to the Roman/curial way of doing things: "I learnt that in Rome you build on the achievements of the past and make as few changes as possible." He was used to desk work and enjoyed composing and editing drafts, all the time keeping a clear goal in mind: an emphasis on pastoral formation instead of exclusively on studies and ascetic life. Hurley had feared the decree would be dry and abstract, but was pleased that through his and other efforts it became very pastoral in its general tone.

He consulted widely, made proposals to bring new periti to the commission and gave interviews on the importance of seminary reform. Within the commission, which had two goals, his focus was on priestly formation while others worked on the future decree on education. The secretary, Mayer, had to oversee both.

Hurley pushed for more pastoral formation in theory and practice, as the basic goal of seminary formation. And here too he was successful. While many others, including the secretary, saw various elements of seminary formation as important: the preaching of the word, solid studies, the seminary as institution, eventually the commission agreed that all priestly formation should be geared to pastoral work, not just as one subject of many, but as a key dimension of the whole programme.

Hurley had not given up on the seminary as an institution but wanted it to be more open. Seminarians should not just be "let out" for an hour a week to give religious instruction, but there should be frequent and ongoing contact with the pastoral reality at all stages of seminary formation.

He defended the inclusion of Thomas Aquinas in the curriculum, as providing solid and systematic content. Usually only the more conservative bishops supported this inclusion. Here Hurley showed his unique insight and a perspective independent of popular "political" positions.

In the course of research for your book "Das Konzil und die Seminare" you must have interviewed Archbishop Hurley quite intensely. What are your memories of those interviews? What were your impressions of him?

Before my visit to Durban Hurley and I had exchanged several faxes in which he had kindly offered me two things: I could come to Durban to interview him, and I could use his material in the diocesan archives.

I had no idea if there would be much in the archives, but sensed that Hurley was of key importance and that I should go despite the costs etc. Well, I found out that Hurley was himself an archivist. He had kept a whole lot of material, especially documents from the commission and letters to friends in Durban, as well as his weekly articles for *The Southern Cross*. All this made my trip to Durban more than worthwhile.

You need to remember that there was hardly any photocopying at the time of the council. Commission documents had to come from its members, the secretary and others. Not all council members kept their documents or notes and in some cases these were thrown out after their deaths.

In March 1997 I had the opportunity to visit Durban for two weeks. The first two or three days I stayed in the presbytery at the Cathedral with the Archbishop who was at that time parish priest there. We had three or four interviews of about an hour each. I remember that one of the days was 17 March – St Patrick's Day. Hurley had a sprig of shamrock on his jacket – and said, "I hope you don't mind me celebrating St Patrick's Day."

I was deeply impressed by his whole personality, by his openness to me – a stranger; his positive outlook on the Church, his enthusiasm for Vatican II, his humour about the ups and downs of church life. For example, he said: "The 1950s was not a time of much new development in the Catholic Church. For me, it was the time to read. I read what I got from the European theologians like Congar and Teilhard de Chardin. The 1960s became the time to act – to have read so much turned out to be very useful in the end."

I came back to Germany after those two weeks saying: I thank God I have had the grace to meet a saint. He was a saint in a very human way. It was Lent when I was there. One evening he said he wanted to watch the news. I joined him. He asked if I would like a beer or a whisky. I said, well, in Lent, I normally don't drink alcohol, but if you give me permission, I will. He said: Oh, I gave myself permission. So we had a whisky.

I must also thank Cardinal Napier and the staff of Archbishop's House for their hospitality during my stay in Durban, when I was working in the diocesan archives.

The Archbishop must have worked quite closely with Augustin Mayer OSB, secretary of the commission, who was later made a Cardinal. Did Mayer comment to you about the Archbishop and his role?

I had many interviews with Cardinal Mayer and I owe him a lot for my work – he and Hurley were major sources of information. As secretary, Mayer was in a key position. Many of the commission members or periti were only working part-time for the commission – the bishops, for example, had to be in the plenary sessions, prepare speeches, etc. The secretary had to carry the burden – without photocopier, computer etc. Most of the commission was absent from Rome for months; the secretary stayed.

Cardinal Mayer always expressed a very positive attitude towards Hurley: grateful for his help, his cooperation, his reading and correcting of drafts. Besides Paola Dezza SJ (later also a cardinal), Hurley would have been one of the key writers of drafts, always having a strong focus on pastoral training. Dezza meanwhile was drafting chapters on studies. All had to be considered by the commission as a whole, but drafts were needed for that discussion. Mayer expressed his thanks in letters to Hurley during the Council (copies in the Durban diocesan archives) and repeated this when I had the opportunity to talk with him between 1993 and 1998.

Hurley at one stage tried to find totally different periti, like Karl Rahner. But they were already engaged with other commissions. I think over the years, he came to appreciate Mayer's work, and during my interviews with him in 1997 he had no criticism, only words of praise. He praised Mayer as a "great strategist and tactician" as shown in the way he had organised a number of speakers from the commission, amongst them Hurley, to defend the decree *Optatam Totius* when it was debated in the council plenaries. As it turned out their efforts weren't needed because the document had been so well drafted that it was received with praise.

I think Mayer tended to see Hurley's contribution as being important in several ways: he valued the fact that Hurley was active in commission meetings, working with drafts, and constantly pushing for a pastoral tone in the whole decree. Thus he was a major contributor, but not the only one. There was Dezza on studies, Mayer himself on the overall text, other members and periti on subsections of all the chapters.

In the course of working on your research for "Das Konzil und die Seminare", did you gain any impressions about the Archbishop's overall role in the Council itself, rather than just in the work of the Seminaries' Commission?

Hurley was prominent during Vatican II on a more general level also. He was one of the most active bishops from Africa. Vatican II promoted interest in bishops from the "margins" of the church via personal contact, and finally also promoted their interests and concerns. Hurley spoke English and other languages, socialised easily, participated in many conferences and meetings, and was also skilled at desk work which proved very helpful for a council. Another advantage was his membership of the Oblate congregation, which gave him easy access to Oblates from all over the world as well as to other religious.

In plenary sessions of the Council he made various speeches on church and politics and these were noticed and discussed – no small achievement when one remembers that there were many speeches, all of them in Latin.

In general, Hurley was regarded as siding with the so-called majority as distinct from the so-called minority. These groups are often associated with church politics – diocesan bishops versus the curia. I personally think the battle line was more on theology and pastoral interest. Hurley had been prepared by his reading, and he saw the need for a new theology in the modern world. And of course he could speak from a highly pastoral and political context.

Is there anything else you would like to say about the Archbishop?

The issues I've discussed in this interview are covered in much greater detail in "Das Konzil und die Seminare" published by Peeters in 2003, so that is a source of further information.

Then I need to say that I got to know the Archbishop from one angle only, as a member of Vatican II. The collected essays *Denis Hurley: A Portrait by Friends* showed me that this was but one of his many strengths. He was of the "old school" in the best way: loyal to his church and his people; with expertise, insight, initiative and faithfulness, common sense and profound faith.

I am very happy that his person and his important contribution to the life of the church through his work for Vatican II are being honoured in this year when we observe the 40th anniversary of the Council's conclusion. Thank you for that!

Denis Hurley and the Reception of Vatican II

Mervyn Abrahams CSsR

Archbishop Denis Hurley described the closing ceremony of the Second Vatican Council in his memoir of the Council: "...then the bishops walked along Bernini's colonnade and made off in their buses for the last time in a volume of vocal farewells and a forest of waving hands. They had begun their journey back to their dioceses where they must endeavour to lead the great effort of bringing the Council decrees to life in the communities they serve."

Returning to their dioceses, the great task that faced Hurley and the other Council fathers was to make the Council known and to implement its vision of being Church. The theological term for appropriating a Church council is "reception" and it refers to the process in which "an ecclesiastical community incorporates into its own life a particular decision, teaching, or practice." [1] This process takes place on various levels of the Church but its ultimate goal is to shape the self-understanding of the Church, which in turn guides it in its evangelising task.

In a sense Hurley had already prepared the groundwork for the reception of the Council during the conciliar process with the 32 articles he wrote for *The Southern Cross* and the numerous talks he gave in his diocese and around South Africa during the intermission periods of the Council. A quick glance at *The Southern Cross* articles reveals Hurley's enthusiasm for the conciliar process and the theological developments that were occurring there. Hurley experienced the Council, in the words of Yves Congar, as a "moment of grace in the life of the Church" and it was that spirit that he communicated in his articles and talks, drawing his readers and listeners into the massive catechetical enterprise that was unfolding within the Church.

Neither Hurley nor any of the other Council fathers could possibly have foreseen how difficult the task of implementing the conciliar reforms would be. How does one impart the spirit of an event to people who had not played an active role therein? The Council called for inner renewal of the Church which would have far-reaching implications but were the priests and the religious who were to spearhead this renewal committed to the vision?

Twenty years after the closure of the Council Hurley had the opportunity to reflect on how this process of reception of the Council had unfolded. The occasion for this reflection was the 1985 Special Synod of Bishops called by Pope John Paul II to assess how the conciliar vision and teachings had been implemented by the universal Church and the local churches and to deepen the application of the Council in the light of new needs which affect the Church. Twenty years is a short period in which to assess a Council: after all it took the conciliar vision of the Council of Trent centuries to filter through the Church and to be assimilated on the popular level. But some assessment was needed because of the changing environment in both Church and society.

In the 20 years since the closure of the Second Vatican Council many of the tensions that had dominated the Council had resurfaced and the very meaning of the Council had become contested. Was the Council to be considered a point of departure or a destination was a hotly disputed question even though Pope Paul VI had reminded the Church that "the conciliar decrees are not so much a destination as a point of departure toward new goals?" What did fidelity to the Council mean? Was it a literal interpretation of the conciliar decrees or was it faithfulness to the conciliar spirit, the desire of the Council fathers to focus the Church away from a tendency to be inward looking and close itself off from the historical processes and from society and other Christian communities and faiths? On the eve of the Synod the British writer Peter Hebblethwaite spoke about an "institutional pessimism" that had taken root in the Roman Curia by 1985, that since the Council the Church had gone to rack and ruin.[2] The atmosphere in the period leading up to the Synod of 1985 was therefore remarkably similar to that in which the Second Vatican Council had met in 1962.

Hurley's response to the questionnaire sent out to prepare the Synod gives us a good insight into his assessment of the reception of the Council both in the Archdiocese of Durban and the Church in South Africa generally. It is that document I will follow in writing this essay[3]. It is clear that two themes guided Hurley as he implemented the Council: that the Church is a communion of the faithful and that the Church is called to evangelise through dialogue with its socio-cultural and historical context. In keeping with these themes Hurley highlights the following developments: liturgical changes in which the faithful could now actively participate; new catechetical books and methods inspired by the theology of the Council; the establishment of diocesan structures and the promotion of lay ministries to reflect the spirit of communion and co-responsibility urged by the Council; a clearer sense of engagement in social justice issues. A closer look at these four areas of development since the Council will help us to assess how the Council was received.

Bringing about the active participation of the faithful in the liturgy had been a concern of the Southern African bishops even before the Council. The use of the vernacular in the liturgy, as a means to greater participation, was the dominant concern of the Southern African bishops in the suggestions sent to Rome in preparation for the Council. Hurley had written in his *votum* that the purpose of the liturgy was the full participation of the faithful in the Christian mysteries and if this was to be realised, then the use of the vernacular was essential. During the Conciliar debate on the liturgy Hurley had, in a written statement, argued forcefully that the primary manifestation of the Church is the full and active participation of the entire holy people of God in the liturgical celebration. If the Church is to be renewed in its apostolic spirit then it is necessary to reform its liturgical life.[4] It is not surprising therefore that within two months of the promulgation of the Conciliar decree on the liturgy the bishops met in Pretoria to begin the process of its implementation. Archbishop Hurley had invited Fr Clifford Howell SJ to give a series of lectures on the reform of the liturgy in order to prepare the South African Church for its implementation. Two years after the Council the liturgical reforms had been introduced in South Africa and the vernacular Mass was a reality. Hurley's contribution to the reception of the liturgical reforms was not confined to the Church in South Africa but continued with his leading role in the International Commission on English in the Liturgy (ICEL).

As with the liturgy, catechesis was also a matter that had concerned Hurley prior to the Council but it was the theological renewal at the Council that Hurley used to guide the catechetical renewal after the Council. At the January 1960 session of the Southern African Catholic Bishops' Conference, Archbishop Hurley, then chair of the Catechetics Department, noted that the faith had been imparted to converts and the young in a rather abstract way, "through dry and defined methods." The result was that the inner value of the Church had been lost and an emphasis placed on the visible Church and obligations to the faith. He suggested that the doctrinal renewal taking place in the Church through the return to scripture and the Fathers of the Church, and the pedagogical reforms in the field of catechetics needed to be introduced into catechesis in Southern Africa.[5] In 1960 Hurley took part in a catechetical conference in Eichstatt, Germany, where he delivered a paper on "The Bishop's Role in the Catechetical Renewal" and in 1963 a new catechetical work, *Africa's Way to Life,* commissioned by the Catechetical Department of the Southern African Catholic Bishops' Conference, was published.[6] This book appeared in 14 African languages and was later translated and reproduced in other regions of Africa.

After the Council the Bishops decided that a new catechetical series was needed in South Africa to meet five needs: to take into consideration the developments and changes in the world and in the Church in the light of the Second Vatican Council; to incorporate new insights in theology and a new understanding of the faith; to flow from the reality of the Southern African context and recognise the multi-racial nature of the Church; to be used for parish catechesis. This series was entitled *The People of God* and the choice of its name and the theological foundation of the series attests to the reception of the ecclesiology of the Council as expressed in *Lumen Gentium.* The first book in the series, written by Mgr. Paul Nadal and Sr Theodula Müller CMM, *You are my Children,* was recommended for use in 1970. When one compares this series with books centred on the question and answer methodology of the penny catechism, the changes are immediately visible. This series was biblical and incorporated both doctrine and liturgy; its methodology was based on the anthropological approach to catechesis.[7] The catechetical renewal that preceded the Council and was affirmed at the Council now shaped the approach of the official catechism in South Africa. Catechesis is one of the constitutive elements that shape Catholic identity and having incorporated the conciliar theology into the new catechism would ensure that the conciliar vision became part of how Catholics understood themselves, the Church and their world.

The third issue Hurley highlighted in his response to the questionnaire for the 1985 Synod was the establishment of diocesan structures and the promotion of lay ministries to reflect the spirit of communion and co-responsibility urged by the Council. Before the Council the laity were often perceived as the ones who filled the pews on a Sunday and put money into the collection plates. Even though Catholic Action attempted to draw the laity into greater activity within the Church they were still considered as helpers of the priests and bishops, not having their own baptismal call to ministry. The ecclesiology of the Council called for a total review of the lay role in the Church. *Lumen Gentium* states unambiguously that the laity shares in the priestly, prophetic, and kingly functions of Christ; as such they have a responsibility for the mission of the whole Christian people to the Church and world.

On his return from the Council Hurley would spend a lot of his energy building diocesan structures to facilitate lay involvement and leadership in his diocese. The structure he implemented was a pastoral council for each parish in the diocese; a diocesan pastoral council that would share responsibility for and help shape the pastoral strategy of the diocese; a diocesan synod that would meet biennially and bring together clergy, laity and religious from across the diocese to discuss diocesan policy with regard to apostolic and pastoral endeavours; and diocesan commissions to publicise and ensure implementation of the diocesan synod's recommendations. The spirit that was to animate these structures was that "clergy and laity share a common mission, for all must work together with Christ for the salvation of the world." For Hurley these structures were a clear expression of the communal nature of the Church and gave effect to collegiality and co-responsibility that the Council called for. He warned that the parish and diocese should not become little Catholic enclaves but be at the service of humanity, echoing the vision of *Gaudium et Spes*. The parish, according to Hurley, was the basic unit of the Church and gathers the people of Christ for worship and enrichment and from there they go out to be a leaven in the world. The sign of a Christian parish is its community spirit and the duty of each parishioner is to contribute to the community and serve the world. Social action for the transformation of the world was therefore integral to the life and evangelizing mission of the Church.[8] In this way Hurley always saw the two great texts of the Council, *Lumen Gentium*, on the Church, and *Gaudium et Spes*, on the Church in the Modern World, as a unity that should guide the post-conciliar Church.

It was therefore not surprising that for Hurley commitment to the struggle against apartheid would have to be crucial for the Church's mission and credibility. In the minds of most people Archbishop Denis Hurley will always be remembered as a person who was committed to social justice and the removal of apartheid in South Africa. It was not the Council however that stirred Hurley into action for he had already been active in the struggle against apartheid since the 1950s. What the Council gave Hurley and the entire Church, was a clear theological foundation for action on behalf of social justice and the basis for a clear and unambiguous stand against apartheid. Hurley considered *Gaudium et Spes* as the conciliar charter that should guide the Church's task of evangelisation. "The joys and the hopes, the griefs and the anxieties of the people of this age, especially those who are poor or in any way afflicted, these too are the joys and hopes, the griefs and anxieties of the followers of Christ", the first sentence of *Gaudium et Spes*, expressed the Council's desire to discern God's presence in the joys and sufferings of human beings in their historical contexts. The Church cannot fulfill its mission in isolation from suffering humanity but must be inserted in its historical context. Making this conciliar vision a reality in apartheid South Africa guided Hurley in his work as president of the Conference and later as chair of its Justice and Peace Commission. Social justice was not an optional extra for the Christian but integral to evangelisation. His work on behalf of detainees, those forcefully removed from their land, those who objected in conscience to joining the apartheid army, was all part of the Church's task of evangelisation. In his submission to the 1985 Synod Hurley writes, "The pursuit of justice in South Africa and the dismantling of Apartheid must become priority number one for the churches, the chief concern of their spiritual, pastoral evangelising effort." A task of such magnitude however demanded collaboration with other churches and bodies, an ecumenical effort, and it was to this end that Hurley played a leading role in the establishment of two important ecumenical organisations dedicated to social action. The first was Diakonia in the city of Durban and the second, the Pietermaritzburg Agency for Christian Social Awareness (PACSA).

In answer to the question as to what the Synod of Bishops should do to ensure that the spirit and letter of the Council be carried out to the full, Hurley replied that the Synod should recommend that "every episcopal conference promote a project of pastoral planning." As the Church moved beyond the second decade of the reception of the Second Vatican Council a pastoral plan should be initiated that would coordinate all its activities, inside and outside the Church. Hurley's concern was that faith and social action were too often seen as different and even as opposites. That attitude contradicted the conciliar teaching that the human person is one entity and that salvation occurs within history. A pastoral plan that clearly showed how these two dimensions, faith and social action, form one unit would move the Church in the direction envisaged in the conciliar decrees.

In fact, the announcement of the 1985 Synod and its focus on the reception of the Council occurred while the Church in Southern Africa was engaged in a comprehensive review of its pastoral practice and working towards a pastoral plan. This review brought the Second Vatican Council into strong focus again for those who were involved in it and were faced with the question of what the Council meant for them. I am of the opinion that the great emphasis on the Second Vatican Council that comes to the fore in the writing of the Pastoral Plan could be traced to this process. The Pastoral Plan, *Community Serving Humanity*, would eventually be launched in 1989 and become the most comprehensive initiative of the reception of the Council in the South African Church and one in which Hurley played a central role.[9]

The Pastoral Plan finds its origin in a commitment by the Southern African Catholic Bishops' Conference in 1977 to "take into account the singular situation and resultant tensions of the Church in South Africa, where 80% of the laity are Black and 80% of the clergy White, and to investigate as a matter of extreme urgency the feasibility of a Pastoral Consultation in which lay people, religious and priests, in large majority Black, may participate with the bishops, in arriving at a policy on Church life and apostolate but not on doctrinal and canonical matters."[10] It was the result of an intensive process of consultation at all levels of the Church and aimed to present practical ways of accomplishing the Church's mission in the South African context in the spirit of the Second Vatican Council. The *Theme Paper for the Pastoral Plan* (1987) put it as follows:

> As the Council pointed out, each local church, each local community has its own character, its own culture, its special talents (LG 13). The special character of each local church also implies that it can have its own special problems. For these reasons, it is desirable that the Church in a particular region should have a pastoral plan designed for it.[11]

The *Theme Paper,* in explaining the concept of pastoral planning, makes it clear that it is "an attempt to work out practical ways of accomplishing the Church's mission in a world of rapid change and increasing complexities." Within this context planning becomes essential. In reviewing the Pastoral Plan, the process that led to its formulation has to be taken into account, as well as its content and effectiveness in the life of communities.

It is clear that the process was one of dialogue in which all sectors of the Church were involved. The process was in itself a manifestation of the Second Vatican Council's understanding of the Church as "people of God", engaged in dialogue and together accepting responsibility for the mission of the Church in their countries. In this process the primacy of baptism could be said to have been operative. This sense of co-responsibility for the mission of the Church was a far cry from the pre-Vatican II model of a passive laity and a directive leadership style on the part of bishops and clergy.

The underlying spirit of the plan is encapsulated in its theme: the Catholic Church in South Africa must be a *Community Serving Humanity.* In order to emphasise the Church as community, the pastoral plan develops the idea of communion as the essence of the community formed around

Christ and "a sign and instrument of communion with God and of unity among all" (LG 1). This community of Christ must seek to foster "God's desire for the entire human race by revealing to it the true depths of that unity" (LG 42). As such, the Church is not meant to be turned in on itself but is called to serve the larger community of humanity. This goal is to imbue the entire life and mission of the Church.

The liturgy must be a community experience so that there is an experience of the full and active participation of all the faithful. Catechesis should be a task of the community and have as its goal a community formed according to the mind of Christ. There needs to be a "deep sense of oneness between bishops, priests and deacons and the communities they serve". Leadership is to be seen as service and to "encourage and enable all members to share in the ordering of the community's life." This concept of community, apart from the fact that it is rooted in scripture, also draws from African cultural concepts. It has been argued that the African concept of humanity implies that a "person is a person through other persons". The idea of community contained in the pastoral plan could therefore be said to summarise the African experience of humanity and provide a focus for the whole conception of humanity. As such, it could be said to involve the cultural dynamics of the communities.

The pastoral plan places a twofold goal before the Catholic Church, namely to become more of a community and to be committed to God's healing and saving work in the world.[12] A serious reappraisal of its mission in the South African context as a "community serving humanity", meant that the Church has moved away from the "the Counter-Reformation view of the Church as a bulwark against Protestantism, from a 'Settler' and 'Mission' Church division inherited from the previous century, and from what has been dubbed the 'sacramental consumerist' view," that was so much part of pre-conciliar Catholic thinking.[13]

As a means to a practical implementation of the pastoral plan in each parish community the Archdiocese of Durban, under the leadership of Hurley, adopted the "Renew process" which originated in the United States of America in 1978 and is described as "a spiritual renewal process to help parishioners develop a closer relationship with Christ, to make an adult commitment to Jesus ... so that they may become more authentic witnesses." In fact Hurley first got to know about the Renew process while attending the 1985 Synod of Bishops in Rome. Hurley writes: "I heard two members of the Synod speak enthusiastically about Renew.... What they said intrigued me as it seemed to contain at least part of the answer to the Durban question of how to pursue and relate community and formation." In 1987 a small team of pastoral workers from the Archdiocese of Durban went to the United States to study the spirit and methods of Renew. The Renew process was launched in the Archdiocese on 30 July 1989 to coincide with the celebration of Archbishop Hurley's 50th anniversary of priestly ordination. The Renew process was followed by the establishment of small Christian communities all over the archdiocese to give effect to the spirit of the Pastoral Plan. Many of them continue to this day, and are being given new dynamism by the "Follow Me" process, which has the same origins as Renew.[14]

A source of great disappointment for Hurley, regarding the reception of the Council, was that the spirit of collegiality that was so evident at the Council and that runs like a thread through all the conciliar documents, seems to be opposed by the Roman Curia. On the diocesan level and regarding the Southern African Catholic Bishops' Conference the spirit of collegiality and co-responsibility has grown and deepened since the Council but regarding the Roman Curia Hurley writes: "The real problem of collegiality seems to lie with the Holy See itself. We are somewhat astonished by decisions that appear to have been taken without regard to collegiality and to criticism of bishops' conferences emanating from a prominent personality in the Curia." The prominent personality that Hurley refers to was Cardinal Ratzinger who had publicly questioned whether episcopal conferences have teaching authority. This was a matter of great concern for Hurley who had argued forcefully at the Council for juridic authority to be granted to episcopal conferences as a local expression of episcopal collegiality. Addressing himself to the Council fathers Hurley had asked: "How do our words sound in the ears of the outside world? Do they sound like the words of people wanting their own way, who on the one hand claim for themselves the right to share in ruling the universal Church, but on the other hand in the running of their dioceses do not wish to impose any limitation on themselves ... or to accept the decisions of brothers in the episcopate?"

For Hurley, collegiality and co-responsibility in the Church flow from our understanding of the Church as a communion of the baptised. When collegiality is ignored it affects the very nature and vision of the Church that the Second Vatican Council placed before us. Hurley returned to this theme in an address he gave a few months before his death. Speaking at a Conference to commemorate the 40th anniversary of the encyclical *Pacem in Terris*, issued by Pope John XXIII while the Council was in session, Hurley described the lack of collegiality in the Church as an unfavourable sign of the times. Collegiality was one of the greatest achievements of the Second Vatican Council, he said, but unfortunately there has been little evidence of its implementation.[15] For Hurley the proper reception of the conciliar teaching on collegiality, especially regarding the relation between the Holy See and local churches and between the pope and bishops remains a task.

When Archbishop Hurley returned from the Council in 1965 he could not have known how difficult it would be to implement the vision of the Council. Assessing his attempt can lead to only one conclusion: that he remained faithful to the spirit of the Council, always seeing it as a moment of grace for the Church, and faithfully worked to implement its vision, both in the Archdiocese of Durban and in the whole South African Church. The reception of the Council remains an on-going process which needs to continue for a long time yet. Hurley's outstanding example should give us energy for the task.

Endnotes

1.   Thomas P Rausch, "Reception" in Joseph A. Komonchak, Mary Collins, Dermot Lane (eds), *The New Dictionary of Theology* (Dublin: Gill and Macmillan, 1992), 828-830, p. 828. See also Yves Congar, "Reception as an Ecclesiological Reality," in *Concilium* vol. 77 (1972), pp. 43-68.

2.   See Peter Hebblethwaite, *Synod Extraordinary. The inside story of the Rome Synod, November/ December 1985* (New York: Doubleday & Co, 1986). See also Xavier Rynne, *John Paul's Extraordinary Synod. A Collegial Achievement* (Wilmington, Delaware: Michael Glazier, 1986).

3.   Archbishop Denis Hurley, "Synod of Bishops. Extraordinary General Meeting: 25 November - 8 December 1985." (Pretoria: Southern African Catholic Bishops' Conference Archives, Box File: Extraordinary Plenary Session, August 1985. Corr/Doc).

4.   See Mervyn Abrahams, "The Second Vatican Council" in Joy Brain and Philippe Denis (eds), *The Catholic Church in Contemporary Southern Africa*, (Pietermaritzburg: Cluster Publications, 1999), pp. 213-245.

5.   See Plenary Session 1960 (Southern African Catholic Bishops' Conference: Pretoria).

6.   For Hurley's address at the Eichstatt Conference see Denis Hurley, "The Bishop's Role in the Catechetical Renewal" in Johannes Hofinger (ed), *Teaching All Nations. A Symposium on Modern Catechetics,* (London: Burns and Oates, 1961), pp. 341-356.

7.   See Prudence Hategekimana, *Setting the Captives Free. The Development of a Catechetical Programme for Southern Africa* (Pietermaritzburg: Cluster Publications, 2002), pp. 26-27.

8.   See Constitution of Diocesan Synod, The Diocesan Pastoral Council, The Diocesan Commissions (Cedara: Missionary Oblates of Mary Immaculate Archives, Hurley Section, Box File: Lay Apostolate – Christian Renewal).

9.   Most of the following section is taken from M. Abrahams, "The Pastoral Plan of the Catholic Church. Receiving the Second Vatican Council in South Africa" in *Studia Historiae Ecclesiasticae,* Volume XXVI (2000), pp. 156-169. For the development of the Pastoral Plan and its theological foundations see Patrick Hartin, Paul Decock, Bernard Connor (eds), *Becoming a Creative Local Church. Theological Reflections on the Pastoral Plan* (Pietermaritzburg: Cluster Publications, 1991). See also, Chris Langefeld, "The Reception of Vatican II in South Africa: A Survey of Themes from the Pastoral Plan" in *Bulletin for Contextual Theology in Southern Africa & Africa*, volume 4/1 (1997), pp. 40-44.

10.   Southern African Catholic Bishops' Conference, *Inter-Diocesan Pastoral Consultation 1980. Report.* (Pastoral Action Series: No 22, 1981), p.4.

11.   Southern African Catholic Bishops' Conference, *Community Serving Humanity: Theme Paper for the Pastoral Plan of the Catholic Church in Southern Africa,* (Pastoral Action Series: No 41, 1987), p.2.

12.   Paul Decock, "Can we call ourselves a Community?" in Patrick Hartin, Paul Decock, Bernard Connor (eds) *Becoming a Creative Local Church. Theological Reflections on the Pastoral Plan* (Pietermaritzburg: Cluster Publications, 1991), 52-64.

13. Bernard Connor, "Arriving at a Pastoral Plan" in Patrick Hartin, Paul Decock, Bernard Connor (eds). *op. cit.*, 35-48, p. 48.

14. Archbishop Hurley, "Renew in the Archdiocese of Durban" (Cedara: Missionary Oblates of Mary Immaculate Archives, Hurley Section, Box File: Lay Apostolate – Christian Renewal).

15. Archbishop Denis Hurley, "Reading the Signs of the Times: 1963-2003" in *Grace and Truth*, vol. 21/1(2004), 9-17, p. 14.

Vatican Council II: Keeping the Dream Alive

Marie-Henry Keane OP

The 10th Archbishop Denis Hurley Lecture, to be delivered at the Glenmore Pastoral Centre, Durban, on 10 February 2005

Naming the Dream

On 25 January 1959, a mere 90 days after he had been elected, Pope John XXIII announced his intention of convoking the Second Vatican Council. After years of relative stability or, as others might think, relative stagnation, the Pope and his Council were calling for an *aggiornamento*, for renewal of a radical kind. Pope Paul V1 later wrote:

> The Council is to be a new Spring, a reawakening of the mighty spiritual and moral energies which at present lie dormant. The Council is evidence of a determination to bring about a rejuvenation both of the inner forces, and of the regulations, by which her canonical structure and liturgical forms are governed. The Council is striving to enhance in the Church, that beauty of perfection and holiness which imitation of Christ and the mystical union with Him in the Holy Spirit can alone confer.[1]

Pope John XXIII spoke of opening the windows of the Vatican to let fresh air in. In his opening speech to the Council fathers, he reminded them that they should "never depart from the sacred patrimony of the truth". He called the Council, he said, not to defend old things, but to relate them to new ones, "to take a step forward", for women and men were on the verge of a new era. "It was for the Council", wrote Adrian Hastings, "so to renew the Church that the tradition of authentic doctrine would be expressed in the forms of modern thought, and that the whole life of the

Church would be related, in the most effective way, to the life of this new era – the quickly developing world of the 20th century."[2]

And that meant change.

Vatican II: Opportunity or Crisis?

Prior to Vatican II, the majority of Catholics regarded the Church as the guardian of eternal truths and values. Things appeared to be written in stone. Renewal was commendable, but radical renewal required enormous changes. The official Church was of two minds: some clerics had been struggling for years for appropriate change, but some were quite happy with things as they were and became alarmed at the proportions these "renewals" were taking. Lay people, even those who regarded themselves as well-informed, were troubled and confused. In all of this few, clerics and lay people alike, seemed capable of distinguishing between essence and form.[3] Too much was happening too soon. In four short years (1961-1965) the familiar ecclesial landscape was being radically transformed. What was even more startling was that the Council had set in motion a process for change which, once started, it seemed powerless to halt. Since the Reformation and even before it, the Church had been seen as a fortress, able to defy the world and its "formidable enemies".[4] The fortress model of Church was psychologically powerful. Peter Hebblethwaite wrote: "Inside the fortress strict discipline was maintained.... Life in the fortress certainly represented one sort of equilibrium, and many remain nostalgic for its apparent peace and tranquillity."[5]

The Church was also seen as a "perfect society" complete in itself. Catholic Christians believed that they had a monopoly of the truth. Uncertainty caused great unease. It was not merely the rank and file who were troubled: Cardinal Siri of Genoa is reported to have said that "the Council was the greatest mistake in recent ecclesiastical history".[6]

Those of us who have taken to heart the spirit and teachings of Vatican II want to keep alive the dream of renewal, of rejuvenation, of appropriate life-giving change, of openness to the world. And among "us" I rejoice to include our great role-model, mentor and friend, our dear departed Denis Eugene Hurley OMI, former Archbishop of Durban. In his memoir on the

Council published in this book he wrote: "The first half of the decade of the sixties presented me with the greatest experience of my episcopal life, indeed, the greatest experience of my whole life: the Second Vatican Council."[7] The Church was being called to greater holiness, to radical renewal. The Church is always in need of reform, *Ecclesia semper reformanda*. Hurley knew that better than most. He was prepared spiritually and intellectually for that great happening. He wrote: "Providentially, the good Lord had provided me with an unforeseen, yet a remarkably apt preparation for this experience, in the form of the reading that came my way during the '50s. As an experience of adult education and spiritual growth I look back upon that decade with fond and appreciative memories."[8]

Pope John XXIII did not wake up one fine morning and say: "Let us have a Vatican Council II." The seeds of renewal were germinating under the soil for a number of years and, although the process of reform within the Church had been slow, the pace was about to accelerate. It was to be a costly and painful process, for there is no such thing as cheap grace.[9] Jesus knew that. Yet the one who paid the heaviest price, wrote not in stone, but in the sand. His Gospel would be etched primarily on the minds and hearts of those women and men who, in faith, could say yes to life-giving change. The Spirit of God remains with the Church, and true prophets like Hurley will continue, moved by the Spirit, to proclaim that "it is Yahweh who speaks", even when they risk being stoned and mocked. Only a few years before the Council, Yves Congar was exiled from Le Saulchoir to Cambridge, and Henri de Lubac was forbidden to teach, or even live in a house where there were students. Before the Council both men were dubbed, "dissenting theologians". Yet at Vatican II both emerged as influential and respected figures. They were simply ahead of their time.

> The old order changeth yielding place to the new
> And God fulfils himself in many ways
> Lest one good custom should destroy the world.[10]

Why did Church people resist the changes advocated by Vatican II? Perhaps because they liked things as they were. They felt secure; in charge.

To talk about renewal or, worse still, reform, seemed disloyal or critical. They saw the Catholic Church as *the* true Church, and outside that Church there was no salvation. To think about radical change appeared like letting the side down.

Theodore Hesburgh offered a more positive analysis of the Council's aims.. He wrote: "The four years of Vatican Council II were years of growing and expanding theological perspectives, as the Church developed a clearer vision of her true nature and her mission in the world of to-day."[11] But there was no getting away from it, a crisis existed. Henri de Lubac defined crisis as "a disturbance in a state of equilibrium, and a search for a new equilibrium. It is the feeling of being knocked off balance that produces a sense of crisis." "The simple reason for this feeling", said de Lubac at the time, "was that the Council had formulated a *new* understanding of the Church which had affected every aspect of its life".[12] Crisis is not necessarily a threat or catastrophe, but a turning point, a crucial period of increased vulnerability and heightened potential.

A story is told of the man who "started all the trouble": John XXIII. He himself was not above feeling the strain. One night he could not sleep. He tossed and turned and then, with characteristic good humour, said to himself: "Relax Angelo, it is not you who is running the Church but the Holy Spirit".

A New Understanding of Church: The Ecumenical Dimension

To see the Second Vatican Council, that is, the 21st Ecumenical Council, as a purely domestic happening within the Roman Catholic Church, would be to underestimate and misunderstand it grossly. All eyes were on Rome: other Christian denominations, the Eastern Churches, Jews, Hindus and Muslims all manifested varying degrees of interest. The world press and the television cameras were there, for what was happening at the Council was newsworthy, and remained newsworthy for four years. Fierce sparring between the Council fathers was seen as a sign of vigour and vitality. One reporter wrote: "Only in a body in which people really cared could disagreement be so keen; the clashing of opinions was better than the anxious imposition of uniformity."

Members of other Christian Churches, invited as observers to the Council, were referred to as "our separated brethren," where previously they had been called heretics! Bernard C Pawley, an Anglican observer to the Council, wrote: "It is one of the first principles of the practice of ecumenism that whatever any one of the members of the Body is doing or thinking is of concern to all the rest. So far at least the Holy Spirit has led us all."[13] Most Christian denominations were represented (with the exception, alas, of the Baptists). G C Berkouwer, a Dutch theologian of the Reformed Church, wrote: "The Vatican Council carries a challenge to Protestant Churches to examine their own faithfulness to the Gospel."[14] Berkouwer suggested that what was good for the Catholic Church (renewal, reform, life-giving change) was good for the Christian Church as a whole. He said that the Catholic Church was being called to examine its own faithfulness, or lack of it; to question its own credibility; to attest to its own genuineness. Berkouwer was in sympathy with the thinking of the Council fathers. He was not alone among Protestants in feeling that way, for they detected a marked change of climate within the Catholic Church, a greater openness to those outside the Church. Berkouwer wrote: "The phrase that most interests us is 'open Catholicism'. This phrase is meant to indicate that Catholicism is no longer preoccupied with itself, that it has thrown open the window of its concern to the whole world."[15]

Vatican II was indeed an ecumenical, or universal Council; it was open-minded and open-hearted. Paul Tillich greeted the more affirmative relations between Catholicism and Protestantism warmly. He continued to believe that the 16th century reformation was necessary, but admitted that besides being a religious gain, it was also a religious loss.[16] It was even suggested that had there been a comparable Council in the 16th century there might not have been the kind of reformation which splintered the Church and severely damaged its unity. We can only conjecture in hindsight.

The partial communion which existed between Christian Churches demanded appropriate expression, so the Council produced a document on ecumenism, *Unitatis Redintegratio*. Much of the inspiration behind this document came from Cardinal Bea and Bishop de Smedt, tireless advocates not only of Christian unity but of unity between *all* God's people.[17]

On Tuesday 7 November, 1962, it was announced that Cardinal Bea would introduce chapter four of the schema *Nostra Aetate* in its first draft. This chapter dealt with the Jews, and it caused a sensation. Xavier Rynne wrote: "This news was greeted with tremendous enthusiasm and applause. In the opinion of some observers there was nothing quite like the spontaneous response on that occasion. Nothing the Council discussed so far had generated so much warmth and feeling."[18] After Bea had addressed the Council "a communiqué of the text was released to the press; (it) received widespread approval among Jews throughout the world".[19]

Within the Council, as elsewhere, there were mixed feelings about the ecumenical issue. The two Spanish cardinals, de Arriba y Castro and Bueno y Montreal were "both basically hostile to the modern movement of ecumenism and were sceptical, as well as fearful, of its possible effects on the Church".[20] Stephanos I Sidarouss, the Coptic Patriarch of Alexandria, Egypt, wanted to drop all mention of the Jews. "If the Council insists on taking up this touchy subject, we shall have to face the music when we (the representatives of Arab Christianity) go home."[21] On the other hand, Cardinal Heenan of Westminster, said: "We (the bishops of England and Wales) are prepared to do anything, outside denying the faith, to obtain the unity of Christians."[22] Of course we would want to add, of all God's people.

Vatican II as the Crystallisation of a Renewal Process

Vatican II has been described as the crystallisation of a renewal process. Those who had been closely following developments in the Church anytime from the death of Pius XI in 1939 to the beginning of Vatican II, would agree that the Council simply intensified and gave official recognition to a renewal process which had already begun. Certainly the ecumenical movement was well under way by 1962; the Council was merely building on what had gone before. As early as 1942 Paul Tillich was described as "an ecumenical theologian". In that year he wrote an article entitled "The Permanent Significance of the Catholic Church for Protestantism".[23] In it he criticised the Catholic Church for its legalism, but at the same time admitted that Protestantism needed a new approach to authority. Tillich praised Catholic theology for its "formal clarity, logical consistency and philosophical exactness".[24] He believed that Protestantism could learn from the Catholic attempt to bring reason and revelation together, from Catholic mysticism and from its sacramental foundations. This is not the place to go into Tillich's article in detail. I merely draw attention to it in order to make a point, namely, that ecumenical thinking was thriving 20 years before the Second Vatican Council. Lively debates between Catholics and Protestants were being conducted in a spirit of freedom around contentious theological issues, at universities and elsewhere. This was ecumenism at its best.

Is it not amazing that Denis Eugene Hurley, one of Vatican II's most committed sons, should have adopted for his episcopal motto: "Where the Spirit is, there is freedom" (2 Cor. 3:17-18) 15 years before the Council? And is it not sad that Mother Church should see fit to "gag" her children, lest they should discuss certain contentious issues? Perhaps she has taken too seriously the mother/child paradigm. Children grow up, they come of age, they are permitted to exercise their God-given gift – freedom of speech. There should be no taboo subjects within the Church. Even as I write this I am reminded of a gem from Hurley's memoir. He, and 50 or 60 French and Spanish bishops, arrived in Rome for the Council. They were ushered into an airport hall set aside for them. There Hurley met Yves Congar for the first time. Hurley writes: "A smiling little Dominican put his hand out and said. 'Congar'. I put mine out and said, 'Hurley'. We fell on each other's necks.... He told me that he was working hard on a book on tradition. It would probably land him in the Holy Office again. Poor Congar! He has suffered severely at the hands of the Holy Office for daring to write the kind of theology that was to influence the Council so profoundly."[25] Hurley, commenting on Pope John XXIII's opening speech wrote: "There were those, the Pope said, who saw everything modern only as ruin and prevarication. He looked upon those, as prophets of doom."[26] Hurley went on: "The Holy Father clearly favoured the progressive camp, but the Curia still had its hands on the controls."[27]

Be of good cheer, those of you who, because you love the Church, dare on occasion, like Congar and our own Catherine of Siena, to criticise the official Church's lack of imagination or courage, or its unwillingness to let go of dead wood for the sake of flowering and fruit-gathering.

What Now?

The question to ask now is not simply, what happened at Vatican Council II more than 40 years ago? The more important question is, what has happened since? What is the climate within the Church today? Is it open to the future? To change? The Second Vatican Council tried to separate essentials from incidentals, the wheat from the chaff. It was dogged by fearful and timid souls who saw in every change a betrayal of the past. They observed developments with profound unease, fearful lest the Catholic faith be twisted to accommodate the needs of the times; lest Christianity itself should become a "cultural phenomenon" subject to the same relativity as everything else. Joan Chittister, among others, distinguishes between the *keepers* of tradition and the *developers* of tradition.[28] "We have not lost the virtues of the past", she writes, "We have simply shaped them into ones necessary to our own times. Now we must own these new ones and form ourselves in them and carry them proudly."[29] There were those who identified with the changing and dynamic model of the Church advocated by the Council. They acknowledged the sincerity of Protestant and Eastern Christians, of members of other faiths, who also desired renewal, reform, appropriate change. This was an opportunity not to be missed, not to be ignored. Between the die-hards and the over-eager a high level of tension existed. The Church survived the so-called crisis. Clearly, the *facts* of history do not change, but how they are *interpreted* is always subject to revision and, consequently, to change. What made the Second Vatican Council so significant was the *extent* of the reappraisal. More changes took place during those four years than in several hundred years previously. So anyone who wishes to keep in touch with what is happening in the Catholic Church should, in my opinion, take as their point of reference not only the teaching, but also the spirit of Vatican II. That means studying the 16 official documents which emerged from it. Bishop Reuben H Muller,

President of the National Council of Churches of Christ in the USA wrote: "The charters for renewal and change in the Roman Catholic Church lie within the pages of this book (The Conciliar Documents). Anyone who hopes to follow the actual developments as we move onward will need to study and discuss and understand the basic documents, as well as the Catholic and non-Catholic commentaries on them."[30]

A Stepping-stone and not a Final Accomplishment

There is no point in trying to canonise Vatican II. Wonderful as it was, it was only a stepping-stone and not a final accomplishment in the long history of the Catholic Church. In spite of all the efforts, at the end of the Council the documents were only paper and ink. They were written in Latin. By themselves they would not be able to renew anything.[31] The Church's *aggiornamento* would consist not in solemn proclamations, but in a spirited and imaginative application of the Council's teaching. The Church was calling, not so much for the changing of some laws, but for a full renewal of minds and hearts. Unless the Council's teaching was both understood in some detail, and applied vigorously, there would be little hope of renewal.

As they were preparing to go home after the Council, Hurley concludes in his memoir on Vatican II: "The bishops walked along Bernini's colonnade and made off in their buses for the last time in a volume of vocal farewells and a forest of waving hands. They had begun their journey back to their dioceses where they must endeavour to lead the great effort of bringing the Council decrees to life in the communities which they served."[32]

Bearers of Good News

As a young Dominican Sister, I, among thousands of others, was blessed to sit at the feet of Denis Eugene Hurley as he proclaimed the good news of the Council's teaching. What I heard was enough to whet my appetite for more. I learned that *Lumen Gentium,* the Dogmatic Constitution on the Church, was hailed with something like unanimity as the most momentous achievement of the Council, both because of its important contents and because of its central place among the Council documents. From his lips I heard for the first time, the opening words of that document: "Christ is the Light of the Nations. It is, therefore, the eager desire of this Sacred Synod, assembled in the Holy Spirit, to enlighten all men (and women) with that brilliance of His which shines on the face of the Church by the proclamation of the Gospel to the whole of Creation."[33] These opening words served as an introduction to the whole Constitution. No document underwent more drastic revision – it was hammered into shape on the anvil of vigorous controversy. The Constitution became a great document even though, being the fruit of the Holy Spirit working in imperfect human beings, it is only a stepping-stone and not a final accomplishment.[34]

Hurley rejoiced in the notion of the Church as "mystery"- as a divine truth inserted into history. It was a long time ago, but I remember Hurley pointing out changes in the Church's perception of herself. She was to be seen primarily in sacramental and not, as previously, in juridical terms. Furthermore, the *inner* fellowship of life derived from union with the Trinity, found *outward* expression in a human community (*communio*). This messianic community was commissioned to witness to and effect the reconciliation of the entire human race to God. We were to do this, not as individuals but as the people of God. When I heard, from Hurley, about the priesthood of all the baptised (a notion dear to Martin Luther), it was like being born again. The baptised participate in Christ's teaching office, for the Spirit teaches the Church through *all* its members. The people of God "celebrated" Mass with the president, they no longer merely "heard" Mass. The ordination of married men to the diaconate was seen to be "pastorally necessary" and raised hopes, at the time, that the gap separating the clergy and the laity was closing.

Coming out of South Africa, where the diabolical system of apartheid affected so many people's lives, Hurley rejoiced that, as never before, the Church fathers were facing up to painful worldwide social problems. They provided the Church with an old/new challenge. The Church could not be satisfied merely with discussing her internal affairs. This was apparent from the dynamic Constitution on the Church in the Modern World, *Gaudium et Spes*, and from the document on Religious Freedom, *Dignitatis Humanae*. After *Lumen Gentium*, the Church no longer had to ask herself whether social and political issues were her concern; she knew they were. Social awareness lay at the heart of the Eucharist: "Truly partaking of the Body of the Lord in the breaking of the Bread" (says article seven of *Lumen Gentium*) "we are partaking with Him and with one another". These were glorious moments, realising for the first time, perhaps, that the Eucharist was not simply about a "heavenly banquet" but about breaking bread with the broken of the world. Scales were being lifted from our eyes.

The Eucharist was also about peacemaking and reconciliation. Hurley records one of the most dramatic and emotional moments of reconciliation within the Council: the Catholic and Eastern Churches had been alienated from each other as a result of the tragic Great Schism of 1009AD. Soon after that the Patriarch of Constantinople, and other Eastern ecclesiastics, were excommunicated in Constantinople by certain Roman Legates and the Holy See they represented. The Patriarch of Constantinople and his Synod responded by excommunicating the Holy See! After a rift of more than 900 years, reconciliation took place at the Council. Hurley records:

> If ever there was a moment when St. Peter's was well nigh bursting with emotion, that was it. Many saw only through their tears the grandeur of the scene as Cardinal Bea standing at the right of the Holy Father read the message of reconciliation. On the Pope's left was the strikingly handsome figure of the Delegate of Athenagoras, Patriarch of Constantinople, Metropolitan Meliton of Heliopolis. And when His Holiness held out the document (of reconciliation) to the Metropolitan and took him in his arms many, and that included me, could not bear to look.[35]

Denis Hurley did not merely communicate the mind of the Council to the people of his diocese. He told us stories and he named names. He gave his message a human face, making us present to the Council and the Council to us.

For Hurley the dream never faded. He wrote:

> She (the Church) had seen the glory of the Word had come to her,
> and the pattern of her worship, and the meaning of her mission. She
> had seen with new pride, what her laity is and what it must do in the
> world. She had seen how all people in some way are hers and must
> be loved accordingly so that in freedom they might seek and find her.
> She had seen how her religious must be renewed and how her priestly
> candidates must be trained for the great pastoral tasks of the future.[36]

That is Hurley at his most prophetic. That is Hurley, faithful son of
Mother Church, doing what he was commissioned to do by the Holy Father:
to return to his diocese and to proclaim the good news of Vatican II. He
later recalled that special moment, the grand finale, when at the end of the
Council, Pope Paul V1 blessed the assembly for the last time: "It ended
with the final invocation and blessing, with the Holy Father's ringing
valediction: 'Go in peace.' The response was the heartiest, 'Thanks be to
God,' that most of us had ever heard". Hurley goes on: "The first step
had been taken in the realisation of Pope John's dream".

"Why the Hurry?" [37]

On Thursday 12 February 2004, the day before he died, two of my fellow
Dominicans and I took afternoon tea with Archbishop Hurley. Yet again
he spoke eagerly about the Council[38] and, more especially, about
Sacrosanctum Concilium, the Constitution on the Sacred Liturgy, a
document to which he had contributed. The Archbishop had long been
Chair of ICEL (The International Commission on English in the Liturgy).
He expressed his sadness at what now appeared to him, and many others
like him, to be liturgical retrogression. To focus on the minutiae of ritual:
a word here, a gesture there; "to correct" worthy practices which had
developed within the liturgy; to keep the laity and women especially, at
arms length, was to diminish the generous spirit which characterised the
Council.[39]

The Constitution on the Sacred Liturgy was the first completed work
of Vatican II. Hurley described it as magnificent. It was the fruit of serious
work done before the Council and followed decades of vigorous liturgical
renewal, particularly in Belgium, Holland, Germany, France, and the United

States of America. Hurley was very familiar with those pre-Conciliar developments. At the Council he had also heard the encouraging words of Pope Paul VI when, on 4 December 1963, *Sacrosanctum Concilium* was promulgated: All rites acknowledged by the Church, said the Holy Father, were to be "carefully and thoroughly revised in the light of sound tradition, and were to be given new vigour, to meet the circumstances and needs of modern times."[40] Such words were music to Archbishop Hurley's ears since, in my opinion, liturgically he always straddled two worlds. He loved Gregorian chant and was loath to part with it, but he knew that the use of the vernacular would make greater participation possible. George Purves OMI wrote: "He loved good liturgy performed with dignity, respect and order, and with the meaningful participation of the congregation".[41]

Farewell, to the Sound of Drums

On Friday 13 February 2004, Archbishop Hurley was at Our Lady of Fatima Convent and Parish. He looked old and frail as he was led off the sanctuary on the arm of Derrick Butt OMI. He had celebrated his last Eucharist; performed his last pastoral duty with characteristic grace, had drunk his last cup of tea, chatted good-humouredly with many who knew and loved him well. We waved him off fondly but, just as he and Fr Derrick reached Sabon House, Denis Eugene Hurley died.

To the end he was the bearer of a dream which he held on to tenaciously for 40 years. He had heard Pope John XXIII's call to the Church to renew itself under God's Spirit, and he had been faithful to that call to the end. So, if there is to be any discussion about erecting a memorial in honour of our dear Archbishop, let that monument be our passion for holiness and renewal, driving us forward, as God's pilgrim people. In my opinion, we would honour his memory best by keeping the dream of *aggiornamento* alive, until the reign of God finally comes.

Denis Eugene Hurley's body lies buried in front of Our Lady's altar in Emmanuel Cathedral, Durban. We count him among the living dead, for no marble slab can hold his spirit down. This great son of South Africa lives on in us. On Saturday 28 February 2004, his dear body was carried in procession into the ABSA Stadium, to the sound of African drums. We came to pay our last respects to one whom we greatly admired and dearly loved. Later, as his body was carried out, the rich sound of the combined Zulu choirs rang out across the stadium: *"O hamba kahle, sihlobo sethu"* – "Go well, our Brother." [42]

Endnotes

1. Pope Paul VI: *Allocution on 29 September, 1963*: Council Daybook, Floyd, Anderson. ed, Sessions 1 and 2, Washington National Catholic Welfare Conference, 1965, p.108.

2. Hastings, Adrian. *A Concise Guide to the Documents of the Second Vatican Council*, (London: Darton, Longman and Todd, 1968) Vols 1 and 2, p.15.

3. The essence of the Church's life does not change: the sacraments, liturgical prayer, the place of the scriptures in the Church; commitment to corporal and spiritual works of mercy etc. The form can and must change according to changing circumstances.

4. This was the post-reformation model of Church to which, for almost 400 years, the Church subscribed. The fortress Church was on the defensive; it kept its enemies at bay. The "enemies" included Muslims, Hindus, Jews and other Christian denominations.

5. Hebblethwaite, Peter. *The Runaway Church* (London: St James, 1975), p.229.

6. *Ibid*. p.12. By "recent" he meant the previous 500 years!

7. Hurley, Denis, "Memories of Vatican II," *Vatican II: Keeping the Dream Alive*, Pietermaritzburg: Cluster, 2005. p. 2.

8. Hurley, *op cit.*, p. 2.

9. See Dietrich Bonhoeffer's *The Cost of Discipleship*, SCM Press Ltd., 1976, especially chapter one.

10. Alfred Lord Tennyson, *Morte d'Arthur*.

11. Hesburgh, Theodore, *Vatican II: An Interfaith Appraisal,* (London: St Paul's Publication, 1966) Prelude, p. VII.

12. De Lubac, Henri, *L'Eglise dans la Crise, Actuelle* (Paris: Cerf, 1969) p. 93.

13. Pawley, Bernard, C. (ed), *The Second Vatican Council: Studies by Eight Anglican Observers,* (Oxford University Press, 1967) p. 4.

14. Berkouwer, GC, *The Second Vatican Council and the New Catholicism*, translated by B Smedes, (Grand Rapids: Eerdmans, 1965) p. 35.

15. *Ibid.* p. 34.

16. Modras, Ronald. *Paul Tillich's Theology of the Church: A Catholic Appraisal* (Detroit: Wayne University Press, 1976) p.125.

17. *Declaration on the Relation of the Church to Non-Christian Religions, Nostra Aetate* was issued on 28 Oct. 1965, *The Decree on Ecumenism* was released on 21 November 1964.

18. Rynne, Xavier, *The Second Session: The Debates and Decrees of Vatican Council II. September 29 to December 4, 1963*, (London: Faber and Faber, 1966) p. 217.

19. *Ibid.* p.223. Note that up to that time the Jewish people were referred to in the Good Friday Liturgy as "perfidious Jews"!

20. *Ibid.*, p. 223.

21. *Ibid.*, p. 237.

22. *Ibid.*, p. 245.

23. Protestant Digest, no. 3, 1943, pp. 23-31.

24. Modras, *op. cit.*, p. 125.

25. Hurley, Denis, *op. cit.*, p. 9

26. *Ibid.*

27. *Ibid.*

28. Chittister, Joan, *The Fire in These Ashes*, (Herts: Fowler Wright Books, 1995) p. 164

29. *Ibid.*, p. 162.

30. Connell, Francis. *The Document on the Church*, in "The American Ecclesiastical Review", no.152. February 1965, p. 84.

31. See Hastings, Adrian. *A Concise Guide to the Documents of the Second Vatican Council*, (London: Darton, Longman and Todd, 1968) vols. I and II.

32. Cf. Denis Hurley: "Memories of Vatican II", p. 18.

33. Abbott, *Lumen Gentium*, art. 1.

34. Cf. Butler, Christopher, *The Constitution on the Church*, foreword. The third chapter was revised 39 times!

35. Cf. Denis Hurley, *op. cit.*, p. 158.

36. *Ibid.* p. 160

37. After about an hour and a half of conversation, we made a move to go. His Grace asked: "Why the hurry?" We sat down again, and continued the conversation for a further 40 minutes.

38. He had just come back from the Community of Sant'Egidio in Rome whose compassion had greatly impressed him. Being in the Holy City (for the last time) he was aware that as an 88 year old, he was one of the last of the Conciliar Bishops to be alive. He mentioned the Englishman, Christopher Butler, another great Council figure who also lived to a ripe old age. When the Council spoke about taking down defences Butler is reported to have said: "Charity has the audacity of the great military geniuses who know by instinct that a strategy of defence can never, in the end, win the campaign".

39. E.g. *General Instruction on the Roman Missal,* no. 308. May a crucifix be put on the altar during Mass? Answer: Yes, but it must not be too big or too small. No objections are made to putting a national flag on the altar.

40. Abbott, *op. cit.*, p. 138.

41. *OMI Update* (Newsletter) Issue 44, March 2004.

42. See Purves, *op. cit.*

Where Are We After 40 Years?

Chrys McVey OP

Every once in a while one uncovers reminders of "what might have been". This happened to me recently when I came across Pope John XXIII's words in summoning Vatican II.

> The Catholic Church leaves many questions open to the discussion of theologians. She does this to the extent that matters are not absolutely certain. Far from jeopardising the Church's unity, controversies, as [Cardinal] Newman has remarked, can actually pave the way for its attainment. For discussion can lead to fuller and deeper understanding of religious truths; when one idea strikes against another, there may be a spark. But that common saying, expressed in various ways, and attributed to various authors, must be recalled with approval: In essentials, unity; in doubtful matters, liberty; in all things, charity.[1]

There is a certain poignancy in reading Archbishop Hurley's Vatican II memoir and recalling these words of John XXIII. In remembering the euphoria of the '60s and the world's astonishing response to the pope's openness, it is hard not to feel that the Church has often turned into a Church of missed opportunities. Where is the excitement that was generated by that tolerant and hopeful vision of 40 years ago? It has, many believe, become clouded and threatened, both from without and from within.

From without, the vision is threatened by a world becoming more violent every day, and a world that has gotten used to it. We have gotten used to the violence – though not everyone calls it such – of the god of the market, where everything and everybody is commodified, where everything and everybody can be bought and sold. In the '80s in countries of the North, greed became a patriotic duty and the resulting poverty of the South inevitable and institutionalised. This institutionalised violence has spawned many local varieties. In Pakistan, where I have lived over half my life, almost every page of the newspaper is a crime page, and few families have remained untouched. Every city and town in the country has experienced ethnic and sectarian violence. The reasons for it are many, but it is most often characterised and fuelled by that "organised anger" that we label "fundamentalism". The 1960s world of excitement, daring and hope has turned into the fear-filled world of 2005.

But fear and anger have also found a home in today's Church. From within, from the centre, fears that those "sparks from ideas" might ignite uncontrollable fires have led to the "official" Church closing itself off from "fuller and deeper understanding," especially of the great religions of Asia.[2] There have been sustained attacks on Indian theologians, by name, and the injudicious – and to many, scandalous – excommunication of the Sri Lankan theologian, Tissa Balasuriya. Discussion has been closed on such a vital topic for the future of the Church as the ordination of women, and adherence to statements of the Magisterium is demanded even when these are not proposed as infallible teachings. When attempts are made to broaden debate, even in response, eg, to the pope's invitation in *Ut Unum Sint,* to discuss the role of the papacy, those who do so, like Archbishop Quinn of San Francisco (on the papacy) or the late Cardinal Bernardin (on a common ground for a polarised Church), are excoriated. It seems that the invitation "to critique and then help improve the exercise of papal ministry" was intended only for non-Catholic Christians and not those within the fold.[3] Anger and fear within the Church have led to bitter and acrimonious antagonism.

The manner in which synods of bishops are prepared is, in a way, paradigmatic of the tension between two ways of thinking. I can only speak from the perspective of Asia, having been involved in responding to the documents of the Asian Synod of 1998, as the Executive Secretary of the Conference of Religious in Pakistan. Reactions to the *Lineamenta,* the "outline" and reflection questions sent by the preparatory commission for the Synod were very critical of many aspects. Individual reservations and fears were echoed by many episcopal conferences in Asia but perhaps the most outspoken was the official response of the Japanese Church to the document.[4]

What is most interesting about the Japanese response is the process. The bishops received the Japanese translation of the *Lineamenta* and the questions and had first asked their priests for a reply to the questions. The reaction from the priests was that "it was not possible to answer those questions... From the way the questions are proposed," they write, "one feels that the holding of the Synod is like an occasion for the central office to evaluate the performance of the branch offices."[5] The bishops then prepared their own questions for the Japanese Church. These were circulated among major seminaries, theology faculties, religious congregations, individual priests and councils of laity. They then composed the official response from the 325 replies submitted to them. The response makes some very important points about methodology, about the way a "working document" should be prepared, and offers special proposals for the Synod in the light of Asian experience.

The response asks for a new paradigm, different from Europe and America, to include the different realities of Asia, and suggests that the global direction of the Synod should not be made by the Roman Secretariat but should be left to the bishops of Asia. The Japanese ask why so little use was made of the work of the Federation of Asian Bishops' Conferences (FABC) over the past *25* years. There are in the *Lineamenta* only two footnotes referring to FABC! It seemed as if the "branch offices" were not even given passing marks.

Andrew Greeley, in a recent article, makes the same point:

> It is not unfair to say that since the bishops went home at the end of the Second Vatican Council there has been little collaborative governance in the Church. The current synod system, for example, is the ecclesiastical version of a Potemkin village. Neither Paul VI nor John Paul II has taken the triennial synod of bishops very seriously. Bishops have no control of the agenda. While bishops may speak, they do not engage in active debate and the proposals that emerge often do not reflect what was said, much less the emphasis with which it was said.[6]

Greeley believes there is no serious collaboration and little tolerance for new thinking and quotes one Roman cleric who said the present pope simply cannot work collaboratively.

Pope John XXIII gave a threefold agenda to the Council: the better internal order of the Church itself; unity among Christians; and the promotion of peace throughout the world. It is hard to overestimate the enormous impact Vatican II had on the life of the Church. There were sweeping reforms of the official liturgy; the Church redressed its relationship with other churches; it showed a greater openness and invited dialogue with non-Christian religions; it demanded the Church work for peace and social justice in the world; and it called for an understanding of the Church as not only a juridical institution but as a Pilgrim Church of the People of God bound in communion. The agenda could serve as a check-list for evaluating where we are now.

A "better internal order of the Church itself" led to the death of the dream of collegiality and a reassertion of curial authority. It is not just that synods are largely ineffective, but national conferences of bishops have been undermined. Bishops are appointed without, and often against, the wishes of the national or regional hierarchy, and orthodoxy takes precedence over orthopraxis. The beatification cause of an Oscar Romero languishes while that of a Jose Maria Escriva is hastened along. The "relationship with other churches," given the rather inept language of some recent documents, is damaged, and the Congregation for Non-Christian Religions was long ago downgraded to a Pontifical Council – and some years ago, the Pontifical Institute for the Study of Arabic and Islamics had to vacate its premises to make room for *Opus Dei*.

In the "work for justice and peace," liberation theology was sabotaged, and the work of progressive bishops in Latin America, like Helder Camara, was cruelly reversed by their successors.

We have moved away from a concept of the Church as a Pilgrim People of God, journeying together, to the reality of conflicting rights and duties between laity, priests, religious and hierarchy, which mirrors the tension between democracy and absolute monarchy. "Modern Catholics," observes Clifford Longley, "are expected to inhabit both worlds, which has generated a serious and debilitating split between the religious self and the political or secular self." [7] "As religious beings," he writes, "lay Catholics are expected to behave like obedient children of a loving father, be it priest, bishop or pope. As citizens they are expected to take active responsibility for the common good and to participate in the political processes with their wits about them." In the same column, Longley believes that this means being sceptical and questioning, holding those who exercise authority to account. It does not really make sense to expect Catholics to switch from being one kind of person to the other in an instant. There are two different personalities required, and a split personality is never a healthy personality. It seems clear that most Catholics have made their choice on what they want to be, and a failure, on the part of the hierarchy or the curia or the pope, to recognise this can only lead to extreme demoralisation. And demoralisation, he believes, ultimately leads to apathy.

There is so often present in official statements from Rome this schizoid element that some, the most notable among them the late Bernard Haring, have described the curial mentality as "pathological." Pope John Paul speaks of dialogue as indispensable, and during the Solidarity years, described loyalty oaths that go against one's conscience and convictions as "the most painful blow inflicted to human dignity". Yet we can all cite church cases where the accused is not part of the dialogue, where there is no due process, and where the individual is presented with a loyalty oath to be signed. There is a discrepancy between the pope's strong, prophetic words of protest against communist authoritarianism and state-sponsored censorship, on the one hand, and his implicit acceptance of similar methods in dealing with theological dissent and disciplinary deviation within the Church's own ranks.[8] Anyone who has had experience of dealing with a paranoid schizophrenic person in family or community knows how exhausting this can be. And knows too how tempting it is to ignore that person.

What all this means for the future is hard to predict. The Council is still alive; religious life more vigorous; the daily commitment of Christians enduring; religion has been rehabilitated, the faithful "owning" it as their own; believers are more articulate and demanding; and theology has been liberated from an exclusively male-seminary model; insights from women theologians have opened up entirely new ways of doing theology. Yet looked at from another perspective, i.e., between Church and world and among the members themselves, more gaps have been created than bridged. Bridging these gaps will take more than dialogue between the "centre" and the periphery. Dialogue is fruitless unless there is a genuine *metanoia,* a "turning of the heart," and more tangible signs of trusting the experience of believers by a listening and learning attitude.

Paul VI, speaking of the hunger for truth in everyone, gives advice worth paying attention to:

> So the search continues and, as you know, in an ocean of truths and mysteries, in a drama in which each one has his own part to play. This is life. Can it be exhausted in this temporal existence of ours? No. In spite of the immense light of our Catholic religion, the search and expectation of future revelation are not complete; on the contrary, they are still at the beginning. Faith is not complete knowledge; it is the source of hope [*Heb 11.1*]. Now we see religious realities, even in their incontrovertible reality, in mystery, in their impossibility of being reduced to the purely rational yardstick; we know these realities "in a mirror dimly". Study, research and – let us say the word that comprises the whole human-religious process – love, remain active and dynamic.[9]

We need study, research, and love, yes, but we also need trust and patience. Trust in the experience of all believers and trust in the Spirit at work in the world. That trust requires of the centre, especially, surrendering the control of events, being patient, awaiting an outcome none of us can predict.

> The kingdom of God is like a person scattering seed on the land. Night and day, while they sleep, when they are awake, the seed is sprouting and growing; how they do not know. All by itself the land produces first the shoot, then the ear, then the full grain in the ear [*Mk 4.26-28*].

Perhaps the best advice to a controlling centre is: Don't worry. Trust in God – and go to sleep. God will do what God does best: make the mysterious divine purposes known and go on surprising us.

Editor's Note on "Potemkin village":

Potemkin (1739-91) was a Russian field marshal and statesman, a great favourite of Catherine the Great, who, it is said, built fake villages to deceive Catherine and impress visitors about his accomplishments. Hence a "Potemkin village" is a false front or façade.

Endnotes

1. *Ad Petri Cathedram,* No 71, 29 June 1959

2. For example, the published remarks in 1994 by the pope about Buddhism being "atheistic," and Cardinal Ratzinger, in an interview two years later describing Buddhism as "autoerotic."

3. Cf Richard P McBrien's review of *His Holiness* by Carl Bernstein and Marco Politi, (New York: Doubleday, 1996), in *Commonweal,* 17 January 1997.

4. *Asia Focus,* 8 August 1997, pp. 7-8.

5. *Ibid.*

6. "Information Deficit, Why the Church's Hierarchy isn't Working," *Commonweal,* 12 March 2004, pp. 11-12.

7. To Bend or to Break, *The Tablet,* 5 June 2004, p. 2.

8. McBrien, *op. cit.*

9. Quoted by Arul Pragasam, "The Uniqueness of Jesus: A State of Affairs in Post-modern Theology", *Vidyajyoti,* 68/4, p. 258.

A Church Alive in the Spirit: The Dynamic of Mysticism and Prophecy

Susan Rakoczy IHM

Archbishop Denis Hurley's episcopal motto was "Where the Spirit of the Lord is, there is freedom" (2 Cor 3:17-18). What a prescient choice he made in 1947: 15 years before the Second Vatican Council and the transformation it set in motion in the Church and one year before the Nationalist Party took power in South Africa and wreaked havoc for 47 years through its policies of apartheid. Both in Church and society the freedom of the Spirit and its gifts of community, unity, peace, prophecy and reconciliation were and are so needed. Archbishop Hurley worked consistently and courageously to make his Church and his country a place of that freedom.

South Africa is now a free and growing democracy, seeking to be a place of justice, peace and reconciliation. Much has been achieved since 1994, yet much more work lies ahead. But in the Church in these early years of the 21st century the situation is so very different and the freedom of the Spirit that Hurley strove so diligently to make real is barely evident.

We are a dysfunctional Church, forbidden (!) by our "father" to discuss issues that are crucial to its ministry such as the ordination of women and celibacy of the diocesan clergy. In this very long papacy of John Paul II the approach of the institutional Church has become ever more authoritarian, centralised and autocratic. Vatican dicasteries make policy as if a law unto themselves; consultation is a forgotten experience. Theologians and bishops who deviate from Vatican orthodoxy in the slightest degree are subjected to an inquisitorial process that violates both their human dignity and makes a mockery of the work of theology as a collegial ministry in the Church.

Bishops are selected as "company men", in agreement with the Vatican list of "thou shalt nots": women's ordination, clerical celibacy, sexuality issues. The sexual abuse scandals around the world have demonstrated how weak and defensive so many bishops are, anxious to protect the clerical club and insensitive to the pain and suffering of the survivors of the abuse. The secrecy and cover-ups which have been brought to light are in utter contradiction to the freedom and light of the Spirit of God.

Bishops' conferences are forced to function as franchises of Rome, with precious little space allowed to shape a local Church according to local needs. The Synod of Bishops has never fulfilled its promise—a collegial body discussing crucial issues—but has become a rubber stamp of papal ideas, with the final document often drafted even before the first session.

People outside Catholicism generally know one definite thing about the Catholic Church: it is anti-sexuality – anti-abortion, anti-contraception, anti-premarital sex, anti-gay and lesbian people. These teachings on sexuality have been shaped almost exclusively by a male, clerical caste. The voices of married people, especially women, are seldom part of the conversation. Although married people through the Christian Family Movement were consulted in the process that led to the encyclical *Humanae Vitae* (1968), their recommendations and the impact of their experience of the Church's teaching on sexuality were completely ignored when the encyclical was written.[1]

The Constitution on the Sacred Liturgy (*Sacrosanctum Concilium*) clearly states that the Eucharist is the central act of the Church: "...the liturgy is the summit towards which the activity of the Church is directed; it is also the fountain from which all her power flows" (*SC* 10).[2] However, in parishes around the world, the possibility of experiencing a Sunday eucharistic celebration is declining each year because of the shortage of clergy. Here in South Africa this has been the experience of rural communities ever since evangelisation began. But now it is affecting urban parishes in the West. Where a parish once had four or five priests, now one priest serves three or four parishes, becoming a "sacramental dispenser" as he rushes from one parish to the next. The intransigence and refusal of John Paul II to even begin discussion of the effects of a male celibate priesthood on the eucharistic heart of the Church is leading to spiritual starvation of the people of God. And much worse times lie ahead unless change happens.

The witness of the Church in the world is an ambiguous one. On the one hand, there has been a very positive response to the call of *Gaudium et Spes* to make the joys and sufferings of humanity the joys and sufferings of the Church. This pope has been outspoken in his condemnation of war and violence wherever it happens and is a strong voice for human rights.

But the Church is not yet a servant Church, washing the feet of the world. It is often an arrogant Church, confident that it alone has the truth. Ecumenical and inter-religious dialogue can go only so far before "Church teachings" are asserted in ways that stifle or end the conversation. This was demonstrated very clearly in 2000 in the document *Dominus Jesus* from the Congregation for the Doctrine of the Faith which sought to assert the primacy of Jesus as saviour in ways which did great harm to ecumenical and inter-religious dialogue.

It is much easier for the Church to denounce human rights violations in Iraq, Sudan, and the Middle East than to look into its own life. The bold statement of the Synod document of 1971, *Justice in the World*, that "While the Church is bound to give witness to justice, she recognises that anyone who ventures to speak to people about justice must first be just in their eyes" (*JW* 40) is in contradiction to its practice.

This perspective is especially in conflict in the issue of women's participation in the life of the Church. Not only has the Vatican stated that the issue of ordination is eternally closed, but women's gifts and experience are not part of the decision-making structures of the Church since ordination and jurisdiction remain bound together. The few women in Vatican offices and the sprinkling of women in diocesan chanceries and on marriage tribunals are certainly not sufficient to witness to the fact that women comprise more than 60% of practising Catholics around the world. And in South Africa, as throughout Africa, they are frequently 70% or 80% of a Sunday congregation.

Only in the area of theology are women beginning to make their impact. And it is significant that while this is an ecclesial ministry, women began to study theology in large numbers after Vatican II with no encouragement from the male hierarchy. They courageously responded to the call of the Spirit and are re-shaping the work of theology.

Must this continue? Must the future be more of the same, a time of stagnation with little of the freedom and power of the Spirit which were the driving forces of Denis Hurley's life and ministry?

I affirm that this need not be so, if the Church refocuses its life and structures to become a community which discerns the Spirit of God together.

A New Pentecost

I was in high school when Vatican II began in 1962. When Blessed Pope John XXIII announced in 1959 that an ecumenical council would be held, the Church was astonished. Even Archbishop Hurley was perplexed by this announcement, since councils are called in times of crisis, and the Church of the late 1950s was not in crisis, but rather was flourishing.[3]

Blessed John XXIII asked the whole Church to pray that the council would be a "new Pentecost". I remember being puzzled by this. Pentecost was described in the Acts of the Apostles, but that was in the past. What could a "new Pentecost" possibly mean? But I dutifully prayed that prayer with my classmates each day. And on the day the Council opened, 11 October 1962, as the small black and white TV in one of the classrooms showed the long procession of bishops enter St Peter's, I had a very powerful sense that I was witnessing the beginning of one of the most important events in the history of the Church.

The Church to emerge in the future must be a Church of a new Pentecost, a Church shaped by the leading of the Spirit. It must become a Church whose inner life and external witness flow from decisions made in different forms of communal discernment processes. It must discover ways to unite its charismatic and institutional dimensions[4] so that they are in a dynamic, creative synergy.

This Church must be a community that walks on the two feet of love, to use St Catherine of Siena's felicitous phrase: love of God and love of neighbour. These two feet are also mysticism and prophecy.

Mysticism: Transformation of the Inner Life of the Church

The great Catholic theologian Karl Rahner stated, "In the future we shall be mystics or we shall be nothing".[5] In the 21st century, mysticism must not be thought of as an esoteric experience of the few, but the full flowering of Christian life.

A central insight of Vatican II on the meaning of the Christian life is the insistence that *all* the baptised are called to the fullness of holiness and the perfection of charity (*LG* 40). This statement abolished the hierarchy of vocations in the Catholic Church which had seen priesthood and religious life, which demand a celibate commitment, as "higher" than marriage or the single life. It summons believers back to the Gospel call to the fullness of life promised by Christ Jesus: "I have come that they might have life and have it to the full" (John.10:10).

Fullness of life in Christ in the power of the Spirit is mystical experience. It is the development of the grace of baptism, lived intensely and deeply. Gospel holiness is not marked by the extraordinary phenomena we usually think of when we consider mysticism, e.g. levitation, trances, visions, etc. but the fullness of love: for God and for others. Rahner's perspective is very important:

> Mysticism ... occurs within the framework of normal graces and within the experience of faith. To this extent, those who insist that mystical experience is not specifically different from the ordinary life of grace (as such) are certainly right.[6]

Every member of the Church without exception is called to live in union with Christ in the power of the Spirit. It is this experience of shared life, of one heart and soul (Acts 4:32) which is the basis of the unity of the community.

This union is described in the vivid image of the vine and the branches (John 15:1-9). *One* life, that of the Spirit, courses through the Body of Christ, whose unity is organic, not functional, and certainly not authoritarian and hierarchical. Each woman and man, girl and boy child, shares the life of Christ and so is gifted for service and ministry. The Spirit does the choosing, not the members, and so gifts can appear in unexpected places, often in people who are poor and of little account according to non-Gospel standards.

Paul's lists of the gifts of the Spirit: prophecy, teaching, healing, miracles, tongues and others (Romans 12:6-9, 1 Cor 12:8-11) reflected the experience of the first Christian communities. Today we can add others such as theologian, artist, musician, administrator. Paul includes the gift of discernment in his list, a vital charism which assists the community in distinguishing gold from dross; movements which may appear to be of God but which are leading the community astray; prophetic utterances which nourish, challenge and strengthen the community, from merely interesting ideas.

The Church is to be a servant Church, after the model of Jesus who washed his disciples' feet (John 13:1-16). Such a community is characterised by self-forgetfulness, with no regard for status and power; utter generosity, hospitality to all, and a care for those most in need of having their feet washed.

The Challenge of Holiness

Pope John Paul II has now named more persons as blessed and saints than any other pope in history. But has the increasing plethora of those designated as models of holiness really made any difference to the people of God?

It does not appear so since most of these new *beati* and saints are founders of religious congregations; few lay people, let alone married couples, have been found worthy of the Church's approbation. Saints continue to be designated as extraordinary persons such as Padre Pio who had the *stigmata*, the wounds of Christ during his passion and crucifixion; or Mother Teresa of Calcutta and her life of heroic charity in some of the worst slums in the world.

The effect on the people of God is very serious since they do not regularly hear the challenge to radical holiness and union with God. This is for the "saints", not for the person in the pew. The Sunday homily is generally woefully inadequate and often gives the assembly only a few crusts of dry and mouldy bread for the week.

What is needed is a radical transformation of the Church community into one body seeking the fullness of life in Christ, which is holiness, and living in the power of the Spirit. In the 1930s Pope Pius XI wrote, "Let us thank God that He makes us live among the present problems. It is no longer permitted to anyone to be mediocre." His words were written in the context of the rise of Hitler and Nazism and the challenges to the Church which this presented. But they are no less true today. Mediocrity and lukewarmness are so often the status quo and expected mode of Christian life that when something different is glimpsed, people are often astonished.

Where do we begin to re-shape the expectations of the baptised? We begin everywhere and with everyone at the same time: from children to Church leaders, from married couples to theologians, women and men, old and young. The language of catechesis and preaching, of ministerial formation, of continuing adult education must make a quantum leap and take seriously the call to radical holiness that is at the heart of the Gospel.

Those who minister in adult formation in a parish, as spiritual directors, or as priests in the Sacrament of Reconciliation, learn very quickly that the people of God are hungry, indeed they are starving, for nourishment in their life of faith. The desire to pray, to experience God more deeply, to be aware of the movements of the Spirit, are strong and clear. Yet the resources are so few.

And often the clergy appear to be uninterested in the call to union with God, the heart of faith, most probably because their hearts are not stirred with desire for God. They preach dry bread because that is what they live on, unaware that there is a banquet table for all. They are unable to teach people how to pray, and to grow in deep relationship with God because they are not persons of deep and profound prayer.

Paul spoke of the need for preachers to be sent to proclaim the Gospel (Romans 10:14-15) in order for people to hear the call to faith. The people of God today must have opportunities to grow in their faith commitment, to be challenged out of mediocrity and comfort, to know that the life of faith has deeper dimensions of the reality of God in their lives than they have ever dreamed. This cannot happen unless those who preach, who teach, who catechise know this from experience and communicate it in every dimension of their ministry.

Currently, the focus on the liturgy by Rome has been to correct "abuses" and to ensure that the translations, especially in English, reflect a certain theological perspective, even if they do violence to the actual Latin text. Lost is what Vatican II proclaimed so strongly: the Eucharist is the heart of Christian life. And if the heart is weak, the whole body is weak. How can we be a holy community if those who preside at the celebration of the Eucharist do not *pray* the liturgy with the people? Faith increases faith; boredom and routine are easily communicated to the congregation who experience "the same old thing" Sunday after Sunday.

A radical renewal of preaching is imperative.[7] Communication techniques are helpful and scriptural knowledge is essential, but those who preach must preach from the heart, from the centre of their own experience of God. The people of God must experience their hearts being warmed by the presence and power of the Spirit. They must learn to recognise that God calls them to more, the *magis* of which St Ignatius of Loyola speaks in his *Spiritual Exercises.*

Rahner's recognition that the heart of faith is mystical experience is a clear call to the Church to transform its approach to ministerial formation, catechesis, preaching and every form of transmission of the faith. The Church will not walk confidently on the foot of mystical experience—the fullness of life in God—unless and until the faithful know that this is their call and that God will truly give them more than they "can ask or imagine" (Eph 3:20-21).

Reshaping Decision-Making: Communal Discernment

One of the very positive fruits of Vatican II has been the growth of parish pastoral councils in parishes around the world. Some dioceses also have diocesan pastoral councils. For the first time in centuries the laity are now involved in shaping the priorities and life of their faith communities. However, these are only consultative bodies and the parish priest reserves the right to make decisions or to refuse to carry out the recommendations of the council, as does the bishop in the case of diocesan councils.

Bishops are organised into national and regional conferences, but the exercise of their authority is severely limited by Rome which reserves the right to approve their decisions and chastises them when they take initiatives for the local Church which do not fit Roman norms. Effective and fruitful collegiality is based on trust, which is not in great supply in Roman offices. Nicholas Lash laments that "I do not believe that anybody, as the Council ended, foresaw the possibility that, only 37 years after the promulgation of *Lumen Gentium*, the Church would be far more rigorously and monolithically controlled by Pope and Curia than at any time in its history".[8]

The Roman dicasteries, Congregations such as those of Divine Worship, Bishops, Evangelisation are now very international, which is a marked departure from the past. But they continue to be totally male since ordination and jurisdiction are joined. Their decision-making and deliberation are done behind closed doors and those most affected are totally left out of the process. Recently a few women have been appointed to the International Theological Commission and the Congregation for Consecrated Life, but their theological positions are in harmony with the extreme conservative mindset of Rome.

Bishops and the pope are selected in secrecy. Even if there is some form of consultation of the priests, religious and laity when a diocese needs a bishop, it has no real authority in the process. Bishops are selected by the pope in consultation with the Apostolic Delegate or Pro-Nuncio and the people of God have to accept whoever is given to them. The pope is elected by a group of elderly cardinals with no consultation of the people of God whatsoever.

All these processes are characterised by lack of trust in the Spirit of God and in people, lack of awareness that the Spirit dwells in the hearts of *all* the baptised, not just the ordained clergy. Secrecy, power politics, imposition of various theological ideologies shape these processes.

What is needed in the Church is a radical transformation of all decision-making procedures into discernment processes. Paul lists discernment as one of the gifts of the Spirit (1 Cor 12:10). In order to respond to the call of the Spirit[9] we need the gift of being able to distinguish which are movements of the Spirit, and which those of the power of evil or of our own spirit.

Discernment is an experience of faith and prayer in which the person or community engages in reflection on their affective experience and the direction it is leading them in order to be able to say, "This is what God asks of us".

The Ignatian perspective of "finding God in all things" describes the dynamic of discernment. We look to Ignatius of Loyola who has given the Church community a precious gift in the Rules for Discernment of Spirits in his *Spiritual Exercises* (313-336). These Rules, which are based on the analysis of one's affective life seen in the light of faith, differentiate between those who are very new to a commitment to Christ and those who have made him the centre of their lives (Rules for the First and Second Weeks).

Central to discernment is a growing freedom and openness to the Spirit. This calls for a recognition of the ways in which we are not free and the bonds which limit our response to the Spirit. There is never a perfect and whole freedom but our response to God allows us to grow in that freedom.

Another significant dimension of discernment is the bond of unity in community experienced by the person. Discernment, even when it involves the decision of one person to respond to the call of the Spirit, is never a private affair since that decision will impact others. This is even more obvious when a group discerns a decision together.

Acts 15:5-23 describes the Council of Jerusalem in which the new community faced the challenge of the application of the Mosaic Law to Gentile converts. The text clearly presents the conflict between James and Peter about this crucial matter (too often in the Church today conflict is denied for the sake of a "false peace") and the final decision was announced in discernment language: "We and the Holy Spirit" (Acts 15:28).

In order to be an inclusive Church, in which the presence of the Spirit and the gifts of that Spirit are honoured in every person, the decision-making at all levels must be reshaped into processes of communal discernment. This would spell an end to the authoritarianism, secrecy, lack of trust and power politics which make the Church no different from other societal institutions, and often a great deal worse.

Communal discernment is based on the following theological principles:

◈ The participation of each person concerned about a decision is vitally necessary because of their baptismal dignity;

◈ Because the Church is a community of faith, its decision-making processes should reflect and embody the perspective of faith;

◈ The Spirit dwells in the heart of each person, not only those who are ordained as deacons, priests and bishops;

◈ Christian life is about living the Gospel, not about the exercise of coercive power;

◈ The gifts of the ordained must form a synergy with the gifts of the whole community for the good of all;

◈ Discerning the Spirit together increases the unity of the community since each one's gifts are recognised as vitally necessary.

Decisions about the life of the Church should be made through communal discernment processes at every level of ecclesial life: parish, diocese, national conferences of bishops, papal elections. In a diocese, for example, when there is need for a new bishop, communal discernment processes must be used to give all the faithful the opportunity to share their insights about the kind of bishop that local Church needs and who might be a suitable bishop. A decentralisation of the process is necessary, with the people of the diocese taking a major role. There have been many calls for a return to the practice of the people of the diocese electing the bishop. If there is a true consultative process in the diocese, then the bishop could be selected and named by the national or regional bishops' conference, and then affirmed by the Congregation for Bishops in Rome.

Women's religious congregations are leading the way in reshaping their chapters and the processes of election of their leaders into experiences marked by communal listening and discernment.[10] The sense of peace and unity which is the fruit of discernment is worth the challenge of learning to listen deeply to each person since each speaks in the power of the Spirit.

This use of communal discernment will not be easy since the past modes of decision-making will have to be abandoned as not worthy of the People of God. Discernment is only as strong and deep as the person with the weakest personal relationship to God and the most distracted listening to the Spirit. Thus the challenge to radical holiness and the use of communal discernment form one coherent whole. Holy people, mystics desiring to live in profound union with God, are those who can discern the Spirit with their sisters and brothers. Communal discernment is not for the faint-hearted nor for those who desire efficiency and expediency at all costs. Rather, it will both transform the Church and call it to greater accountability and transparency to the extent that all are invited to listen and speak their truth in the Spirit of God.

Making Discernment Practical

Reshaping the Church community into one which discerns the Spirit together will lead to the transformation of the ministry of leadership in the Church. This leadership is now often characterised by domination and authoritarianism. When a different model is shown, as in the example of the late Bishop Kenneth Untener of Saginaw, Michigan in the United States; it is so striking because it is so rare. As priests, bishops and the pope recognise that they are in the midst of the community, not outside or above it, they will hopefully experience a closer bond with the people of God. Often authoritarianism is a sign of insecurity; when Church leaders know and trust the faithful, the people will know and trust them. Decisions made together are everyone's decisions.

A Church seeking the Spirit together will necessarily be inclusive since everyone's prayer and voice is important. No branch on the vine is forgotten nor forbidden to flourish. The Spirit is the Spirit of courage and openness, and thus the presence and voices of women, of gay and lesbian people, of the disabled, of children (some parishes have Children's Parish Pastoral Councils), of the elderly, will be welcomed and celebrated. As the world-wide Church becomes ever more multi-cultural, not just in the growth of the Church in Africa for example, but also in Western Europe and the United States, the diversity of cultural experiences which are brought to communal discernment processes of all kinds will enrich and strengthen the whole Body.

Discernment of ministry will also be transformed by the use of communal discernment. A young man (eventually a young woman) who is beginning to sense a call to ministry in the Church will first consult with their parish community, for it is that community who know the person and their gifts. Too often at present a man appears to "call himself" to ministry, and present himself to the diocese or religious congregation, who in a frantic focus on numbers are only too willing to accept any warm male body. His call is disconnected from the community. And when the local community affirms this initial sense, it has a continuing responsibility to support and continue to discern this call with the person as the years of formation unfold. As the young person does pastoral ministry as part of the formation experience, these communities too are responsible to add their insights to the discernment process so that when a person is ordained as deacon or priest, these Christian communities can truly affirm that he or she is called to serve the people of God.

Mysticism Leads to Prophecy

The transformation of the expectations of the people of God from living a mediocre life of faith to a full-hearted response to the call to radical holiness will transform the Church into a prophetic community. Vatican II radically reshaped the Church's attitude towards the "world", stating that "The joys and hopes, the griefs and anxieties of the men (sic) of this age, especially those who are poor or afflicted, these too are the joys and hopes, the griefs and anxieties of the followers of Christ. Indeed, nothing genuinely human fails to raise an echo in their hearts" (*GS* 1). This prophetic stance flows from Jesus' own sense of his call:

> The spirit of the Lord is on me,
> for he has anointed me
> to bring the good news to the afflicted.
> He has sent me to proclaim liberty to captives,
> sight to the blind,
> to let the oppressed go free,
> to proclaim a year of favour from the Lord.
> (Luke 4:16-19)

The phrase "reading the signs of the times" has become part of the vocabulary of the Church in the last 40 years. What are the signs of the times today that call for the Church's prophetic response?

Globalisation

The world is now a global village, an interdependent community in ways not dreamed about in the 1960s. Global capitalism and the "free" flow of money to the strongest bidder has intensified and widened the divide between rich and poor nations and rich and poor people in a country. The massive protests of the last few years at international meetings such as the G8 or World Trade Organisation demonstrate that at least some people in the world community sense deeply that there is definitely something wrong with global economic structures.

The Catholic Church is a global community and thus should build on this strength to help the world make sense of globalisation which has very real detrimental effects and yet also very helpful dimensions such as ease of global communication through the internet. Church leaders in various parts of the world, North and South, have no real way to communicate with each other in a formal way because of the extremely centralised Church structures mandated by Rome. What communication there is internationally on major social issues by bishops' conferences is only informal and without authority. And frequently an international community such as the Community of Sant'Egidio, based in Rome and with members around the world (with which Archbishop Hurley had a strong and loving relationship) has a much clearer sense of the relations between the rich and the poor internationally than do ecclesial leaders.

The Church must model an effective and caring global faith community in its patterns of communication, sharing of resources (not only money but people) and in its prophetic denunciation of the harmful effects of globalisation. A number of years ago Walbert Bühlmann in his book *The Coming of the Third Church*, accurately described the shape of the Church in the 21st century: a shift from the North to the South. He also argued that trying to maintain unity in the Church through an increasingly centralised administration and uniformity of discipline, is a human means when what is needed is "something deeper, more sublimely and biblically expressed as *koinonia* and trust to the action of the Holy Spirit to achieve it".[11]

He also made a most intriguing suggestion that the papacy should move from country to country every ten years, so that the pope would experience the richness of Christian life in diverse cultures. His proposal would involve a radical shift in the Church's self-understanding: from a highly centralised bureaucracy in Rome to a stripped-down curia/cabinet travelling with the pope around the world. Advances in communication in the last 30 years make this idea much more feasible than it was in the 1970s. And the sense that we are a "global village" makes Bühlmann's suggestion thoroughly in harmony with contemporary experience.

The Desire for Unity

Within the energy, both positive and negative, of globalisation, is the hope that the world can live together as an interdependent community. The 20th century saw the birth of the ecumenical movement and achievements in dialogue, respect and common action which were both dramatic and imbued with the presence of the Spirit of God. This was especially important for Catholics who were late-comers to the conversation.

The early 21st century is seeing something of a reversal of this passion for unity which so marked the past 100 years. Controversies over sexuality issues, e.g. the ordination of gay and lesbian people in the Anglican Communion and other Church bodies, is a particularly contentious issue. Formal dialogues such as those between Roman Catholics and Anglicans, and Lutherans and Catholics do continue, but at times there is a sense of "how much further can we go?" when there are seemingly intractable issues such as the role of the papal office and women's ordination on the agenda.

A prophetic Church is full of courage and daring; it does not rest on what has already been achieved but steps forward into the unknown. Can the Catholic Church respect and learn from the decisions of other Christian ecclesial bodies on issues such as the ordination of women? Or must it forever put up a sign that says "Not to be discussed"? It can only do the first if it is confident of the presence and power of the Spirit acting in the whole Christian community, not only in the Catholic Church.

An important example is Eucharistic sharing with members of other ecclesial communities, a practice which occurs with increasing frequency. The official Roman position is that Eucharistic sharing will be the fruit of structural unity and thus may not occur (except on very rare occasions) until this unity is realised. But people who have experienced Eucharistic sharing know that this practice actually strengthens the bonds of unity which already exist because we are baptised in the one Spirit. A prophetic Church is called to recognise this "sign of the times" and discern its fruits carefully, not smother the new buds on the tree of Christian life

The Spirit is the Spirit of unity (Eph 4:4-6) and the Spirit calls the Church to a passion for unity, for new forms of ecclesial relationship, for continuing sorrow that the one Church of Jesus the Christ is so fragmented. It rejoices in every effort at common understanding, common worship, common action for justice and peace.

A Listening Church

Linked to the ecumenical movement within the Christian Churches is inter-religious dialogue. The movement of peoples around the world has increased dramatically in the last 40 years, both as the result of wars and the desire of persons to seek a "better" life somewhere else. This has meant that areas of the world which have been predominantly Christian for centuries, such as Europe and North America, now have many Muslims, Hindus and Buddhists within their borders. Inter-religious dialogue has come home.

The "Declaration on the Relation of the Church to Non-Christian Religions" (*Nostra Aetate*) was a dramatic reversal of the Church's traditional position that "outside the Church there is no salvation". It spoke in positive terms of the world religions and said that "the Catholic Church rejects nothing of what is true and holy in these religions" (*AE* 2).

The Church today appears to be ambivalent about this sign of the times. On the one hand, Pope John Paul II initiated the days of prayer for peace at Assisi, inviting persons of every religious conviction to pray for peace, each in their own way. But *Dominus Jesus* was a very unfortunate example of a Vatican document which disregarded the religious sensibilities of millions of people by asserting the uniqueness of Jesus the Christ in ways which offended them.

A listening Church listens and learns. It speaks too, but it speaks in dialogue and conversation as it learns what the other is saying and feeling.

The world is becoming much more multi-religious each year. The voice of the Church must be respectful, aware that the Spirit is present in the hearts and minds of all those who seek God.

Sexuality Issues

A second area of listening is that of sexuality. Here Church leaders have almost no practice in listening to the Spirit in the experience of the laity. Teaching on sexual issues is defined by a male, celibate clergy. The voices and experience of married couples form no part of its vision. John Paul II's theology of sexuality, focused on a theology of the body, is beautiful but abstract and does not reflect the experience of married couples who find many challenges in their sexual union. Absent in the teachings on contraception and abortion are the voices of women. The focus is put on the pre-born child and the mother is generally forgotten.

It does the Church no good simply to condemn abortion, contraception, sexual activity outside marriage. People make these decisions for all kinds of reasons. Where is the Church of compassionate listening and loving response? Where is a practical, positive theology of sexuality?

The sex-drenched cultures of the West and increasingly of South Africa need a different approach than condemnation. In the many years since the encyclical *Humanae Vitae* was issued by Pope Paul VI in 1968, the Church's moral authority on sexual issues has been totally eroded because this teaching does not find a home in the experience of married couples. This is not because of "bad will", sinfulness or selfishness, but because the teaching does not relate to the experience of married sexual love. A listening Church, sensitive to the Spirit in all the baptised, would and must speak differently.

Listening to Women

The male leadership of the Church seldom listens to women in the Church and it definitely does not pay heed to women's voices in the wider community. A truly prophetic Church would break the silence on the abuse of women and their children, on the increasing sexual slavery of young girls and women, of the use of rape as a weapon of war. The women of the world seldom find friends and allies amongst the leaders of the Catholic Church.

Prophetic words and action on these heart-rending issues come from women themselves, occasionally with assistance from male allies. In South Africa the book *Silent No Longer: The Church Responds to Sexual Violence*[12] began its journey to publication as a position paper on sexual violence written under the auspices of the Theological Advisory Commission (TAC) of the Southern African Catholic Bishops' Conference (SACBC). When neither the SACBC nor the TAC agreed to its publication, a coalition of women produced the book. At the press conference at the launch of the book, the secular media were astonished that the Catholic Church was speaking out on this issue, a striking testimony to the silence of Church leadership on these issues.

Gay and Lesbian People

Listening to women is difficult; listening to gay and lesbian people appears to be beyond the ability of Church leaders. Many gay and lesbian people are faithful members of their parish communities; others have voted with their feet and hearts and moved to other Church communities or out of Christian communities altogether because of the prejudice and exclusion they experience.

The documents of the Church on social teaching speak about the call to stand with the poor and the marginalised, but gay and lesbian people experience precious little welcoming and loving pastoral ministry.

Care for the Earth: Peace and Sustainable Community

The first photos taken of the earth from the moon by American astronauts in 1969 showed us our home: a shining blue, round sphere. It is, so far, the only home humanity has. In words and actions the Church must prophetically care for our home through its unceasing work for peace and reconciliation and its vision of a sustainable earth community.

From *Pacem in Terris* to the latest speeches of Pope John Paul II denouncing the war in Iraq, the official teaching of the Catholic Church on war and peace is strong and clear. Here prophetic words are evident and abundant.

But this teaching has not yet made its home in the hearts of believers. Why do Catholics continue to support war and violence as ways to solve problems, especially on the international and regional levels? Gandhi, whose conversion to non-violence took place in South Africa, lived a consistent non-violent life and his witness has influenced persons of all religions. Yet people often claim that "non-violence doesn't work". But when it is used, the results are striking: the non-violent revolution in the Philippines in 1985 which ended the rule of the Marcos regime and the generally non-violent end to Communist rule in the Soviet Union and Eastern Europe beginning in 1989.

Here is an issue in which mysticism and prophecy become wedded since it is only in the conversion of a violent heart to a peace-making heart that the world and all its small communities will know peace. It is the gift of Christ's own peace (John 14:27) which makes possible a life of peace in every relationship.

The Church should be seen as a creative force for peace on earth. The witness of the Sant'Egidio community, which negotiated the peace process in Mozambique in the 1990s, is a clear example of prophetic peace-making. But this should be the norm, not the exception. The creative Spirit longs to teach the world community new ways of conflict resolution which will end the deaths of millions in war as the human community wakes up to its responsibilities to make its home a happy, peaceful one for all.

As we make peace together for our present happiness and the future of the human community, the wise words of the 19th century Native American Chief Seattle challenge us clearly. He spoke of making decisions with the perspective of seven generations ahead—decisions for peace and decisions to care for our earth. This applies both to the fruits of sound ecological decisions and the destruction of ecosystems which can continue for generations. He also described the inter-relationships of all living things: "All things are connected like blood that unites us all. Man (*sic*) did not weave the web of life ... whatever we do to the web, we do to ourselves".[13]

Prophetic ecological action is also part of our responsibility as disciples of Jesus.

Our Church communities, our buildings, our consumption patterns should strikingly witness to the care we have for the earth. We are called to model sustainability in every way we interact with our environment in order that our descendants seven generations after us will have a flourishing world in which to live and grow. This is not a "green" option for those whose hobby is recycling. Rather, it is the living out of our commitment to the earth in which the Word and Wisdom of God dwells among us.

Conclusion

Forty years is a sufficient amount of time to assess a very significant event such as the Second Vatican Council which was one of the defining events in Denis Hurley's life. The hope and promise of the Council as a "new Pentecost" has slowly and thoroughly been eroded by ecclesial leadership which is much too frequently self-serving and authoritarian.

Yet the Spirit promises so much more, as Hurley expressed in his motto: a Church of freedom in the one Spirit. Today the Spirit calls the Church to remember that it is called to walk on the two feet of mysticism and prophecy. It is to be a community living its call to radical discipleship and radical holiness, announcing truth and denouncing injustice and oppression as it reads the signs of the times in the light of the Gospel. It is to be a Church which embodies the peace, reconciliation and compassion of Jesus the Christ.

The Church is called by the Spirit of freedom to reshape its communal life and its decision-making processes so that they become experiences of communal discernment, of seeking the Spirit together. It is in this experience of discernment that the Church will know when it is faithful to the Spirit of freedom, joy, peace and compassion and when it is not. Archbishop Denis Hurley knew this and lived according to his motto for all the years of his episcopal ministry. The Spirit asks no less of us now and in the future.

Endnotes

1.   Patrick and Patty Crowley were the "lead couple" in the Christian Family
      Movement in the United States and were involved in the preliminary
      discussions of the Vatican commission which led to the encyclical *Humanae
      Vitae* in 1968. See Robert B Kaiser, *The Politics of Sex and Religion*
      (Kansas City, Missouri: Leaven Press 1985), pp. 70-98, 177, 195 on the
      involvement of the Crowleys. Kaiser describes how the Crowleys were
      informed about the encyclical: "A night editor in New York started phoning
      American members of the commission. He woke the Crowleys in Chicago,
      gave them the news and asked for their reaction. Patrick had no comment,
      but then, not knowing whether to laugh or cry, he hung up the phone and
      said to Patty, 'Mom, just what in hell did we go to Rome for?' " (p. 195).

2.   Quotations from the documents of Vatican II are from Austin Flannery
      (ed). *Vatican Council II: The Conciliar and Post Conciliar Documents*,
      volume 1. (Northport, New York: Costello Publishing Company, 1975).

3.   Archbishop Hurley recalled receiving a letter from the Cardinal Secretary
      of State asking for suggestions for the Council. This letter was sent to all
      bishops throughout the world. "I looked at mine and I wondered why the
      Church needed a Council. There seemed to be no special crisis. Many
      bishops, I think, felt the same, especially in English-speaking parts of the
      world where the Church seemed to be in good shape, with churches well-
      attended, schools flourishing and vocations multiplying." Denis E Hurley
      OMI, "The Second Vatican Council", in *We give thanks: Ukwanda
      Kwaliswa Umthakathi, St Joseph's 1943-1993*, ed. Susan Rakoczy (Cedara:
      St Joseph's Theological Institute, 1993), p. 24.

4.   See the Dogmatic Constitution on the Church (*Lumen Gentium*) which
      speaks of the charisms given by the Spirit which are "fitting and useful for
      the needs of the Church". Those "who have charge over the Church should
      judge the genuineness and proper use of these gifts, through their office,
      not indeed to extinguish the Spirit but to test all things and hold fast to
      what is good (cf Th. 5:12 and 19-21)" (*LG* 12).

5.   Karl Rahner, "The Spirituality of the Future," in *Theological Investigations*,
      volume 20, trans. Edward Quinn (London: Darton, Longman & Todd, 1981),
      p. 149.

6.   Karl Rahner, "Mysticism: Theological Interpretation," in *The
      Encyclopaedia of Theology,* ed. Karl Rahner (London: Burns & Oates,
      1975), pp. 1010-1011.

7. Andrew Greeley comments that "If the Congregation for Divine Worship were truly interested in the quality of the liturgy, it would launch a worldwide campaign to improve sermons." "Information Deficit: Why the Church's Hierarchy Isn't Working". *Commonweal* (March 12, 2004), p. 15.

8. Nicholas Lash, "Vatican II: Of Happy Memory- and Hope?" in *Unfinished Journey: The Church 40 Years after Vatican II*, ed. Austen Ivereigh (London and New York: Continuum, 2003), p.17.

9. For background on the meaning and practice of discernment see William A Barry, "Toward a Theology of Discernment". *The Way Supplement* 64(1989): 129-140; John English, *Spiritual Freedom*, 2nd ed. (Chicago: Loyola University Press, 1995); Thomas H Green, *Weeds Among the Wheat*. (Notre Dame, Indiana: Ave Maria Press, 1984); David Lonsdale, *Listening to the Music of the Spirit: The Art of Discernment* (Notre Dame, Indiana: Ave Maria Press, 1992); Joan Mueller, *Faithful Listening: Discernment in Everyday Life* (Kansas City, Missouri: Sheed and Ward, 1996); Brian O'Leary, "Discernment and Decision Making", *Review for Religious* 51 (1992): 56-63; Susan Rakoczy, "Discernment and Desire", *The Way* 39 (1999): 269-280.

10. For a description and analysis of the use of communal discernment processes by a women's religious congregation see Susan Rakoczy, "A Congregation Chapter Report", *Human Development* 22, (2, 2001), pp. 43-48.

11. Walbert Bühlmann, *The Coming of the Third Church* (Slough, England: St Paul Publications, 1976), p. 188.

12. Edited by Susan Rakoczy IHM (Pretoria: SACBC, 2000).

13. http://www.ecolivingcenter.com/articles/favorite_quotes.html (24 May 2004).

Contributors

Mervyn Abrahams is a Redemptorist priest and graduate of the Katholieke Universiteit Leuven. He teaches Church History and Moral Theology at St Joseph's Theological Institute, Cedara.

Philippe Denis is a Dominican brother. He is Professor of the History of Christianity at the University of KwaZulu-Natal and Director of the Sinomlando Centre for Oral History and Memory Work in Africa.

Alois Greiler, member of the Society of Mary (Marists), was ordained in 1988. After pastoral work he went to Leuven, Belgium, for further studies in 1993. In 1995 he received his licentiate in theology, followed by his doctoral degree in June 1998, which deals with the genesis of the Vatican II decree on priestly formation, *Optatam Totius* (1965). During his research he had the opportunity to interview various members of the commission that drafted this decree. This was followed by two years of historical research for his congregation. In 2003 his doctoral thesis was published under the title *Das Konzil und die Seminare*. At present, he is a parish priest in Germany.

Marie-Henry Keane is a Newcastle Dominican and currently Prioress General of her Congregation. She lived in South Africa for many years where she was Associate Professor in Systematic Theology at the University of South Africa before being recalled to England in 1993. Thereafter she taught Ecclesiology and Feminist Theology at Oxford. She has delivered lectures and presented seminars in England, Scotland and Ireland as well as in North and South America and has written numerous articles, contributed to several books and has been interviewed on television and radio.

Paddy Kearney trained as a Marist Brother and taught at Marist schools in Durban, Port Elizabeth and Johannesburg. A graduate of Natal,

Witwatersrand and Toledo, Ohio, he has lectured in Education at Natal University, Pietermaritzburg. He led the staff team at Diakonia and the Diakonia Council of Churches from 1976 to 2004. He is now a consultant to the KwaZulu-Natal Christian Council and is researching the life of Archbishop Hurley.

Chrys McVey, Dominican, was born in the USA but has spent over half his life in Pakistan in pastoral work, teaching and administration. His articles and talks on Pakistan, Islam, mission and inter-religious dialogue have appeared in journals in England, Ireland, Pakistan, India and the Philippines. He presently resides in Rome as the Socius, to the Master of the Order, for apostolic life.

Allan Moss is an Oblate of Mary Immaculate. After completing studies for the priesthood in South Africa, he specialised in catechetics at Corpus Christi College, England. Later he studied at Lyon University in France and at Berkeley (United States of America), where he obtained his doctorate in theology. He also holds a masters degree in philosophy, from the University of South Africa. His pastoral experience includes serving as a parish priest in various urban and rural situations in the Archdiocese of Durban. He has also taught at St. Joseph's Theological Institute, Cedara. At present, he is Provincial of the Oblate Province of KwaZulu-Natal.

Albert Nolan entered the Dominican Order in 1954. He studied theology at St Nicholas Priory, Stellenbosch, and from 1961 to 1963 was a postgraduate student at the Angelicum in Rome. The author of two books, *Jesus Before Christianity* and *God in South Africa*, as well as numerous articles and booklets, Albert Nolan is well-known as a speaker at conferences and other gatherings. He has taught theology and religious journalism. In the heyday of the struggle against apartheid he was a student chaplain and worked for the Institute for Contextual Theology. Later he edited the ecumenical magazine *Challenge* and until recently was Provincial of the Dominicans in Southern Africa.

John Page served on the staff of the International Commission on English in the Liturgy (ICEL) from 1972-2002. In 1997 he was the recipient of the McManus award from the U.S. Federation of Diocesan Liturgical Commissions, and in 2003 the Pax Christi Award from St. John's Abbey in Collegeville, Minnesota.

Susan Rakoczy IHM, PhD was born and educated in the United States. Since 1982 she has lived and worked in Africa, first in Ghana and, since 1989, in South Africa. She is a lecturer in Spirituality and Systematic Theology at St Joseph's Theological Institute, Cedara and Honorary Professor of Theology in the School of Theology and Religion of the University of KwaZulu-Natal. Her academic research is focused on the interface between spirituality and psychology, feminist theology and mysticism and social commitment. She has published several books and her articles have appeared in South African, European and North American publications. Forthcoming in 2005 is *Great Mystics and Social Justice: Walking on the Two Feet of Love* (Paulist Press). She is a member of the Sisters, Servants of the Immaculate Heart of Mary (Monroe, Michigan, USA).